Tennyson and Clio

Alfred Tennyson

Henry Kozicki

Tennyson and Clio
History in the Major Poems

The Johns Hopkins University Press
Baltimore and London

The Johns Hopkins University Press, Baltimore, Maryland 21218
The Johns Hopkins Press Ltd., London

Library of Congress Catalog Number 79-10979

ISBN 0-8018-2197-5

Library of Congress Cataloging in Publication data will be found on the last printed page of this book.

For Melissa and Pam

Contents

ACKNOWLEDGMENTS   ix
INTRODUCTION   xi

   I   Clio at Somersby   1
  II   Clio at Cambridge   13
 III   From Cambridge to the Death of Hallam   32
  IV   The English Idyls and *The Princess*   53
   V   *In Memoriam*   70
  VI   The Political Poems and *Maud*   98
 VII   The Rise of Camelot   112
VIII   The Decline and Fall of Camelot   128
  IX   The Final Stage: Poems of the Sixties   150
   X   Epilogue: Beyond Clio   164

WORKS CITED   171
INDEX   179

Acknowledgments

I WOULD LIKE TO thank John Reed of Wayne State University for his Tennysonian expertise and for his encouragement over the years. I am also grateful to Robert Canary of the University of Wisconsin-Parkside for his general support and for his interdisciplinary scholarly enthusiasm.

Summer Research Grants from the University of Wisconsin system for 1971, 1974, and 1975 are appreciated, as is a Grant-in-Aid from the American Council of Learned Societies that allowed study at the Tennyson Research Centre in Lincoln, England, during the summer of 1974.

I am grateful for the work of the editors and readers of the journals where my essays have appeared and for the efforts of The Johns Hopkins University Press. Without their help, this book might not have appeared. The following journals kindly granted me permission to draw on my published essays. A bit of "Tennyson's *Idylls of the King* as Tragic Drama," *Victorian Poetry* 4 (1966): 15–20, appears in chapter 3. Most of "Wave and Fire Imagery in Tennyson's *Idylls*," *Victorian Newsletter* no. 43 (Spring 1973): 21–23, is woven into chapters 7 and 8. "Philosophy of History in Tennyson's Poetry to the 1842 *Poems*," *ELH* 42 (1975): 88–106, formed the basis for chapters 1, 2, and 3. A large part of chapter 4 is "The 'Medieval Ideal' in Tennyson's *The Princess*," *Criticism* 17 (1975): 121–30. If chapters 7 and 8 were condensed, they would approximate "A Dialectic of History in Tennyson's *Idylls*," *Victorian Studies* (and the Trustees of Indiana University), 20 (1977): 141–57. Chapter 5 contains a large part of "'Meaning' in Tennyson's *In Memoriam*," *Studies in English Literature* 17 (1977): 673–94.

The Samuel Laurence portrait of Tennyson that appears as the frontispiece to this volume was provided courtesy of the National Portrait Gallery, London.

Introduction

ARNOLD SAID IN "The Scholar Gipsy" that Tennyson occupied an "intellectual throne" for the Victorians. Later, in the first part of the twentieth century, the overriding impression was of a certain Tennysonian simplicity. Since World War II, Tennyson's mental stock has been bullish indeed, and today Priestley calls his intelligence "wide-ranging, penetrating and profound."[1] Yet, there is a good deal of critical disparity about the intellectual content of Tennyson's work, with much more of a tendency to credit him with penetrating emotional and spiritual insights than with some central and important conceptual order. We see him too much as an emotional fox and not enough as intellectual hedgehog. The present study is based on the idea that the major poems of Tennyson—individually, in groupings, and collectively—contain that "aesthetic effect of intellectual cogency" that Trilling says we find in the work of poets who make a great impression on us.[2] Further, it is argued that the intellectual order that unifies Tennyson's major poems comes out of his sense of history, specifically his "philosophy of history" in the speculative, metaphysical, nineteenth-century sense of this term.

Philosophy of history customarily is defined as a more-or-less systematic attempt to understand the "meaning and purpose of the whole historical process."[3] To begin with, we must be persuaded that a

---

[1] F. E. L. Priestley, *Language and Structure in Tennyson's Poetry*, p. 181.
[2] Lionel Trilling, *The Liberal Imagination*, p. 291.
[3] As, for example, by W. H. Walsh, *Philosophy of History*, p. 26.

"Passion of the Past"[4] is characteristic of Tennyson early and late, from the 1827 *Poems by Two Brothers* to the last of the *Idylls* in the eighties. If any single interest appeared to dominate Tennyson's work and thought, it was his concern about the whence and whither of human affairs. And if any single muse is to be assigned to him, it must be Clio, the muse of the "meaning and purpose" of history. *Meaning* is a critical concept that will be developed in the pages that follow, but here we might merely observe the intellectual content of this kind of "speculative" philosophy of history, which, just because it is characterized by highly charged emotional affirmations usually involving the "ultimates," contrasts with "analytic" philosophy of history, which is scientific and pragmatic. On the other hand, speculative philosophy of history differs from a merely simplistic faith in God's will and from a general euphoria about the inexorable purposefulness of the universe insofar as it contains a consciously understood frame of reference.

It follows that in such a context the "meaning and purpose"[5] of the past cannot obtain without both a conceptual system and intense convictions. And we cannot interpret properly a poem in which we deem Clio's influence operational unless we are able to identify both idea and emotion. For example, the presence of the notion of historical cycles does not bring meaning to a poem unless we can discover what the poet felt about that notion. The intellectual order that is a philosophy of history in Tennyson's major poems is, thus, an inextricable compound of concepts and convictions that must be determined in its totality, as a lifelong development, before it may be used as a sounding board to enhance any note elicited from a particular poem. Lest this be taken as an intentionalist intent (and a disregard of everything we have learned from the new criticism) I can only say, with Brooks, that "my basic concern has been to read the poem," but to note that, in order to do this, the critic must select "from scholarship those things which will help him understand the poem *qua* poem."[6]

This philosophy of history as a complex of ideas and emotions will be established in three ways. First, the philosophy of history will be

---

[4]The phrase is from Tennyson's 1885 "The Ancient Sage" (l. 219) but also essentially appears as a reference to Tennyson's "passion for the past" in an 1831 letter from Hallam to Tennyson ([Hallam, Lord Tennyson], *Alfred Lord Tennyson*, 1:81; hereafter cited as *Memoir*).

[5]*Meaning* in such a context is clearly a complex idea. The chapter "The Meaning of Meaning," with its sixteen groups of definitions, in C. K. Ogden and I. A. Richards, *The Meaning of Meaning*, 8th edition (New York: Harcourt, Brace and World, 1946) may be consulted. On the other hand, my understanding of the term, however rudimentary, might be postulated for purposes of practical criticism.

[6]Cleanth Brooks, "Literary Criticism: Poet, Poem, and Reader," p. 112.

argued as a genuine structural underpinning of Tennyson's major poems. Second, this philosophy subsumes and codifies Tennyson's statements, readings, beliefs, and feelings about the historical process, thus basing itself upon the poet's life. Third, this complex of ideas and emotions is representative of a way of thinking about history in the nineteenth century and so it rises from the thought of the age. For the purpose of practical criticism, the philosophy of history will be considered as consisting of three primary clusters of ideas and emotions. These will be called simply God, history, and man.

God is the sense of some kind of divinity, something more than human that is involved in the affairs of men. This may take the form of the Biblical God, of providence in various guises, or of something symbolic, such as a great Angel Mind confronting the poet. That is, this divinity may be something apart from history but overseeing it, it may settle (and be incarnate) in the historical process, or it may be a divine "analogue" within the individual human spirit. It does not follow, though it would appear it should, that such conceptions are signs of sanguineness or optimism. There may be despair or an existential, tragic courage attending these ideas, or, indeed, the concepts may be exhilarating.

History in such a context means the workings or mechanics of the historical process, either free or determined in various ways. Thus, history may be superintended providentially, either through direct intervention, or through the medium of the prophetic and active spirit, or even through paradoxical causalities like the "private vices-public benefits" mechanism. History may be bound up in natural law (which may or may not be seen as God's province) and so occurring in inexorable cycles, in an upward-and-onward progress, or in spirals or disjunctive ascents. On the other hand, history may be so freely within man's control as to be accidental, chanceful, mere fortune. Or, there may be a complex dialectic between historical necessity and historical freedom. Again, specific emotional affirmations do not automatically attend any of these concepts. It can be documented readily that cycles may be of infinite comfort and progress a torment, that a free universe may be a joy or an agonizing purposelessness. A private vice like that of Caligula may be at work wonderously preparing the womb of the Christian faith. Freedom may be the lock-step of perfect service. We shall simply never know what a poem that contains one of these ideas "means" unless we determine the emotion that envelops it.

Man, finally, is the term here for all individual and collective historical imperatives, either in the making of history or the intuition of such patterns as may be in it. Man may be a unique individual moving history out of selfish motives, a symbolic representative of the historical process, or a victim of impersonal historical forces. Man may be a group of the elect, a nation, or humanity at large, knowingly or unknowingly either making history or sensing its nature. Man may be the individual perceiver of the historical "analogue" that exists at the interface of man and God, or the perceiver of historical anarchy in a free field of chance. The convictions that attach themselves to any of these conceptions are as varied as those that attend the other two clusters of ideas: despair or confidence, peace or restlessness, dissolution or renewal.

This frame of reference—the ideas and the emotions that constitute Tennyson's philosophy of history—is not a constant. Like everything, it has a beginning, an end, and a flux throughout. An essential identity, however, runs through it all. The poems of Tennyson's early youth and those of his old age may differ markedly as life, attitudes, and craft alter through time, but rudimentary ideas and convictions that developed early can be recognized at the end even after they have undergone extreme metamorphoses. Because he was a representative Victorian—a very social man in a circle made significant by the presence of important men and women—his intellectual life has a contiguous relationship with contemporary political movements that were based on a certain idea of history. In an effort to convey the limits and transformations of this collective mental "structure" and to understand the ways that it evolved, assimilated, and regulated that portion of the world within its formative power, the commentary is laid out in stages that follow laws of association. Each step depends to some degree upon the preceding one, and at each stage we may see the play of component elements seeking equilibrium and forming aggregates and mutations in the passage of time.

These stages are as follows. First, the fundamentals of Tennyson's philosophy of history are introduced in chapter 1 through references to early readings, influences, and attitudes. This amalgam of concepts and convictions is animated by intuitionalism, an intense empathy with the passions of the past that is almost a putatively divine prophetic faculty. Here history is directed providentially by the Biblical God, an anthropomorphic "other" working out his nature. History occurs in invariable cycles, with a focus on the disastrous nature of the decline of states. The hero, both the individual and the collective spirit, somehow is a free agent of this divinity, yet unwittingly he is a bringer of the cyclic decline of states. The convictions that attend these conceptions include an unthinking acceptance of the Biblical scenario, a zestful exhilaration at the colorful pageant of the past, and a certain melancholy at mankind's ordained, disastrous condition. God is a mysterious unknown, history does not "teach" anything, and man's actions offer no easy moral judgments.

A second stage is the period 1827–33, covered in chapters 2 and 3, from Tennyson's entry into Cambridge and the circle of the "Apostles" to the time of Hallam's death. Out of Tennyson's access to the most sophisticated thought about history then available, his intuitionalism can be seen to some degree as wedded to a scientific understanding of history, one that involves a special distinction between active providence (whose power is available for "progress") and ordinary providence (the plane of mere natural process). History is in continual change and its present transformation is not benign to the fortunes of the hero class. The hero suffers obsolescence in the turn to a bourgeois-commercial phase of society. For the poet, identifying his own prophetic faculty with the heroic intuitionalism of the providential intent, the meaning of history becomes beset with contradiction. On the one hand, there is an emotional affirmation of a new progressivism in the affairs of men, and on the other a despair about the fate of heroic spirit.

One way of reconciling these contradictions works itself out in a third stage (chapter 4) that covers the English idyls and extends into *The Princess* of 1847. Divinity suffuses itself into the historical process and appears as an archetype of social order: the Great House paradigm of the medieval ideal that animated the period. History is "progressive" but only as a series of materializations of this ideal under the aegis of heroes in whom, however, the prophetic faculty is either atrophied ("weird seizures") or nonexistent, insofar as those heroes embody rather than effect a benign social transformation. At this stage, Tennyson emotionally affirmed, if with some ambiguity, the meaning of history by the "end-determined" frame of reference implicit in the idea of progress.

The resolutions of a fourth stage are on a different, though complementary, plane than those of the third. Chapter 5 deals with the protagonist facing both the total unknowability of divinity and the condition of cyclic disaster on personal, natural, and historical planes. In the absence of all divine sanction and all traditional frames of reference, the resolution that runs through "Locksley Hall" and into *In Memoriam* finds the meaning and purpose of history not in the "end-determined" frame of either the Biblical eschatology or secular progressivism, but rather in an "open-ended" expansion of an apocalyptic present: the phoenix death-birth of all things. The affirmation in this case is not joy in the benignity of history, but an acceptance of the sorrow of the free human condition. Divinity is realized in the metamorphosis of the persona of *In Memoriam* (the "human race") as a form of divine self-creation and so an imitation of God, particularly as the God of mind in history (in the Hegelian sense). This kind of hero also can be seen as the transfiguration of the vatic poet (who goes forward sanguine, beyond the tragic existentialism of the 1833–34 time).

The fifth stage—roughly the decade 1850–60—contains the main drift of Tennyson's thought, which can be seen as an extension of strategies developed during the fourth stage. Under the stimulus of new historical and metaphysical studies and a general sense that the material prosperity of the age carried the seeds of spiritual decline, Tennyson undertakes in the political poems, the Wellington ode, and *Maud* (chapter 6) to work with aspects of the cyclic decline of the human condition. The field of history becomes progressively anarchic. Divinity becomes a mysterious Universal Mind that works through human agents who, in war and self-discipline, bring a temporary ideal into realization. In the *Idylls* (chapters 7 and 8) a full range of men enlist themselves in the freedom of perfect service to wrench civilization out of anarchy. Once Camelot's full historical form is attained, however, the will to perfection flags and the makers of history fall away from the ideal into the "freedom" of the merely sensuous life. This "freedom" in turn brings a dissolution of historical form.

Chapter 9 deals with a sixth and final stage of Tennyson's philosophy of history as an underlying structure in three poems of the sixties. In "Enoch Arden," "Aylmer's Field," and "Lucretius," the historical cycle has come full tilt onto the natural field of chance and animal anarchy. Redemptive forces do not appear. Heroes embody debased social qualities and, accordingly, morbid suicidal proclivities. The epilogue (chapter 10) notes the fragmentation of Tennyson's philosophy of history into poems that confirm the hopelessness of contemporary history, that work with primal beginnings divorced from any context in current affairs, and that celebrate pure spirit, now totally disentangled from history.

It may be gratuitous to observe that no particular approach to a body of poems today seems canonical in this critically ecumenical age. The commentary that follows seeks to incorporate whatever appears appropriate to explain past "meanings" while remaining aware that present "significance" mediates the selectivity.[7] The literary work must be explained in terms of the conditions of its genesis, and yet also in terms of a great set of significances that have accrued since the very earliest interpretations. The work means both what the poet and what the audience thought it meant at the time it was written and what readers have thought it meant ever since. From this perspective, the work is an historical "event" whose nature is a continual interaction between its own imperatives and those of subsequent periods. The whole composes a kind of expanding *Weltanschauung*, which is "not a mere nexus of causes," to cite Hirsch's words about an integrity of thought without a direct intercourse, but "an organic system, a cultural selfhood with a logic and autonomy of its own."[8]

[7]The terms, of course, are from E. D. Hirsch, Jr., *Validity in Interpretation,* p. 8 passim.
[8]E. D. Hirsch, Jr., *Wordsworth and Schelling,* p. 5.

Tennyson and Clio

1 Clio at Somersby

ON THE EVIDENCE of his early poems, Tennyson as a youth was much inspired by providential, apocalyptic history: a Biblical God ordaining events, momentous battles, and the thoughts and acts of heroic warriors and kings at such moments. Some eighteen of the forty-five poems attributed to Tennyson in the 1827 *Poems by Two Brothers* were on such subjects, coming mostly from the Bible. Tennyson's "Armageddon" suggests his apocalyptic view of all human history: the "gathering of nations / Unto the mighty battle of the Lord," as he put it.[1] The apocalyptic moment seems useful to the young poet to carry three convictions: at such times, providence interjects itself into history most decisively, power is transferred from one nation to another, and passions well forth most abundantly for the literary palette. The corollary to these three ideas of a philosophy of history is that the poetic temperament is uniquely qualified to establish an intense empathy with such passions and, in this way, to understand the nature of God and of history.

It is a truism that the Biblical God is a God of history. "The very existence of a philosophy of history and its quest for a meaning," as Lowith points out, "is due to the history of salvation; it emerged from

---

[1] All of Tennyson's poetry quoted from Christopher Ricks, ed., *The Poems of Tennyson*. The composition and publication dates of poems are taken from this edition, except where noted.

the faith in an ultimate purpose."[2] There is no indication that the young Tennyson was deficient in this faith. In addition to such a conviction, however (as argued in the Introduction), an intellective understanding of history is necessary if a philosophy of history is to obtain. History was, in fact, a central part of a classical education at the time, and under the tutelage of his father Tennyson became a good scholar. He (and his brother) were pleased to exhibit their considerable historical learning in fashionably extensive footnotes to their work in the 1827 *Poems*.[3]

Dr. Tennyson was a "grim teacher, driving the boys hard" with "fierce concentration," as Charles Tennyson says, "but he was really fond of them and could be a delightful and stimulating companion."[4] The early education Tennyson received has been studied so well by Paden that there is no point in going over the same ground. Tennyson knew his Bible, of course, and he was familiar with the classical poets, particularly Horace and Vergil, with the great English figures of Shakespeare and Milton, and with modern poets like Byron, Moore, Scott, and "Ossian" (also with Sir William Jones). What is important here is that Tennyson also was familiar with the great historians: Herodotus, Tacitus, Xenophon, Suetonius, Rollin, Voltaire, Hume, Gibbon, and "travelers" like Savary. With regard to what can be called history in its mythic mode, Tennyson shows knowledge of the work of Jacob Bryant, Faber, and Davies.[5]

A study of Dr. Tennyson's library indicates "the Historians are almost fully represented," classical and modern, church histories, classical antiquities.[6] By a rough count, some 64 titles in that portion of Dr. Tennyson's library preserved at the Tennyson Research Centre are histories but, according to the sales catalogue at his death, it appears that at least 56 other titles were lost. These history books together made up 120 titles or nearly 300 separate volumes of historical writing.

But beyond the pedagogical imperative to historical knowledge and

[2] Karl Löwith, *Meaning in History*, p. 5.

[3] Thomas R. Lounsbury, *The Life and Times of Tennyson*, pp. 47–48, calls the boys' learning "multifarious"; they had been "omnivorous readers." W. D. Paden, *Tennyson in Egypt,* pp. 109–10, observes only that the boys "were well enough read in the polite literature." Jowett called Tennyson "very much of a scholar" (*Memoir,* 2:463).

[4] Sir Charles Tennyson, *Alfred Tennyson*, p. 31.

[5] See Paden, especially the Appendix, pp. 99–110.

[6] George Moore, "A Critical and Bibliographical Study of the Somersby Library of Doctor George Clayton Tennyson," pp. 12–21.

the library in which it is presumed that this was exercised, it might be assumed further that the Tennysons participated in the general interest in history in the period. Much historical writing of the eighteenth and nineteenth centuries—the work of Hume, Smollett, Gibbon, and Robertson particularly (all in Dr. Tennyson's library)—was popular to the point of being used as family entertainment. Emily Tennyson evokes a good time when she records in her journal for 1858 that Tennyson "begins reading Motley [*The Rise of the Dutch Republic*] to me. A feeling of the freshness of youth comes over me. History read aloud recalls the feeling of the days when my Father used to read it aloud to me & my sisters."[7] She also wrote in her "Narrative for Her Sons" that "in whatever respect I was fitted to be your Father's wife I owed it to my father who had so lovingly trained me by reading to me the best historians and poets and encouraging me to read them myself, and books of science and theology and all that could help life besides." She wrote elsewhere that in youth her favorite time of day had been the evening, from half-past eight to ten, when her father would read aloud from Gibbon, Macaulay's *Essays*, and the novels of Sir Walter Scott.[8] Such practices were common in the time.

People bought history books in large quantities and read them as if they were novels. These histories had enhanced literary qualities that brought the immediacy of the past into close juxtaposition with the concerns of the present. But in contrast to the Enlightenment "interest in universal man with its corollary of relative indifference to national history" and to the Augustan tendency to attribute "laws, states, religions, and art to rational design,"[9] these histories probed the mysterious inner workings of society, both collectively and individually. "The English historians of the second half of the eighteenth century, Hume, Gibbon, and others," an early nineteenth-century German historiographer wrote, "have become the models for the rest of Europe; their excellence is due to their attempt to live up to Tacitus's demand that the historian make history intelligible by penetrating into the condition of society and into the inner life of man."[10] In this, these historians were but preparing the "underlying historical premise of the

---

[7] Quoted from Emily Tennyson's unpublished "Journal 1850–74" at the Tennyson Research Centre, Lincoln, England by kind permission of Lord Tennyson and the Lincolnshire Library Service.

[8] James O. Hoge, "Emily Tennyson's Narrative for Her Sons," pp. 99–100, note 18.

[9] Sherman B. Barnes, "The Age of Enlightenment," p. 160.

[10] George H. Nadel, "Philosophy of History Before Historicism," p. 61. The quotation is a paraphrase of words by Ludwig Wachler.

historiography of Romanticism," which was, as a modern study shows, the "doctrine of the gradual and unconscious nature of cultural evolution in any nation. . . . Great emphasis was laid upon national traditions and the alleged 'ideas' which go to make up this spirit of the age and of the nation."[11]

The literary sensibility was peculiarly suited to achieving, through poetical feeling and imagination, an intense empathy with the ideas and passions of historical protagonists. And so people also bought large quantities of literary works and read them as if they were histories, or at least as works that brought genuine history to them. "Without belittling the great influence of Gibbon, Hume, and Robertson," writes a modern assessor of the "historical mind" in the nineteenth century, "it can rightly be said that the Romantic movement gave a strong impetus to interest in history in England and on the continent in the first half of the century and that the most important figure in this respect is Sir Walter Scott."[12] Carlyle noted in his 1838 essay "Sir Walter Scott" that Scott's "Historical Novels have taught all men this truth, which looks like a truism, and yet was as good as unknown to writers of history and others, till so taught: that the bygone ages of the world were actually filled by living men, not by protocols, state-papers, controversies and abstractions of man. . . . History will henceforth have to take thought of it. Her faint heresays of 'philosophy teaching by experience' will have to exchange themselves everywhere for direct inspection and embodiment."[13] Whether or not Carlyle exaggerates this Romantic break with the immediate past, at about the age of eleven Tennyson "fell under the spell of Scott's poetry and composed an epic of six thousand lines in the style of Marmion."[14] Tennyson himself recalled, "When I was 17 & my brother Charles 18 I wrote an Epic in three books. It was full of furious battles a la Scot. . . . I never felt so inspired."[15]

Tennyson felt this kind of history on the pulse, and it follows that a visionary capacity is required to realize it. A poet possesses this power in full measure, and Tennyson never doubted he should be a great poet, nor did his father who, as Tennyson relates, "thought so highly of my first essay that he prophesied I would be the greatest Poet of the

---

[11] Harry Elmer Barnes, *A History of Historical Writing*, p. 178.

[12] Richard A. E. Brooks, "The Development of the Historical Mind," p. 133.

[13] *The Works of Thomas Carlyle*, 16:160.

[14] Tennyson, *Alfred Tennyson*, p. 32.

[15] Trinity Notebook 0.15.34. All references to Trinity Notebooks are by kind permission of the Master and Fellows of Trinity College, Cambridge.

Time."[16] A poet for the time, in fact, was one of those "unacknowl-
edged legislators of the world," as Shelley wrote in "A Defense of
Poetry." He was one who not only plumbs to the heart of men's actions
but also formulates such truths in the only way they can be apprehended. "The mind of a poet of the highest order is the most perfect
that can belong to man," observed F. D. Maurice in 1828. (Maurice was
the founder of the "Apostles" whose company Tennyson would join
shortly in Cambridge.) He noted further that "There is no intellectual
power, and no state of feeling, which may not be the instrument of
poetry.... his mind is a mirror which catches and images the whole
scheme and working of the world. He comprehends all feelings.... He
cannot be untrue, for it is his high calling to interpret those universal
truths which exist on earth only in the forms of his creation."[17]

Tennyson always is credited with feelings of visionary power.
"Angels have talked with him, and showed him thrones," Tennyson
asserted in his 1830 "The Mystic"; "In intellect and power and will"
the poet hears "Time flowing in the middle of the night, / And all things
creeping to a day of doom." By this power the mystic poet enters that
last circle which "Investeth and ingirds all other lives," and especially
the lives of the past. In the poem "In deep and solemn dreams,"
probably begun at Somersby and finished at Cambridge, the poet comes
into virtual telepathic communication with the inhabitants of Alexandria
just before a disastrous invasion:[18]

All adown the busy ways
Come sunny faces of lost days,
Long to mouldering dust consigned,
Forms which live but in the mind.

Then methinks they stop and stand,
And take each by the hand,
And we speak ...

But the poet also sees the future. "Armageddon" dates probably from
Tennyson's fifteenth year and opens with an apostrophe to the

Spirit of Prophecy whose mighty grasp
Enfoldeth all things whose capacious soul

[16]Trinity Notebook 0.15.34.
[17]From *The Anthenaeum*, quoted by Paden, pp. 149–50.
[18]Identification with Alexandria by Paden, p. 147.

> Can people the illimitable abyss
> Of vast & unfathomless bottomless futurity
> With all the Giant Figures that shall pace
> The dimness of its stage.[19]

The young poet is standing, as a matter of fact, "upon the mountain which o'erlooks/The valley of Megiddo"—the traditional plain of decisive battles in Hebraic history. Here he encounters the anthropomorphic projection of his prophetic faculty, the "great Angel Mind." In its presence, his soul grows "godlike" and "winged with knowledge and the strength/Of holy musings and immense Ideas" as he faces the "annihilating anarchy/Of unimaginable war." His every sense "thrillingly distinct and keen," the poet even obtains insight into extraterrestrial life, "the hum of men/Or other things talking in unknown tongues,/And notes of busy Life in distant worlds."

"Hail holy Light," Tennyson in effect says with Milton. Tennyson sees working in the world the Biblical divinity whose history, as Rollin (from whose work Tennyson took most of his subjects) observed, "proclaims universally the greatness of the Almighty, his power, his justice, and above all, the admirable wisdom with which his providence governs the universe." It is plain that "God disposes all events as supreme lord and sovereign; that he alone determines the fate of kings and the duration of empires; and that he, for reasons inscrutable to all but himself, transfers the government of kingdoms from one nation to another."[20]

The early poems demonstrate Tennyson's full faith in this Old Testament God of history and of dreadful apocalypse. The prophet Ezekiel tells Nebuchadrezzar in "God's Denunciations against Pharaoh-Hophra" that the "Lord leads thee on . . . thy guide" to such slaughter that the Nile's "stream shall be red/With the blood that shall gush o'er thy billowy bed." Titus works with a similar commission in "The Fall of Jerusalem" so that there remains "not one stone above another"; "Signs on earth and signs on high," the poet tells Jerusalem, "Prophesied thy destiny." Over the poem "The High-Priest to Alexander" brood the lines "Bloodshed in the whole globe of the earth,/Arms, fury, and new war,"[21] yet Alexander is the agent of the Lord in such a scenario. The *vates* of the poem shows him that his conquest of four empires had been

---

[19] From Trinity Notebook 0.15.18.
[20] Charles Rollin, *Ancient History*, 1: iii.
[21] Translation given by Ricks, ed., *Poems of Tennyson*, p. 139.

predicted by the prophet Daniel. He is encouraged with, "Go forth, thou man of force!/The world is all thine own." But, the prophet warns Alexander, "spare Jerusalem./For the God of gods, which liveth/Through all eternity,/'Tis he alone which giveth/And taketh victory."

The early poems also demonstrate Tennyson's belief in God's transfer of power from one nation to another without any particular progressivism being involved. Such a notion of the historical process is in the mainstream of Christian thought. Critics sometimes represent the Judaic-Christian vision of history as progressive and (thus) exhilarating and the Greco-Roman as cyclic and (therefore) depressing and pessimistic. But the idea of disastrous cyclicity always has gone along comfortably with millenarianism. To Thomas Browne, for example,

> All cannot be happy at once, for because the glory of one State depends upon the ruine of another, there is a revolution and vicissitude of their greatness, and must obey the swing of that wheele, not moved by intelligences, but by the hand of God, whereby all Estates arise to their Zenith and vertical points, according to their predestined periods. For the lives not onely of men, but of Commonweales, and the whole world, run not upon an Helix that still enlargeth, but on a Circle, where arriving to their Meridian, they decline in obscurity, and fall under the Horizon againe.[22]

And so go the nations in Tennyson's early poems. In the 1827 "Persia," just as Persia's "thunder" once had rolled "O'er lone Assyria's crownless head," so now "stormy Macedonia swept/Thine honours from thee one and all." Here, Alexander is contrasted with Cyrus, "the one founder, the other destroyer, of the powerful empire of Persia," as Rollin observed in his *Ancient History*.[23] Nadir Shah and Persia triumph as India is "bowed to the dust of the plain" in the poem "The Expedition of Nadir Shah into Hindostan." Spain conquers Peru in the "Lamentation of the Peruvians." In "The Druid's Prophecies," Rome raises the "eagles of her haughty power" over the Druids, but "Soon shall come her darkening hour" when the Goths will "leave their frozen regions,/Where Scandinavia's wilds extend;/And Rome, though girt with

[22] L. C. Martin, ed., *Religio Medici and other Works* (Oxford: Oxford University Press, 1964), p. 18.

[23] Quoted by Paden, p. 29.

dazzling legions,/Beneath their blasting power shall bend." Nations rise and fall and, as Browne noted, "the glory of one State depends upon the ruine of another."

With such an inscrutable God ordaining, in Tennyson's view, an equally mysterious chain of national cycles, it but remains to examine the third fundamental idea of his philosophy of history in this youthful period: the role of man in the providential scheme, specifically his function in the transfer of power from one nation to the other. There are so many references to pride in Tennyson's early poems that we might see him working with a kind of historical irony, almost a sacred version of the "private vices-public benefits" formula. Cyrus has a "proud spirit" yet Alexander, God's special chosen, is "doubly proud." Pizarro dwells "in the halls of thy pride." Caesar "sits in glory,/ Enthroned on thine hills of pride" in the poem "The Druid's Prophecies." Tennyson's footnote in "God's Denunciations against Pharaoh-Hophra" refers to Egypt's "vain and foolish pride." But because such heroes, in the paradoxical freedom they enjoy within God's omniscient plan, are unwitting weavers of the divine fabric, Tennyson unsurprisingly is reserved about any judgments to be passed on historical conduct. To begin with, for the most part he uses persona to utter any denunciations that seem to be in order. For another, the heroes are attended too closely with transcendent omens for their ruthlessness to be condemned summarily. Finally, a sense of heroic tragedy attends historical protagonists as they carry out their national destinies. Thus, although their conduct is fearsome, it is also ambiguously "admirable."

In the "Lamentation of the Peruvians" Pizarro seems to be condemned, cursed for "crimes and thy murders" (and presumably for using cannon, like Satan in *Paradise Lost*): "foully ye threw/Your dark shots of death on the sons of Peru." But, then, the speaker is a Peruvian and naturally he would feel this way; besides, he asks the heavens:

> Why blew ye, ye gales, when the murderer came?
> Why fanned ye the fire, and why fed ye the flame?
> Why sped ye his sails o'er the ocean so blue?
> Are ye also combined for the fall of Peru?

Sadly, the answer would seem to be, yes, considering the providential scheme. The speaker asserts to Pizarro that "remorse to thy grief-stricken conscience shall cling" but we may presume to doubt the truth of the matter.

In "The Fall of Jerusalem" Ezekiel reviles neither Titus nor Rome "whose sway/All the tribes of earth obey." In the poem "Mithridates Presenting Berenice with the Cup of Poison," this fiercest of Rome's antagonists does not vilify "Proud Rome's triumphal car" even though he and Berenice by death are avoiding "slavery's pangs and tearful anguish." The native speaker in "The Expedition of Nadir Shah into Hindostan" calls the Persian monarch's hosts the "fiends of destruction" with a "vulture behind them." He also terms them "the dauntless, the bold" and notes something akin to the Peruvian's sense of aerial transcendence: "the spirits of death, and the demons of wrath,/Wave the gloom of their wings o'er their desolate path." Some of the emperors in "The Druid's Prophecies" are blamed but others are praised. Nero is depicted as "by heartless anguish driven," but Rome's eastward conquests are carried by "Five brilliant stars": "The five good Emperors," as Tennyson's footnote reads, "Nerva, Trajan, Adrian, Antoninus Pius, and Marcus Aurelius."[24] And the last Caesars are merely "hapless monarchs" who "fall together,/Like leaves in winter's stormy ire," in what could be taken as a reference to the naturalness of it all. All the Caesars are subsumed more or less indifferently under the cultural development that is Rome, with its destiny to fulfill.

Such heroes engage the divine intent willfully, conquer as the occasion arises, and of course suffer conquest and death when their turn comes to leave the stage. Paden argues that these poems show that "aggression is almost always connected, not with triumph, but with suffering, despairing revolt, or certain death," and that aggression is always (except in the case of Alexander) connected with "remorse."[25] It is hard to see this. Heroes enact historical roles beyond their understanding, and they do so with no particular emotions save those attributed to them by the unreliable personae of the poems. They simply indulge their pride and power with a certain exaltation over the monumentality of their deeds. In "The Old Sword," the poet evokes associations that are hardly remorseful. To the weapon clings the memory of "triumph's fierce delight,/The shoutings of the victory." With it, the warrior had "cloven his foes in wrath" so that "heroes' blood was spilt." On it, writes the poet, is "venerable rust." In the poem "The Vale of Bones," the speaker is fairly ecstatic over the heroic memories of the battleground. "Ye would not change the narrow

[24] Quoted by Ricks, ed., *Poems of Tennyson*, p. 107.
[25] Paden, pp. 74, 75.

space," he tells the fallen heroes, "For realms, for scepters, or for thrones." In the poem "The Old Chieftain," the warrior says that in his "bosom proudly dwells/The memory of the days of old,"

> When our enemies sunk from our eyes as the snow
>   Which falls down the stream in the dell,
> When each word that I spake was the death of a foe,
>   And each note of my harp was his knell.

The ones who are remorseful are the losers, and we may presume that they would be as exalted as the Old Chieftain had they won the battle.

Even when they know, or may suspect, their own wretched deaths, heroes are consoled by the glory of their enterprises. They may not be aware that they are furthering the development of providential history, but we may assume that Tennyson's approbation results from his own understanding of their role as divine agents. In "King Charles's Vision," the monarch is shown the usual pictures of bloody historical success (and his own death), but Tennyson caps his career with, "Yet in every clime, through the lapse of all time,/Shall my glorious conquests be known." In the early poem "Alexander," this "Warrior of God" secures his dread mission from the Chamian Oracle of "unapproached mysteries." Upon learning the extent of the warfare in which he will engage on behalf of divinity (even, we may presume, his own fate in the process), Alexander is simply exalted by the "High things" that "were spoken there . . . from the secret shrine/Returning with hot cheek and kindled eyes." This reaction is consistent with Tennyson's attitude throughout these poems. Why should not furthering God's design kindle his eyes? As Rollin had observed in the *Ancient History*, Alexander "was, like Cyrus, the minister and instrument of the Sovereign Disposer of empires." As in the case of all such ministers and instruments, this "Power conducted their enterprises, assured them of success, protected and preserved them from all dangers, till they had executed their commission."[26]

Tennyson also entered the mind of a collective hero in the intriguing ninety-odd lines he wrote on Napoleon's retreat from Moscow (in a notebook watermarked 1823). The Russian soldiers together make up the national culture opposed to Napoleon, who is beaten by the superior strength of a collective will. This is the hallmark of the Romantic sense of history, the sense that it is the inner spirit of man

---

[26]Quoted by Paden, p. 28.

within the context of national traditions that moves the affairs of men. Napoleon's "eye shall quail/Before a fierce frown" (initially "sterner frown" in the manuscript), and the victory of Russian spirit will go "thrilling thro'/Ages on Ages of undying fame" as a type of reservoir of heroic potentials. In the victors,

> There was a thought of former Victory
> A hope of future. All the trophied Past.
> The days of flowing Conquest thick and fast
> And brilliantly on the expanded brain
> Came flashing thro' the Night of thought again.[27]

The "expanded brain" of the soldiers in contact with their cultural past is much like that of the speaker in "Armageddon" who says, "My mental eye grew large/With such a vast circumference of thought . . ." In addition, the fire imagery suggested by the "flashing thro' the Night of thought" is similar to "Armageddon"'s reference to the poet becoming a "scintillation of Eternal Mind,/Remixed and burning with its parent fires." We might almost equate the Christian God of history with his own objectification in this "trophied Past," insofar as the inner life of historical man intuits the providential intent.

In these early poems, Tennyson may be indicating that for him pageantry, high passion, and monumentality possess the brightest colors on the literary canvas. But he also takes pride in an exact knowledge of of his subject matter and, further, looks without squeamishness or illusions upon the ordained ways of the world (unless Christian orthodoxy is taken for illusion). He wants to understand history. And in this understanding, as it is revealed in these early poems, we may see the basic characteristics of Tennyson's philosophy of history. A divinity of some sort is working out its nature in history. History is occurring in apocalyptic cycles. The hero, either as individual or as collective spirit, somehow is a "free" agent of this divinity.

Significantly, he wrote no poems on pious or undocumentable historical themes (like Jesus and Herod, for example), nor was he tendentious about the dreadful scenes he portrays, merely accurate. He also wrote no poems on mythological subjects, either of Christian, Greco-Roman, or modernist persuasions. This may seem surprising in light of his knowledge, as Paden shows, of such new Helio-Arkite

---

[27]Trinity Notebook 0.15.19. This poem is printed in full by Ricks, *Times Literary Supplement*, 21 August 1969.

theories as those in Bryant's *New System, or, an Analysis of Ancient Mythology* or Faber's *The Origin of Pagan Idolatry*.[28] For his poems he is not yet interested in such diffused figures of myth and legend as Arthur, even though Tennyson noted that "when little more than a boy, I first lighted upon Malory" (*Memoir*, 2:128). This disinclination to myth was to change when he went to Cambridge, however, and his philosophy of history was to undergo considerable refinement.

[28] See the references in Paden's Index and in chapter 6.

II Clio at Cambridge

TENNYSON WENT TO Cambridge in November of 1827 and he found formal study there "so uninteresting, so much matter of fact" (*Memoir*, 1:33–34). His suppressed sonnet "Lines on Cambridge of 1830" indicts those "that do profess to teach/And teach us nothing, feeding not the heart." It was a different matter among the company of the "Apostles" where, as Buckley observes, he "obtained his real education." His fellow Apostle, Kemble, claimed, "To my *education* given in that society I feel that I owe every power I possess."[1] In a context of intense Apostolic interest in history, Tennyson's basic philosophy of history underwent confirmation and sophistication. Here, he found a sanction for visionary empathy as a mode of thought. His belief in God's superintendence of the historical process was confirmed, but he now encountered a crucial distinction between active and ordinary providence: between divine potentials available for spiritual and, therefore, societal progress and the natural forces available for mere growth and decay. And under the impress of the age's new respect for myth, Tennyson's heroes became figures in a special kind of historical symbolism. Tennyson's early (and suppressed) poems "Timbuctoo" and

[1] Buckley's observation and Kemble's words in Jerome Hamilton Buckley, *Tennyson: The Growth of a Poet,* p. 28. Peter Allen shows how little Tennyson attended formal Apostolic gatherings, "as distinguished from the almost daily gatherings in one man's or another's room," but concludes that Tennyson "was greatly influenced by some of the Apostles' characteristic ideas" (*Cambridge Apostles,* pp. 133–35).

"The Hesperides" (both 1829-30) contain these new perceptions in imperfect form, yet we may see in them the frame of reference that would stay with Tennyson throughout his life.

The "Apostles" was one of several clubs formed at Cambridge after 1815 under the stimulus of the "many questions, political, religious and literary, which were agitating the youth of the day."[2] Their leadership during Tennyson's time was in the hands of Julius Hare and Connop Thirlwall (successors to the founders, John Sterling and F. D. Maurice). At this time Hare and Thirlwall "were probably the only Englishmen thoroughly well versed in the literature of Germany"; whatever Hare "wrote or thought was coloured through and through with German research and speculation."[3] Under these mentors "Coleridge and Wordsworth were our special divinities," wrote the Apostle Merivale, "and Hare and Thirlwall were regarded as their prophets." Merivale mentions also how these prophets led them to a "lofty pedestal for Kant and Goethe."[4] Edward Fitzgerald wrote of how "College Days, when the German School, with Coleridge, Julius Hare, etc., to expound, came to reform all our notions."[5]

But among them, even more than Coleridge, Wordsworth, Kant, or Goethe, the great German historian Barthold Niebuhr was the "god, who for a lengthy period formed all their sentiments."[6] The "first commanding figure in modern historiography, the scholar who raised history from a subordinate place to the dignity of an independent science, the noble personality in whom the greatest historians of the succeeding generation found their model or their inspiration,"[7] Niebuhr was an inspiration to the Apostles as well. Hare and Thirlwall translated his seminal *The History of Rome*, Thirlwall was preparing a *History of Greece,* Merivale a *History of the Romans under the Empire*, and Kemble was on his way to becoming a leading authority on Anglo-Saxon history and literature. Beyond this immediate circle, Hare and Thirlwall

---

[2] Sir Charles Tennyson, *Alfred Tennyson*, p. 67. Many debating clubs, no doubt the Apostles among them, were stimulated by the zest of wringing from the authorities concessions for freedom of discussion. In 1817, for example, the vice chancellor dispersed the Union Society (est. 1814) and it did not meet again until 1821. Not until Tennyson's time at Cambridge was debate permitted without hindrance. See D. A. Winstanley, *Early Victorian Cambridge* (Cambridge: At the University Press, 1955), pp. 25-27.

[3] "Archdeacon Hare's Last Charge," *Quarterly Review* 97 (1855): 17-18.

[4] Quoted by Harold Nicolson, *Tennyson: Aspects of his Life, Character, and Poetry*, p. 73.

[5] In his annotated copy of volume 1 of Tennyson's 1842 *Poems*, p. 144: Cambridge University Library listing Adv d/11/26. See also *Memoir*, 1:36.

[6] Frances M. Brookfield, *The Cambridge "Apostles,"* p. 8.

[7] G. P. Gooch, *History and Historians in the Nineteenth Century*, p. 14.

were members of what was later to be called the "Liberal Anglican" school of history. It consisted of Hare, Thirlwall, Thomas Arnold, H. H. Milman, Richard Whately, and A. P. Stanley,[8] all devoted followers of Niebuhr, whom they saw as the guide to both advanced Germanic speculation and Broad Church Anglican theology.[9]

Out of what we may assume was an excitement about providential history in the making, some of the Apostles even became active revolutionaries (outside of England of course). Tennyson, who in 1827 had composed "Written During the Convulsions in Spain," went with Hallam to the Pyrenees in the summer of 1830 to deliver money to rebels against the brutal King Ferdinand VII. Both could have lost their lives. In November, 1831, Sterling's cousin Boyd and a few other enthusiasts did lose theirs, shot in Spain with the liberal leader Torrijos and fifty native revolutionaries. For a time it was feared that John Kemble—the "soldier-Priest" of Tennyson's 1829-30 sonnet "To J. M. K."—was a member of this company (*Memoir*, 1:51-54).

Niebuhr's religious cast of mind, his wide learning and scientific rigor, and the new methodology he formulated were intensely stimulating, whether applied to Biblical or to secular historical documentation. That Tennyson was aware of the former might be gathered from his mid-century remark to Jowett that "the true origin of modern Biblical Criticism was to be ascribed not to Strauss, but to Niebuhr, who lived a generation earlier" (*Memoir*, 1:36). His awareness of the latter might be deduced from the relationship between certain Niebuhrian sentiments and Tennysonian attitudes in those poems involving a visionary empathy with the passions of the past. This empathy has been described in chapter 1 as a corollary to Tennyson's philosophy of history. Indeed, Niebuhr's celebrated method of understanding history grew out of so passionate an identity with the past that his critics complained of it as an "occult faculty of historical divination."[10] "When a historian is

---

[8] See Duncan Forbes, *The Liberal Anglican Idea of History*. For a general survey of German historical thought in England, see Klaus Dockhorn, *Der deutsche Historismus in England* (Göttingen: Vandenhoeck & Ruprecht; Baltimore: Johns Hopkins, 1950).

[9] "Hare, Thirlwall, and Arnold were the earliest English defenders of Niebuhr's ideas": "As clergyman of the Broad Church persuasion, they were searching for a *via media* between the 'bibliolatry' of the evangelicals and the dogmatic pronouncements of the High Church party. It seemed to them that Niebuhr's philological method provided the basis for a proper study of the biblical narratives. As classical philologists they were in a position to judge Niebuhr's competence and respect his achievements. As disciples of Coleridge and Burke, they applauded a writer who spoke of himself as a 'German Burkean' and took pains to emphasize the spiritual welfare as well as the material well-being of the nation" (Robert Preyer, *Bentham, Coleridge, and the Science of History*, p. 33).

[10] Gooch, p. 20.

reviving former times," Niebuhr wrote, "his interest in them and sympathy with them will be the deeper, the greater the events he has witnessed with a bleeding or a rejoicing heart . . . as it all were going on before his eyes," and "when he is thus moved his lips speak, although Hecuba is nothing to the player."[11] His disciple Thomas Arnold wrote similarly of "that sense of reality about the Romans—that living in a manner amongst them, and having them and their life distinctly before our eyes—which appears to me so indispensable to one who would write their history."[12]

Tennyson's 1829 "The Idealist" addresses just such an "interchangeable supremacy" (in the phrase of that "special divinity" of the Apostle, Wordsworth: *The Prelude*, XIV, 84) between the historical past and the perceiving imagination: "I am the spirit of a man,/I weave the universe,/And indivisible divide,/Creating all I hear and see." In this poem, Tennyson runs through the natural objects of Wordsworth's "Tintern Abbey"—sun, ocean, air, sky—but then significantly adds the historical dimension:

> I am the earth, the stars, the sun,
> I am the clouds, the sea.
> I am the citadels and palaces
> Of all great cities: I am Rome,
> Tadmor, and Cairo: I am Place
> And Time, yet is my home
> Eternity . . .

It was in such a context that Tennyson touched up the Somersby poem "In deep and solemn dreams," in which the poet sees in his mind "sunny faces of lost days" and he takes "each by the hand,/And we speak."

This visionary ontology may be said to have a natural home at Cambridge, long a center for Neoplatonic thought. Wellek observes that the three ideas he regards as typical of Romantic thought—organic nature, creative imagination, poetry as prophecy—have descended "from Neoplatonism through Giordano Bruno, Boehme, the Cambridge Platonists, and some passages in Shaftesbury."[13] And "beginning about 1790," Harper observes, "Taylor's translations were responsible for a

---

[11] Barthold Georg Niebuhr, *The History of Rome*, 1: xiii.

[12] Arthur Penrhyn Stanley, *The Life and Correspondence of Thomas Arnold, D.D.*, 1:52.

[13] René Wellek, "The Concept of 'Romanticism' in Literary History," p. 171.

'revival of Platonic studies' in Cambridge, the traditional home of Platonism in England."[14] In a study of this Platonic tradition, Inge points out that, along with F. D. Maurice, Julius Hare "was a worthy successor of the Cambridge Platonists. He laid great emphasis in his sermons on the work of the Holy Spirit." Inge further observes the close relationship between Plato the religious mystic and Plato the social reformer.[15] Such a combination also was characteristic of Maurice, the founder of the Apostles and later one of the founders of the Christian Socialist movement. Later still, in the fifties, Maurice became one of Tennyson's closest and most valued friends.

"That Tennyson was something of a mystic has long been a critical commonplace," notes Benziger in associating him with "religions of the inner light."[16] But Tennyson was vehement about the intellective nature of his visionary state: "By God Almighty, there is no delusion in the matter! It is no nebulous ecstasy, but a state of transcendent wonder, associated with absolute clearness of mind." Tyndall describes Tennyson's mysticism as "that 'union with God' which was described by Plotinus and Porphry" (*Memoir*, 2:473–74). The "candle of the Lord" for the Cambridge Platonists of the seventeenth century was a revelation of the infinite "reason" about mankind not confined to the pages of Holy Writ.[17] And Plotinus himself, translated by Taylor in the 1790s, wrote that "eternity is a deity shining and unfolding himself in intelligible light."[18]

Such intuitionism, combined, unparadoxically, with rigorous learning, was characteristic for the period. It was often described in fire-and-light imagery. Carlyle, for instance, described his best thinking as a "blazing, radiant insight into fact, blazing, burning interested about it."[19] Charles Tennyson writes that Jowett "grasped truth intuitively, apprehending one aspect of it after another, but making little effort to trace their logical connexion—'I put down my thoughts like sparks,' he once wrote, 'and let them run into one another'."[20] Prophetic insight

---

[14] George Mills Harper, *The Neoplatonism of William Blake*, p. 13. See also John H. Muirhead, *Coleridge as Philosopher*, p. 38.

[15] William Ralph Inge, *The Platonic Tradition in English Religious Thought*, pp. 95, 96–97.

[16] James Benziger, *Images of Eternity*, p. 141.

[17] See, for instance, the brief description in Basil Willey, *The Seventeenth Century Background*, pp. 133–38.

[18] The seventh treatise of the third Ennead: given by Harper, pp. 135–36.

[19] Quoted in James Anthony Froude, *Thomas Carlyle: A History of His Life in London 1834–1881*, 1:197.

[20] Tennyson, *Alfred Tennyson*, p. 267. G. Wilson Knight notes some spark-as-intuition imagery in Byron, Browning, and Arnold in "'The Scholar Gipsy': An Interpretation," *Review*

in Tennyson's poems was often suggested by the same imagery. The poet in "Armageddon" was in revelation a "scintillation of Eternal Mind,/Remixing and burning with its parent fire." In "Timbuctoo" he possessed "a maze of piercing, trackless, thrilling thoughts,/Involving and embracing each with each,/Rapid as fire, inextricably linked." In Tennyson's 1830–32 "Oenone," a "fire dances" before "wild Cassandra" in the throes of prophecy. Nor is such a mode of "mythic thinking" unrelated to the understanding of the historical imagination today.[21]

Not only was Tennyson's visionary intellection confirmed, his early belief in providential history, the first element in his philosophy of history, also was verified in the Apostolic circle. Niebuhr, the Apostles, and the Liberal Anglican historians alike saw a transcendent purpose as an unquestionable reality in history; without it history was meaningless. Niebuhr almost repeats Augustine's words when he observes, "All the virtues of the state and of the people would have been ineffectual, unless destiny had saved Rome in her perils. . . . these are the events in which we cannot but recognize the finger of God. . . . the union of the Roman world was necessary to the spreading of religion."[22] But providence is of two types: active and ordinary.[23] Active providence had been much in evidence as a special dispensation in the early ages of the world, in the Christian revelation, and in miracles. It is present now in extraordinary events like earthquakes and plague and in such historical events as the outcome of the Punic Wars (necessary for Roman hegemony) and Napoleon's retreat from Moscow.

Ordinary providence, on the other hand, covers the laws of nature at large and such racial and geographical differences as explain national

---

of *English Studies* 6 (1955): 57-58. The scholar gipsy waits the "spark from heaven" (l. 120).

[21] "All genuine historical reflection, instead of losing itself in contemplation of the merely singular and nonrecurrent, must strive, like the morphological thought of Goethe, to find those 'pregnant' moments in the course of events where, as in focal points, whole series of occurrences are epitomized" (Ernst Cassirer, *Language and Myth,* p. 27). Such thinking is to occur in what Langer points out is Cassirer's "mythic" mode of thought, wherein an "intense feeling is spontaneously expressed in a symbol, an image seen in something or formed for the mind's eye by the excited imagination" (Susanne K. Langer, "On Cassirer's Theory of Language and Myth," p. 395). As R. G. Collingwood said some time ago, the historical imagination is "properly not ornamental but structural" (*The Idea of History,* p. 241).

[22] Niebuhr, *History of Rome,* 1:xxviii. Consider Augustine: "The cause, then, of the greatness of the Roman empire is neither fortuitous nor fatal. . . . In a word, human kingdoms are established by divine providence. [Through Rome] God was pleased to conquer the whole world, and subdue it far and wide by bringing it into one fellowship of government and laws" (Marcus Dods, trans. and ed., *The City of God,* 2 vols. [New York: Hafner, 1948], 1:177-78, 2:241).

[23] See Forbes, pp. 72-73.

character and circumstance in history. On this plane, the nation transcribes laws of normal history or the whole cycle of a nation's existence as merely a "natural" phenomenon. Man can lift his collective life out of nature, however, by tapping the powers of active providence. As Hare wrote, "It is the idea of God that lifts us out of the eddying flux and reflux of time,"[24] but "when a nation loses its hold on religion it collapses back into the natural cycles of growth and decay, and, like a plant, dies inevitably."[25] It dies on the level of ordinary providence whose laws a nation must, nevertheless, determine and observe reverently, for they too are part of the providential scheme of things.

The historical process is informed by this complex, Janus-like divinity. Progress in general, salvation in extraordinary historical circumstances, and thrusts upward out of the welter of the merely natural are all spiritual efforts that tap the potentials of active providence. Without this spiritual effort, a collective life transcribes merely organic form on the level of ordinary providence. But, given man's flawed nature, spiritual effort flags; the nation then sinks into the natural life. Misunderstanding may exist over the organic metaphor used here, for it may suggest an implicit inevitability. The Liberal Anglican historians, however, took pains to elucidate the notion that with effort and resolve man can transcend the entrapment of deterministic process. The "corporeal analogy," wrote Stanley in an 1840 essay, was an "error"; what was "truth" was the "moral analogy which forms the basis of belief in a national providence"; this "furnishes a complete answer to the error which would substitute for it belief in a national fatalism."[26] Burkean ideals of organic change were gaining acceptance both generally and among the Apostles.[27] These ideals agree entirely with Liberal Anglican positions, particularly two of them: that the state was the "known march of the ordinary Providence of God" and that the counter-dynamic was Original Sin.[28] But man is free to choose between the ways. Nothing is inevitable.

---

[24] Quoted by Forbes, p. 83.

[25] Forbes, p. 98.

[26] Quoted by Forbes, p. 58.

[27] See note 9 above. Jerome Hamilton Buckley, *The Victorian Temper*, p. 74, suggests that Burke's ideas came to Tennyson especially through the Apostle Spedding.

[28] The quoted words are from Frederick L. Mulhauser, "The Tradition of Burke," p. 162, citing Burke's "Letters on a Regicide Peace." Mulhauser also quotes C. Crane Brinton as saying that Burke "fully accepts the pessimistic Christian doctrine of original sin" (p. 160). Clyde de L. Ryals credits Tennyson with a tenet of "Original Sin" (*From the Great Deep*, p. 198).

Given the proposition that history occurs in cycles because of man's flawed nature (the second idea of Tennyson's philosophy of history), there would be and was in Niebuhr and for the Liberal Anglicans a basic antipathy to the idea of inevitable progress. It follows that they disliked the French philosophes in particular. Niebuhr condemned their atheism, abstract intellectualizing, and ideas of mechanical "Progressivism," while the Liberal Anglicans and the Apostles rejected French "organic" history. They had no quarrel with the concept, given in Voltaire's *Essay on Manners*, of "Mind in History" as the total inner life manifesting itself in the growth of religion, art, science, and philosophy—as humanity seeking a consciousness of itself. But irresistible growth through scientifically determinable law was hateful to them because the implicit determinism denied God's providence and the freedom of the human will.[29] We cannot extrapolate too much from the course of history, argued Hare: "Even if we assume the human race to have been constantly advancing or receding hitherto, this will not warrant a conclusion that it must necessarily continue to move in the same direction hereafter; for that it may have just reacht a tropical point, and may be verging on its perihelion, or its aphelion, from which its course would be reverst."[30] The Liberal Anglicans were not to be persuaded of inevitable "progress" in universal history.[31] Accordingly, as Forbes summarizes the Liberal Anglican positions, "'Civilization' and the 'March of Mind' were assumptions which the Liberal Anglicans could

[29] Cassirer confirms this Apostolic judgment in summarizing Voltaire's view of historiography: "The natural scientist and the historian have the same task; amid the confusion and flux of phenomena they seek the hidden law. Neither in history nor in natural science is this law to be considered as a divine plan" (*The Philosophy of the Enlightenment*, p. 220).

[30] [Julius Charles and Augustus William Hare], *Guesses at Truth by Two Brothers*, p. 337. This volume was published first in 1827 and was revised and enlarged in 1838. Much new material was added for the second series in 1848 (in the edition I cite, that of 1897, the second series begins on p. 291—hence the difficulty of locating data precisely). This work is characterized by René Wellek as "an early influential miscellany which shows considerable knowledge of German philology and philosophy" (*Confrontations*, p. 198).

[31] Today, speculative philosophers of history and historians of a religious persuasion are dubious that "progress" is a meaningful term. Toynbee, for example, is sceptical that "a set of objective criteria for the measurement of the progress of civilization" is obtainable, it being his belief that "every judgment of progress, in whatever field, is subjective intrinsically and incurably" (*A Study of History*, 12:267). Jaspers says that "there is progress in knowledge, in technology, in the prerequisites for new human possibilities, but not in the substance of humanity. Progress in substance is refuted by the facts. The peoples which had reached the highest levels perished, succumbing to those inferior to them" (*The Origin and Goal of History*, p. 252). Compare Hare's awareness of this relativity of standards: even when men surpassed their ancestors, "they deemed that the accessions in wealth or knowledge were more than counterbalanced by the decay of the integrity, simplicity, and energy" of man (*Guesses*, p. 314).

not accept, because they dispensed with God's Providence."[32] The various Apostolic and Tennysonian expressions of disdain for the progress-oriented Saint Simonists during the crisis-period 1830–32 are well documented.[33]

Besides, the very idea of periodicity was becoming deeply held. Warton's neoclassic progression (ages of imagination, reason plus imagination, and then reason) underlies the notion of cyclically alternating periods in a nation's history as found in the critical writing of men like Hazlitt, Southey, De Quincey, and Peacock. Hallam in his 1831 review of Tennyson's *Poems, Chiefly Lyrical* deals with an implicit cyclicity when he speaks of "youthful periods" of literature and then of a "period of degradation."[34] Also entering this general understanding of cycles in the time were the influential ideas of Vico, who influenced Burke through Shaftesbury. Hare, Thirlwall, Arnold, and other Broad Church leaders knew Vico's work, as did Coleridge, who disseminated his ideas.[35] In Vico's thought, the historical cycle consists of "successive ages of gods, heroes, and men." Providence is behind it all, but man's freedom is given in the concept of "course and recourse," a kind of trial before an anthropomorphic judge, the overseer of providential history.[36]

Man in this process (the third idea in Tennyson's developing philosophy of history) may engage the divine potentials of a providential imperative either singly or collectively. "Whenever any of the great changes ordained by God's Providence in the destinies of mankind are about to take place," wrote Hare, "the means requisite for the affecting of those changes are likewise prepared by the same Providence." These means may consist of individual heroes but, as Hare noted further, the means may also be "learning" in general (and archeological discoveries

---

[32] Forbes, p. 8.

[33] The views of various Apostles, including Tennyson, on the St. Simonians are given by John Kilham, *Tennyson and "The Princess,"* pp. 24–27.

[34] Given in *Tennyson: The Critical Heritage*, pp. 40–42.

[35] In 1831, Hare and Thirlwall founded the short-lived journal *The Philological Museum*, which, in 1833, printed a long article by John Kentrick on Vico that was the "best exposition and criticism of Vico's doctrines in English prior to Flint's book in 1884" (Max Harold Fisch and Thomas Goddard Bergin, "Introduction," *The Autobiography of Giambattista Vico*, p. 87; this Introduction contains a description of Vico's general influence in England). See also Forbes, pp. 154–58. Arnold called Vico "profound" in a work of 1830 ("Appendix I," *The History of the Peloponnesian War, by Thucydides* [Oxford: Parker, 1840], p. 504).

[36] Giambattista Vico, *The New Science of Giambattista Vico*, pp. 335, 336. Vico's providence and the mechanics of his cycle are in line with other concepts of the eighteenth century: his idea of the partnership between man and providence is "closely akin to B. Mandeville's thesis set forth in his *Fable of the Bees: Private Vices, Public Benefits* (1714)" and is not unrelated to Adam Smith's "invisible hand" (Giorgio Tagliacozzo, ed., *Giambattista Vico: An International Symposium* [Baltimore: Johns Hopkins, 1969], p. 73).

specifically). He cites Niebuhr's thinking that "many remains of Antiquity have been brought to light, as Providential dispensations for the increase of our knowledge of God's works, and of His creatures."[37] The conceptual drift here is from change effected by the individual hero to change brought about by the group, even by the "people."

Then too, the age was no longer content with a simple identification of mythic figures and historical heroes. Manuel argues that the "Vichian theory broke the limits of Euhemerism and bordered on historical allegory, a new symbolism. Myth was at once the language of primitive man and a hieroglyphic record of major developments in the history of humanity."[38] "Every ancient gentile nation had a Hercules as its founder," claimed Vico, with Hercules the "heroic character of the founder of peoples."[39] Vico influenced Wolf, who in 1795 argued for the collective authorship of Homer (insofar as the *Iliad* resembled folk epics, Homer was the Greek "people"). And in about 1810 Niebuhr himself became convinced of the collective authorship of early legends, ballads, and poetry.[40] Grote called the heroes of myth and legend the "popularized expression of the divine and heroic faith of the people."[41] Insofar as "Westcott may be considered a follower of Maurice,"[42] Westcott's assessment of the significance of myth also bears on the Apostolic understanding: "the myths were accepted by common consent as the text for the deepest speculations of the later Platonic schools, and so have contributed, through them, more largely than any other part of Plato's writing to the sum of common thoughts. . . . the Myths mark also that shape which a revelation for men might be expected to take. The doctrine is conveyed in an historic form: the ideas are offered as facts, the myth itself is the message."[43] Besides sounding like Marshall McLuhan, Westcott indicates how ideas of divinity and history may intersect in symbol.

[37][Hare], *Guesses*, pp. 61, 62. Consider how ancient the idea of divine potentials is. To Augustine, "God has placed in matter a latent treasure of forces, constituted according to the eternal exemplars or divine ideas corresponding to the material essences. These are the seminal reasons, *rationes seminales* (Stoicism, Neo-Platonism), the successive germination of which when the opportune circumstances are realized, *acceptis opportunitatibus,* give rise to particular beings" (Augustine's thought summarized by Maurice De Wulf, *History of Mediaeval Philosophy,* Ernest C. Messenger, trans., 3rd ed., 2 vols. [London: Longmanns, 1935], 1:90).

[38]Frank E. Manuel, *The Eighteenth Century Confronts the Gods,* p. 160.

[39]Vico, *New Science,* pp. 174, 45. See the discussion in Manuel, pp. 255–56.

[40]See Emery Neff, *The Poetry of History,* pp. 98–99.

[41]George Grote, *History of Greece,* 1:445. Grote started writing his history in 1823 and the volumes were published originally in 1846–56.

[42]Inge, p. 97.

[43]Brooke Foss Westcott, *Essays in the History of Religious Thought in the West,* pp. 46, 49.

In brief, heroes who symbolize the spirit of mankind stand before providence and choose between its active and ordinary powers, much as Hercules chose between duty and pleasure. These heroes embody the "gradual and unconscious nature of cultural evolution in any nation," to use words cited before in regard to the "underlying historical premise of the historiography of Romanticism."[44] God presents these heroes with what Hera (as Vico explained) presented to her son Hercules: challenges and trials; hence the name *Heras kleos*, the glory of Hera. "If glory be properly esteemed," wrote Vico, "as Cicero defines it, as 'widespread fame for services to mankind,' how great a glory must it have been for the Herculeses to have founded the nations by their labors!"[45] But heroes also may fail the challenge and then the nation slides into natural decline. We may see in the proposition an ancient idea in Judaic-Christian thought celebrated by Toynbee as the key to the rise and fall of nations.

The idea originates, according to Toynbee, in "the Israelites' anthropomorphic vision of God as a person with whom persons have personal encounters" within "history as a series of acts in each of which God presents a challenge to some human being individually, or collectively to the participants in some human community or society." But, man being free, it follows that "the outcome of a response to a challenge is not causally predetermined, is not necessarily uniform in all cases, and is therefore intrinsically unpredictable." "God reveals Himself in encounters."[46] Shinn maintains that "God's self disclosure is mediated, not through propositions but through historical events in which men are confronted with a responsibility and a demand for decision, with a judgment and a promise coming from the divine Lord."[47] Life is a "trial," such as in the Vichian idea of *corso-recorso* or the Hegelian notion that the "history of the world is the Last Judgment."[48] And, in being a confrontation with a divinity of terrible judgment, the situation is naturally the apocalyptic moment that is Tennyson's basic posture before history, as stressed in the preceding chapter: a moment both of disaster and of revelation.

[44] See Chapter I, note 11.

[45] Vico, *New Science*, pp. 174-75.

[46] Toynbee, *Study of History*, 12:255. The tradition of the idea may be suggested by Toynbee's statement that, after he had formulated the idea of challenge-and-response, he found the same notion in the fourth stanza of Browning's "Master Hugues of Saxe-Gotha" (*Study of History*, 10:231-32).

[47] Roger Lincoln Shinn, *Christianity and the Problem of History*, p. 17.

[48] For the equatability of Vico and Hegel on this point, see the discussion in Fisch's "Introduction," Vico, *New Science*, pp. xliii–xliii.

Clearly, in suggesting that such ideas about God, history, and man were present in the Apostolic circle and that Tennyson was nourished in this intellectual "soup," I am disagreeing with critical conclusions that "it would be easy to exaggerate the intellectual and spiritual influence which the Apostles had upon Tennyson" and that his "opportunity to understand England's political and economic state had been limited at College."[49] But the proof of the soup is in the eating, and I submit that we can profit by examining the poems of Tennyson from this vantage and, further, that we can trace these ideas in various forms throughout his life. At the moment, we can approach "Timbuctoo" and "The Hesperides" with the following elements of the poet's philosophy of history before us: a god of history is manifested anthropomorphically to peoples in an apocalyptic moment; the challenge offers engagement with and judgment before an active providence working its will in the world; and the national spirit is embodied in leader figures who respond (or fail to respond) to this challenge. The corollary is that a visionary faculty of historical divination is incumbent both on the actors in the historical drama and on the poet (vicariously, his own hero) who records it.

In 1829 Tennyson won the Chancellor's prize-poem contest with his "Timbuctoo." Presumably the subject was chosen because there were then underway in Africa various quests for the remains of the ancient city of Timbuctoo. As Lounsbury points out, "During the decade from 1820 to 1830 special interest had been awakened in the city itself. It had flourished for centuries, it had been the seat of successive kingdoms and the prize of contending nations."[50] Timbuctoo, in short, was much like the Babylons, Jerusalems, and Persepolises lost in historical apocalypse in Tennyson's early poems. Recognizing this, Tennyson sent home for the manuscript of "Armageddon" and scaled down its archetypal "gathering of nations/Unto the mighty battle of the Lord" to reflect the demise of one specific civilization.

Critics are prone to take Timbuctoo as a "dream-city" of the imagination, a personal "vision" of the "ideal," a "fair city of the ideal."[51] But Timbuctoo can be the ideal in an historical sense as well: an archetypal city, an objectification of the heavenly city, even

---

[49] Respectively, Christopher Ricks, *Tennyson,* p. 31; and Mary Joan Donahue, "Tennyson's *Hail Briton!* and *Tithon* in the Heath Manuscript," p. 399.

[50] Lounsbury, p. 79.

[51] Respectively, Nicolson, *Tennyson: Aspects,* p. 85; Johnson, *The Alien Vision of Victorian Poetry,* p. 6; and Buckley, *Growth of a Poet,* p. 32.

civilization itself. The Angel Mind, a kind of local God of history, speaks of Timbuctoo as "my city." Insofar as he is the force "to sway / The heart of man: and teach him to attain / By shadowing forth the Unattainable," his worship embodies the ideal in real terms of brick and mortar. He is the apotheosis of the heroic will to historical form, because "it is the idea of God that lifts us out of the eddying flux and reflex of time," as Hare was cited earlier in saying.[52] In visiting his votaries' "eyes with visions" this mind is the genius of the rise of civilization anthropomorphically portrayed because, as Hare also pointed out, all religions "must of necessity be anthropomorphic. The idea of God must be adapted to the capacities of the human imagination."[53] As we know, Tennyson always insisted that "our highest view of God must be more or less anthropomorphic" (*Memoir*, 1:311).

But he is also the spirit of fable:

The permeating life which courseth through
All the intricate and labyrinthine veins
Of the great vine of *Fable*, which, outspread
With growth of shadowing leaf and clusters rare,
Reacheth to every corner under Heaven,
Deep-rooted in the living soil of truth.

There is no critical strain here in taking the vine for that commonly used symbol of the human race in the period, Igdrasil, the World Tree (a knowledge of Nordic myth is not too much to expect in the Apostolic circle). Besides, as Westcott was quoted above as saying, "Myths mark that shape which a revelation for men might be expected to take."[54] In brief, the Angel Mind is an agent of active providence. By communion with it man can learn "step by step to scale that mighty stair / Whose landing-place is wrapt about with clouds / Of glory' of Heaven." Tennyson's footnote to these lines, "Be ye perfect even as your Father in Heaven is perfect,"[55] suggests that the city that

---

[52] See note 24 above.

[53] [Hare], *Guesses*, p. 209.

[54] See note 43 above.

[55] Tennyson's footnote suggests he is indebted to Hare, who wrote warning against French progressivism—"the belief in the perfectibility, or even in the progressiveness of mankind . . . [has] much of errour . . . mixt up with it"—and made it plain that true progress is spiritual, because God "set His own absolute perfection as the aim of our endeavour before us, by that blessed command,—*Be ye perfect, even as your Father* in heaven is perfect" (*Guesses*, p. 347). Given such sentiments, the fact that both Hare and Thirlwall were examiners for the prize poem contest could not have hurt Tennyson's chances for the prize nor for being elected to the Apostles in the following May, 1829 (Paden, p. 139, n. 158).

results from such empathic union with the divine is a type of "perfect": the ideal, but an historical ideal.

The critical problem of "Timbuctoo" lies in the spirit's lament that

> the time is well-nigh come
> When I must render up this glorious home
> To keen *Discovery*: soon yon brilliant towers
> Shall darken with the waving of her wand;
> Darken, and shrink and shiver into huts,
> Black specks amid a waste of dreary sand,
> Low-built, mud-walled, Barbarian settlements,

and the poet's concomitant feeling of loss: I "was left alone . . . the Moon/Had fallen from the night, and all was dark!" Critics tend to assume that Tennyson laments discovery (which "threatens to darken and destroy the fair city of the ideal," as Buckley notes).[56] Further, they argue that this is a typical Tennysonian attitude toward the world, that, as E. D. H. Johnson observed with regard to "The Mystic," Tennyson is "aggressively disposed to repudiate the world and to seek immunity from its disturbances in the depths of his own imaginative being."[57]

But the idea that Tennyson resented discovery is troubled by his manifest appreciation of discovery in general. As mentioned before, Niebuhr believed that discovery in archeology was dispensed providentially, while Hare believed that God provided discoveries to foster ordained changes in mankind's destiny. Tennyson's 1833 "Mechanophilus" speaks glowingly about mechanical discovery:

> Far as the Future vaults her skies,
>   From this my vantage ground
> To those still-working energies
>   I spy nor term nor bound.
>
> As we surpass our father's skill,
>   Our sons will shame our own;
> A thousand things are hidden still
>   And not a hundred known.

---

[56] Buckley, *Growth of a Poet*, p. 32.
[57] Johnson, *Alien Vision*, p. 4.

In Tennyson's poem "The Mystic," the anthropomorphic "imperishable presences" (surely kin to the great Angel Mind) are with "shining eyes/Smiling a godlike smile" precisely because "the innocent light/Of earliest youth" is "pierced through and through with all/Keen knowledges of low-embowèd eld." Tennyson's keen knowledge of lost Babylons and Alexandrias had produced no such lament about discovery in the historical poems he wrote at Somersby. He surely knew what Hare pointed out in his *Guesses at Truth* sometime later, that the "ultimate tendency of civilization is toward barbarism."[58] Nor is Tennyson's outlook toward such historical destruction timid in the poem he wrote at Somersby entitled "Time: An Ode." The track of time's "scythèd car" is "Strewed with the wrecks of frail renown,/Robe, sceptre, banner, wreath, and crown," yet

> Those splendid monuments alone he spares,
>   Which, to her deathless votaries,
> Bright Fame, with flowing hand, uprears
> Amid the waste of countless years.
> "Live ye!" to these he crieth; "live!
> "To ye eternity I give—

Fame and "eternity" Timbuctoo surely has, and these are as good reasons for addressing it as is the historian's criterion: the "monumentality" of the situation. (The latter is the reason why Thucydides wrote about the Peloponnesian War. It was simply "more worthy of relation than any that had preceded it.")

If, then, Tennyson neither resents discovery nor shrinks from knowledge of the way things really were, what is the spirit (and Tennyson) lamenting, especially given his faith that history is directed providentially? As he says in the poem, history is "Seraph-trod" in regard to all legendary cities, "Filled with Divine effulgence." I believe the young Tennyson, before the fact of man's fallen nature, simply is applying the rhetoric of the "thus pass the splendors of the world" formula toward the past. This is perhaps more keenly felt now by virtue of a certain inevitable maturing, a Wordsworthian wisdom in hearing more acutely now the "still, sad music of humanity" that chastens and subdues. Yet this lament fundamentally is no different than the lugubrious elegiacs toward the bloody past found in many of the poems Tennyson wrote at Somersby: the "woe to thee, Tanis! thy babes shall be thrown/By the

[58] [Hare], *Guesses,* p. 459.

barbarous hands on the cold marble-stone" sentiments of "God's
Denunciations against Pharaoh-Hophra," for example.

As an agent of active providence, the spirit is lamenting the sad fact
that for inscrutable reasons the Lord giveth and the Lord taketh away.
But insofar as he is also the projection of the poet's prophetic faculty—
the same role the great Angel Mind occupied in the earlier "Armageddon"—he is the embodiment of the same perception on the part of
Tennyson. What both the spirit and the poet see is the apocalypse that
overtakes the city as a result of man's falling away from active
providence. "Armaggedon" had put this disaster in terms of a "red
eruption from the fissured cone" of a volcano, which had brought up
"Witchcraft's abominations." In what I suggest is Tennyson's growing
education in such matters, "Timbuctoo" depicts civil tumult as caused
by one manifestation of providential judgment, an earthquake. The
"walls/Shake" not before the demonic, but before some "subterranean
voice" from the "streets with ghastly faces thronged"; it is merely a
"fearful summoning," perhaps before the world court of justice. In
Tennyson's mind the precise cause of such a disastrous end for the city
is not clear, but it may be deduced from the lines about the priestess
worshiping. Once the spirit had been worshiped on a "throne of fiery
flame" by "multitudes of multitudes." Now she is alone before "marble
knees," a mere graven idol with "eyes which wear no light but that
wherewith/Her phantasy informs them." It is not plain that the
people's faith had departed, yet neither is it unreasonable to see that
this is so. They had failed the idea of God, so the old order had begun
changing. God fulfils himself in many ways, though the results are
grievous to those on the downward phase of the historical cycle.

"The Hesperides" is found by most recent criticism to be based on
the "situation of the artist," the "mind devoutly dedicated to the
imaginative life," the "stasis" of the "poet's task."[59] Few critics even
notice Hanno. Green mentions that the gardens seem "existing apart
from historical vicissitude and unpredictably glimpsed only by a few
exceptional spirits, such as Hanno, the Carthaginian navigator who
overhears the song."[60] Joseph interprets Hercules (and, by implication,
Hanno) as man in quest of immortality.[61] But the way into the poem is

[59] Respectively, G. Robert Stange, "Tennyson's Garden of Art: A Study of *The Hesperides*,"
p. 100; Buckley, *Growth of a Poet*, p. 47; and Elton Edward Smith, *The Two Voices*, pp. 122-
23.

[60] Joyce Green, "Tennyson's Development During the 'Ten Years' Silence (1832–1842),"
p. 668.

[61] Gerhard Joseph, "The Idea of Mortality in Tennyson's Classical and Arthurian Poems,"
p. 138.

by following up Croker's 1833 remark that Tennyson, "with great judgment, rejects the common fable" to work with a "comparatively recent period—namely, the voyage of Hanno" (though he failed to say why he found satisfactory the substitution of an historical for a mythic figure).[62]

While on a voyage of exploration Hanno suddenly enters a visionary state in which "came voices, like the voices in a dream." This is the dream state that in Tennyson's poems is always an "essentially spiritual experience," as Charles Tennyson points out.[63] Unlike Hercules, however, Hanno does not land and secure the apples. He seems to be presented with a challenge by anthropomorphic symbols of transcendence, but he does not respond in the apocalyptic situation of a world "wasted with fire and sword." In not ravishing the golden fruit, Hanno freely chooses not to engage the divine plan. It is therefore most appropriate that he is representative of Carthage, soon to be wasted in the world court of justice, as was Timbuctoo and so many other cities in Tennyson's *Poems by Two Brothers.*

The gardens, and especially the apples and the tree on which they grow, symbolize from this critical vantage the reservoir of all potential historical forms as these forms are intuited by the human intelligence. The Neoplatonic doctrines of the time approved of the apple "as one of the symbols used in the rites of the Eleusinian Mysteries. According to Sallust, 'the Hesperian golden apples, signify the pure and incorruptible nature of that intellect, or Dionysius, which is participated by the world; for a golden apple . . . is a symbol of the world.'"[64] The poem indicates that "Honour comes with mystery" and somehow the apples contain the mystery of why "Kingdoms lapse, and climates change, and races die." In "Oenone," another Tennyson poem of this period, the "fruit of pure Hesperian gold" (l. 65) that Paris holds in his hand contains the potential destruction of Troy. This is made particularly explicit in the original version of 1832:

> Behold this fruit, whose gleaming rind ingrav'n
> "For the most fair" in aftertime may breed
> Deep evilwilledness of heaven and sere
> Heartburning toward hallowed Ilion.[65]

[62] Given in *Tennyson: The Critical Heritage,* pp. 75, 76.

[63] "The Dream in Tennyson's Poetry," p. 248.

[64] Harper, pp. 175–76, who adds that the "one tree which Blake never speaks of in a derogatory sense is the apple" (p. v).

[65] See W. J. Rolfe, ed., *The Complete Poetical Works of Tennyson* (Boston: Houghton Mifflin, Riverside Press, 1898), p. 800.

But the cataclysm is only potential, as the *may* suggests. Man makes his own choices in beauty and history alike. The gardens and its apples are, as Stange notes, a "source of creativity,"[66] although he would place this in the world of art. Yet we may view the longing for a paradise as simply that blessed command that Tennyson appended to "Timbuctoo": Be ye perfect, even as your Father in heaven is perfect—on earth as it is in heaven. The gardens are an ideal as well as a challenge, but the call is to historical form.

One way to get there is to climb the tree. Hercules did so and fulfilled the mandate of heaven, whether this is to be taken symbolically as the harvesting of grain or the stealing of sheep or, on more recondite levels, as attaining to pure intellect or to knowledge of historical good and evil. "The Hesperian tree bearing golden apples was a type of that in Eden," observes Paden.[67] Though free to stand or fall, Adam and Eve brought about both history and the fulfillment of a larger scheme by which humanity attained heaven as the higher Eden. From the vantage of modern comparative mythology, Eliade describes the shaman's ascent to heaven, while in a state of ecstasy, "by the instrumentality of a tree or upright pole, symbols of the Cosmic Tree or Pole." The tree here symbolizes the belief that in the "mythical time of 'Paradise,' there was a Mountain, a Tree, a Pole, or a Vine which connected Earth with Heaven and that primordial man could readily pass from one to the other by climbing them." Eliade also stresses the "complete ideological continuity between the most elementary forms of mystical experience and Christianity."[68] The poet in "Timbuctoo" "stood upon a Mountain." In "The Hesperides," a "golden tree" of "charmèd root" and "flowering arch" is featured prominently; in line 19 it is likened to a mountain peak.

The Apostles' knowledge of Gothic myth was argued above in reference to considering "Timbuctoo"'s vine of fable as Igdrasil, the World Tree. In fact, a drawing of the Gothic cosmography is a veritable illustration of "The Hesperides": Yggdrasill, the World Ash, is on an island promontory and its three roots reach Asgard, Midgard, and Niflheim; the World Serpent encircles the earth and the dragon Nithoeggr gnaws the roots.[69] "When King Gylfi visited Asgard," writes Branston, "and enquired 'Where is the headquarters—the holy of holies

---

[66] Stange, "Tennyson's Garden of Art," p. 101.
[67] Paden, p. 155.
[68] Mircea Eliade, "The Yearning for Paradise in Primitive Tradition," pp. 65, 67, 73.
[69] Brian Branston, *Gods of the North*, pp. 297, 215 (plate 6).

of the gods?' he was told 'That's at the Ash Tree Yggdrasill: you'll find the gods giving judgment there every day'."[70] The point is that Hanno encounters a symbol of active providence. He is challenged to climb the tree and to ravish its secrets, failing which he will be judged wanting in human history. This history is what Igdrasil represents traditionally. Rather than climbing, however, Hanno significantly is down below that "highland leaning down a weight/Of cliffs" on which the sacred tree stands.

Probably in response to its poor critical acclaim—Mill liked the "fine sonorous opening" of the poem but considered the rest a comparative failure when scaled against the other poems in the 1830 volume[71] — Tennyson suppressed "The Hesperides," although he later said to his son that "he regretted that he had done away with it from among his 'Juvenilia'" (Memoir, 1:61). The mix of mythology and history in this poem was methodized as insufficiently as it had been in "Timbuctoo" and the whole was too impacted with complex meanings. There is a strange element of humor in the poem, too. This element is difficult to describe. It is a kind of serious jesting, like that of "The Poet's Mind": "Dark-browed sophist, come not anear;/All the place is holy ground . . . your ears are so dull . . . you are foul with sin." This tone, along with the "awful mystery" and the cryptic numerology of "The Hesperides," comes, perhaps, from the emblematic nature of the Neoplatonic Eleusinian mysteries. In Taylor's words, "It was the custom of Pythagoras and his followers, amongst whom Plato holds the most distinguished rank, to conceal divine mysteries under the veil of symbols and figures, to dissemble their wisdom against the arrogant boastings of the Sophists; to joke seriously, and sport in earnest."[72] If this humor is in the poem, it grits against Tennyson's sense of the pathos in history. It also grits against his realization (in his remaining year at Cambridge) that in real life the English heroic class may be failing the challenges of the time, and (insofar as he identifies the poetic faculty as "heroic") against his fear that the poet too can become obsolete in the providential transitions.

---

[70] Branston, pp. 73–79.
[71] Given in Tennyson: The Critical Heritage, p. 95 n. 2.
[72] Quoted by Harper, p. 48.

III From Cambridge to the Death of Hallam

THE PREVIOUS CHAPTER focused on two poems that contained a unified philosophy of history whose elements, native to Tennyson's mind, were honed and sophisticated in the intellectual atmosphere of the Apostolic circle. Tennyson's thinking may appear to contain a contradictory outlook insofar as during 1830–33 he wrote poems that can be classed in two ways. Stout, sanguine (and forgotten) declamations like the 1830 "National Song" ("There is no land like England") and the 1833 "You ask me, why" ("land that freeman till . . . A land of settled government") are side by side with troubled, pessimistic (and famed) poems like "The Lotos-Eaters" and the four he wrote just after Hallam's death in late 1833: "Morte d'Arthur," "Ulysses," "Tithon," and "Tiresias." A principle of plenitude is a kind of truism in Tennyson criticism; Kemble did say that "in Alfred's mind the materials of the greatest works are heaped in an abundance which is almost confusion" (*Memoir*, 1:122). There is also lately a sense of mirrorings, oppositions, contradictions, a "radical incommensurateness,"[1] but the apparent contradiction in Tennyson's outlook on history can be seen not as paradox, but as the complementary sides of a consistent understanding.

The one side encompasses poems that result from his confidence

[1] Applied to the symbolism of the *Idylls* by John D. Rosenberg, *The Fall of Camelot*, p. 102.

that the providential imperatives are settling down into the national culture, that history is progressing, and that heroic properties somehow are being carried forward by gifted groups like the middle-class Apostles and even by the people as a whole—and all without a disastrous, apocalyptic moment. The other side contains the works that result from Tennyson's uneasiness about the role of the traditional heroic class in this process. The providential turning of the historical wheel seems to be rendering them and their qualities obsolete, and they exist in an apocalyptic stasis, locked into union with symbols of an indifferent or even an inimical divinity. To anticipate the argument, the first attitude leads to the sanguineness of *The Princess*; this is the substance of the next chapter. The second attitude leads down a far more difficult path, the effort to reintroduce the hero (and the heroic poet) into national affairs. Tennyson resolves this dilemma in the works leading to *In Memoriam* (beyond this, to the *Idylls*) and this is the substance of chapter 5.

One part of Tennyson's mind was certainly at ease about what was happening in history. The early thirties commonly are taken to be a momentous time of unusual stress for Englishmen as the debates about the Reform Bill (to be passed in 1832) wound their paranoid way. Tennyson's sanguineness about the bill is suggested by the celebration of its passage in Somersby. Tennyson and "some of his brothers and sisters at once sallied out into the darkness, and began to ring the church bells madly" (*Memoir*, 1:93). Some Tennyson poems of the period 1830–33 show the power of active providence "trickling down" from ancient divinatory heights (such as the mountain of "Timbuctoo" and the high promontory of the "Hesperides," a promontory that heroes had to climb for power). "Freedom slowly broadens down," Tennyson wrote in "You ask me why," no longer informing mere heroic self-realization but the hurly-burly of ordinary active life. Tennyson's 1833–34 "Love thou thy land" announces this investiture as a "motion toiling in the gloom—/The Spirit of the years to come/Yearning to mix himself with Life." The great Angel Mind descends the mount. Shapes like the Hesperides mingle with ordinary men. In the 1833 poem "Of old sat Freedom on the heights," the divine protagonist—for she "God-like, grasps the triple forks,/And, King-like, wears the crown"—comes down:

There in her place she did rejoice,
    Self-gathered in her prophet-mind,

But fragments of her mighty voice
    Came rolling on the wind.

Then stept she down through town and field
    To mingle with the human race,
And part by part to men revealed
    The fulness of her face—

The hero of this process is no longer the historical titan engaging transcendence at the limit but instead a leader working with slow prudence within established institutions, a leader who, if he climbs that "mighty stair" (of 'Timbuctoo") at all, climbs it as a leader into Westminster. The poem "I loving Freedom for herself" suggests the end of that mighty stair, that "landing-place . . . wrapt about with clouds," as a place of mundane, self-transfiguring institutions:

I trust the leaders of the land
    May well surmount the coming shock
By climbing steps their fathers carved
    Within the living rock.

The state within herself concludes
    The power to change, as in the seed,
The model of her future form,
    And liberty indeed.

Neither a conquering force like Alexander or Ulysses nor an impotent one like Hanno, the hero is an embodiment of general social change brought about by all the people. Insofar as Tennyson will show the hero in such poems, he will be a symbol like a Scott hero: "not precisely Everyman, but every gentleman—not in some supercilious social sense, but in the profound conviction that society is a compact of independent owners of property."[2] These heroes, like Sir Walter of *The Princess*, are not masters but enlightened superintendents of historical change, with the whole people acting as God's agents, a democratic trend in thought as in politics. A whole people achieve progress in science and industry. "This Earth is wondrous, change on change," Tennyson wrote in some lines of 1833. The 1833 "Mechanophilus" praises the mechanical wonders that are to be:

---

[2] Alexander Welsh, *The Hero of the Waverley Novels,* p. 57.

Far as the Future vaults her skies,
   From this my vantage ground
To those still-working energies
   I spy nor term nor bound.

As we surpass our father's skill,
   Our sons will shame our own;
A thousand things are hidden still
   And not a hundred known.

. . . my brothers, work, and wield
   The forces of today,
And plow the Present like a field,
   And garner all you may!

All work in the vineyard of the Lord.

These poems lack the apocalyptic setting. Plowing suggests the "natural" way that divinity and man "mix" and "mingle." History "broadens," is "slow-developed." Three other poems of this period— the 1830 "Ode to Memory," the "Ode: O Bosky Brook" (written at Somersby but revised at Cambridge), and the 1833 "The Progress of Spring"—while "not explicitly historical" have a "degree of historical consciousness insofar as they are progress poems. . . . time is marked by gradual transitions rather than catastrophies . . . a progressive expansion of thought rather than an abrupt ascent to transcendency."[3] Society is is conceived romantically as organic form or "culture," a result of cultivation and tillage. This is the Burkean "idea of continuity" in a nation made by people as a "deliberate election of the ages and of generations," not "a tumultuary and giddy choice." Williams notes that Burke is describing the "spirit of the nation" or what later in the century came to be called a national "culture."[4] So Tennyson says that the state contains within herself "as in the seed,/The model of her future form" ("I loving Freedom"). Yet, as was argued in the previous chapter, all this organic imagery is to be applied to spiritual matters, for only the idea of God lifts man out of the natural law of ordinary providence.

On the other hand, the important poems from this 1830–33 period seem to be invested with the deepest gloom and despair. The pessimism, however, is not about the historical process but about the role of heroes

[3] Andrew Fichter, "Ode and Elegy: Idea and Form in Tennyson's Early Poetry," pp. 406, 412.

[4] Comment, and Burke's words quoted, by Raymond Williams, *Culture and Society*, p. 11.

in the providentially directed transitions. The protagonists of the 1831 "The Lotos-Eaters" and of four poems written upon Hallam's death are in apocalyptic situations. Except for "Ulysses," which is a transition piece, they also close with anthropomorphic symbols of transcendence inimical to their heroic properties. These heroes are blighted, morbid, disturbed—and obsolete in the scheme of things. As such, their despair is decorous and fundamentally ironic. To carry this historical irony Tennyson invented the genre of the dramatic monologue, a device particularly suited to distancing, ambiguity, and relativity. Providential history requires that Romes be sacked and that heroes depart when their work is done. This does not make sacked cities and heroes feel good, but splendid agony should not cast doubt on the divine imperative at the heart of history.

"The Lotos-Eaters" contains a situation that can be compared with that of "The Hesperides." Ulysses and his mariners, like Hanno and his, are voyaging in historical time when suddenly they encounter timelessness, a "challenge" (decorous also in the Odyssean context). Hanno hears "voices, like the voices in a dream" but he sails past this Hesperidean correlative of his interface with active providence (as was argued in chapter 2) and so returns home to await the Carthaginian apocalypse. But Ulysses cries "Courage!" and the mariners respond to the challenge by coming ashore to ravage not the golden apples, but the lotos fruit. This is a complex irony, for the heroic impulse by which they once made a providentially ordained history (conquering Troy on Zeus's orders) is the very means by which they are withdrawn from a history that continues with presumed normality without them (as Ulysses will find when he gets to Ithaca). That is, the heroic nature that in an earlier time engaged active providence is the social mechanism that immobilizes them on the plane of ordinary providence. This is the "invisible hand" of God in the historical process. Because they are obsolete now, the mariners hear dream-like voices but the voices are their own, "thin, as voices from the grave," and the grave is where they are (historically speaking).

"All round the coast the languid air did swoon,/Breathing like one that hath a weary dream." The whole island, in fact, is a correlative for the inner light now seen through the providential glass darkly: the symbolism of ordinary providence. The mariners sit on the beach enchanted with lotos and with "Music that brings sweet sleep" (Hanno heard not the "melody of the Lybian lotosflute"). They are far below the "Three silent pinnacles of agèd snow" that might have contained the

Hesperidian sisters (the 1832 version indicated that some of the mariners sat "On the ancient heights divine" but significantly the line was stricken for the 1842 version). In "The Hesperides" the immortal golden apples hung over the sea (the "deep") eternally, but in "The Lotos-Eaters" the apples are mortal. They are part of the natural process, "sweetened with the summer light,/The full-juiced apple, waxing over-mellow,/Drops in a silent autumn night." "Slumber is more sweet than toil," the mariners say and they too, over-mellow, drop into silence. They join the realm of mere organic purposefulness, the cyclicity of leaf, apple, and flower (and lotos) that "ripens in its place,/Ripens and fades, and falls, and hath no toil,/Fast-rooted in the fruitful soil." Their compost will be "fruitful," neither guilty nor innocent, for they move into the past as heroic memory to make the national soil. This idea will be central to such later poems as *In Memoriam* and the Wellington ode. In "The Lotos-Eaters," the "minstrel sings . . . of the ten years' war in Troy,/And our great deeds."

To be sure, they suspect he sings of these "as half-forgotten things," but the material is in an ironic mode, and it is not clear that their deeds will be half-forgotten. "Is there confusion in the little isle?" they ask wearily, but we suspect that there is no confusion at all. They think that maybe "Our sons inherit us . . . Or else the island princes over-bold/Have eat our substance." This is true. "'Tis hard to settle order once again," they complain, but if Tennyson's Ulysses is any measure, it is *their* order that is at issue, not "order." What they encounter on the island is the symbolic equivalent of the passing of their order in history. Their disengagement from active providence is suggested by their disinclination to act in life's "trial." "What pleasure can we have/To war with evil?" they ask. What kind of evil? The lines immediately preceding these—"All things are taken from us, and become/Portions and parcels of the dreadful Past"—suggest an enforced loss. The loss is perhaps something like the result of the 1830 summer elections, which weakened the Wellington antireformist government and brought in a parliament that Croker described as bearing in it the "seeds of the most troublesome and unmanageable Parliament since that of 1640 which overturned the monarchy."[5] What was taken away from aristocratic landowners who resisted liberalist change was a considerable portion of of their power, with political "sons" inheriting that power.

The argument was made above that in "Timbuctoo" the God that

---

[5] Quoted by Michael Brock, *The Great Reform Act* (London: Hutchinson, 1973), p. 86.

the protagonist imagines—the great Angel Mind—was but a projection of his own prophetic faculty: man creating God in his own image. In another truism, the Lucretian gods the mariners imagine always have been taken critically as a correlative of their spiritual state, instances (in de Vere's words) of an "aloofness from all human interests and elevated action, an Epicurean and therefore hard-hearted repose, sweetened not troubled by the endless wail from earth" (*Memoir*, 1:504). But seldom is it appreciated how much these gods have in common with the hard-hearted aristocrats who opposed the Reform Bill (from a liberal perspective, of course). "Careless of mankind," the divine aristocrats "lie beside their nectar" in "golden houses" and "smile in secret, looking over wasted lands,/Blight and famine" and the "ill-used race of men that cleave the soil." This warrior class is not interested in alleviating the plight of the common man but takes pleasure only in ancestral memories of "Clanging fights, and flaming towns, and sinking ships, and praying hands."

Critics perceive in "The Lotos-Eaters" instances of "selfish irresponsibility" and of "escape from the claims of duty and effort," of "life-weariness, a longing for rest through oblivion," and of "inclinations toward tranquillity and lassitude."[6] These are quite proper except that they should have historical referents, but even here things are much more complex than they seem. If it is true that, based on the "private vices-public benefits" formula, Tennyson portrays in "The Lotos-Eaters" a providential abstention from heroic felicity, critical judgments about the mariners are as hard to come by as are judgments about the heroes in the historical poems Tennyson wrote at Somersby, for example. Alexander, Pizarro, and Nebuchadrezzar were doing the Lord's bidding, and the ambiguity of their moral status for the young poet was noted in chapter 1. Similarly, the mariners effected the divine scheme in disposing of Troy, but that was in another part of the historical cycle. Now they dispose of themselves, all unknowingly (*felix culpa*) by enacting their heroic natures. Locked into ordinary providence, they vegetate deliriously and dream of warrior gods. Such responsibility and duty as they would bring to Ithaca are no longer required, would indeed be wrong given the nature of their "order."

As a matter of fact, the Liberal Anglicans had given considerable thought to the role of the hero class in normal historical transitions. In

---

[6]Respectively, Douglas Bush, *Mythology and the Romantic Tradition in English Poetry*, pp. 207–208; Robert Langbaum, *The Poetry of Experience,* p. 89; and George O. Marshall, Jr., *A Tennyson Handbook,* p. 71.

his *Thucydides* (1830), Thomas Arnold wrote, "The guilt of all aristocracies has consisted not so much in their original acquisition of power as in their perseverance in retaining it: so that what was innocent or even reasonable at the beginning has become in later times atrocious injustice; as if a parent in his dotage should claim the same authority over his son in the vigour of manhood, which formerly in the maturity of his own faculties he had exercised naturally and profitably over the infancy of his child."[7] Such intransigence in the political "parent" is Tennyson's very concern in "Hail Briton!" (worked on 1831–33): that "in the land diseases grew/From want of motion which is meet,/And power that still should change and fleet/Had festered in the hands of few" (ll. 29–32). Thus, if England's leaders, over-mellow late in the heroic age, are exercising impious repression over political children long grown to manhood, then this historical contradiction could well be portrayed poetically as disturbed old men, symbols of the dotage described by Arnold. This rupture with providential intent also would be suggested well by union with deadly anthropomorphic shapes. The society they control would, then, properly be malformed or descending in apocalypse. In these circumstances, any divinatory perceptions that are displayed would be morbid and cloudy as well.

A deadly deformation is found in the "Morte d'Arthur," which contains the as yet unqualified Malory matter: Modred is Arthur's son and, in killing each other and in the death of all, a mighty state founders on an inability to reconcile internal differences. In "Tiresias," the deformed cycle is implicitly (and decorously) in the Greek matter, where Tiresias, the epitome of helpless prophecy, warns that the "tyranny of one/Was prelude to the tyranny of all . . . the tyranny of all/Led backward to the tyranny of one." This is the standard, menacing sequence of the French Revolution so ominous to the Apostolic mind: aristocratic oppression, revolution, mob rule, and finally dictatorial tyranny, probably by the same aristocracy. The result of such mismanagement is the same as in "Morte d'Arthur" and in Tennyson's early history poems: a violent cycle of "civil outbreak . . . Would each waste each, and bring on both the yoke/Of stronger states." Internecine aristocratic struggle and inept transitions of power are implicit in this legendary matter as well. Eteocles, the elder son of

---

[7]Quoted by Duncan Forbes, *The Liberal Anglican Idea of History*, p. 23. And as the cycle moves on, Tennyson moved with it: in 1847 he said that one of the great social questions impending in England was the "housing and education of the poor man before making him our master" (*Memoir*, 1:249).

Oedipus, breaks a political agreement and illegitimately seizes power; he and Polynices kill each other on the battlefield; all die in the civil war and the invasion; and Thebes itself is destroyed later by the Epigoni.

In "Tithon" (that "pendent" of "Ulysses") the themes of historical upheaval are present also in the allusive material. As a matter of mythological record, Tithon was a brother to Priam and father of a son killed in the Trojan battles. He therefore can be taken to represent in his immobility both aristocracy and Troy dead in history. As Bryant made clear in his *New System of Ancient Mythology* (in the Somersby library), Tithonus was just a name for "tower"[8] and he is thus a synecdoche for Troy or the archetypal city lost to history. Tithon's ineffectuality is in stark contrast with the cyclic return of Eos on "silver wheels," seemingly the symbol of a divine, recurring, animating principle that is unavailing to Tithon now.

"Ulysses" is a variant and a poem that suggests a certain Tennysonian resolution of history's dilemmas. Implicit in the matter is the destruction of Troy, a destruction through which Ithaca succeeds to prominence but, in doing so, displays subsequently a seemingly peaceful internal transition to the bourgeois, constitutional monarchy phase under Telemachus. Those that "hoard, and sleep, and feed" and "pay / Meet adoration" to household gods replace without civil war the heroes of battle, travel, "honour," and "work of noble note." Considering Apostolic convictions about the imperative to such a phase (and this is to be said of "The Lotos-Eaters" as well), we cannot avoid the not-so-paradoxical conclusion that it was the blessed absence of Ulysses and his heroes that made such a "normal" transition possible.

As a complement to the fiery historical decline, these four poems show the deadly union between hero and anthropomorphic transcendence. In history on the ascendant, Arthur in the *Idylls* will be embraced by a covey of such figures at the inception of his reign: the supernatural Lady of the Lake, the three Queens (which are like three Hesperides, a triplicated Eve, or "three Guineveres," as Paden notes)[9], and (from this mythical perspective) even Guinevere herself as a symbol for what makes Camelot possible. With history on the decline,

---

[8]Bryant said that Tithonus "was nothing more than one of these structures, a Pharos, sacred to the sun, as the name plainly shews"; quoted by Christopher Ricks, ed., *Poems of Tennyson*, p. 1117. It is also, then, one of those ancient heights divine on which Tennyson's protagonist now withers.

[9]W. D. Paden identifies the Hesperides as a "type of the triplicated Eve" of Faberian notions (*Tennyson in Egypt*, p. 155). King Arthur, having three Guineveres, appears, in a Tennysonian sketch for a religious allegory in the *Idylls*, written in the late thirties (*Memoir*, 2:123).

however, the union appropriately is disastrous. The sorrowing and long-absent queens receive Arthur dismally into the reservoir of future potentials. If the godhead of Arthur is divorced from, but sorrowful over, his fallen agent, that of "Tiresias" is actively inimical in two guises. Ares, whose curse dogs the history of Thebes since Cadmus unknowingly slew his sacred serpent (no Hercules, Cadmus wins only trouble and no golden apples); and Athene, who blinded Tiresias as he chanced upon her bathing. Both are anthropomorphic aspects of the "more than man/Which rolls the heavens, and lifts, and lays the deep,/ Yet loves and hates with mortal hates and loves." The great god Ares cries, "I loath/The seed of Cadmus," while Pallas Athene "in anger" blasts Tiresias with "Henceforth be blind." No great Angel Minds, both can be seen as the divine, terrible judgment roused by historical and divinatory presumption. Cadmus founded a city with the dragon's teeth; Tiresias was driven by "some strange hope to see the nearer God." Surrogate for both Cadmus and Tiresias, Menoeceus sacrifices himself to the malign unknown but procures only a temporary respite for Thebes.

Tithon's union with godhead is frightful, for he is supinely passive within a divine corrosion. He "lay wooed" and is her "choice" (the 1860 word of "Tithonus"), her "chosen" in a perversion of the relationship between God and the "Elect." He says, "I wither slowly in thine arms" where once, in love-union with Eos, he had been a part of the inception of history. Tithon refers to "that strange song I heard Apollo sing,/While Ilion like a mist rose into towers," much as all legendary cities were built. But now the result of the love union, as with all those associated with Troy—Zeus and Leda, Paris and Helen—is disastrous for both Tithon and, of course, Troy. Ulysses and his men also once "strove with Gods" in love and war on the "ringing plains of windy Troy," responding successfully to challenge and making great history in fulfillment of the divine plan. But his role is a variant one. He is closed with no inimical goddess but is, on the other hand, apart from Penelope, as Arthur will be from Guinevere at *Idylls'* end. Within these extremes, the dissolution of their union brings him to death but at least it spares disaster to Ithaca.

Within a distorted cycle and a corrupted sacred union, the four protagonists are broken suitably in what the imagery suggests is an historical way. At the feet of the Queens, in images that evoke ruined Camelot, "Like a shattered column lay the King . . . his brow/Striped with dark blood . . . his face was white/And colourless . . . like the withered moon." Just as Troy was sacked and burned, Tithon is blasted in Eos's fire; in the poem's adjectives, he is withered, cold now his wrinkled feet, and, in the 1860 version, he is "ashes, marred, wasted, maimed." Tiresias is ancient and blind. Ulysses, though old, is the physical exception, as if reflecting in his strength Ithaca successfully passing through change. Further, the condition of prophetic insight of each hero corresponds to his physical one. Arthur is defeated and numbly resigned in the debacle, "Like one that feels a nightmare on his bed." He asks Bedivere to "Pray for my soul," wonders "if indeed I go—/(For all my mind is clouded with a doubt)/To the island-valley of Avilion," and hopes only "that which I have done/May He within Himself make pure." Tithon despairs and longs for the "ground . . . my grave." Tiresias too says, "I would that I were gathered to my rest." Ulysses is bitter, resentful, and, as has been observed often, suicidal.

"Ulysses" should exercise us. Most criticism identifies the issue in the poem as the disjunction between a societal and an "existential" frame of reference wherein, depending on critical sympathies, the Ulyssean condition is assessed as somewhere between admirable and contemptible. The problem lies in finding a vantage point that will unite simultaneous yet contradictory perceptions of social and individual imperatives. It is true that Ulysses "cannot be justified in any but the most individualistic terms" and that "life without faith leads to personal and social dislocation,"[10] but where do we stand to admire Ulysses' nobility and at the same time decry his morbid life weariness? Kincaid argues that "there is no way we can sensibly assume a secure place in a moral station with signs" through the "ironic rhetoric" of the poem, but from the viewpoint of irony we can recognize the "sloughing off" of all "communal values" to achieve "undefeated will," "heroic but naked endurance," and "existence of the self."[11] Perhaps ironic perspectives ultimately cannot be focused, but an historical rather than a moral station has the signs more plainly in place.

The question is what in history is good and bad or, put another way, what is the "meaning" in history? From the critical vantage being proffered here, the meaning of history comes "from the faith in an ultimate purpose," to use Löwith's definition of the necessary condition

---

[10] Respectively, E. D. H. Johnson, *Alien Vision*, p. 41; and E. J. Chiasson, "Tennyson's 'Ulysses'—A Reinterpretation," pp. 165, 172–73.

[11] James R. Kincaid, "Rhetorical Irony, the Dramatic Monologue, and Tennyson's *Poems* (1842)," pp. 222, 228–29.

for a philosophy of history.[12] This faith in Tennyson is his belief in providential history. From this standpoint, it is good that Ulysses is leaving a phase of history that no longer can use his naked, self-willed heroism and too bad that these qualities must eat inwardly to produce morbid behavior. Ulysses is disdainful about presiding over the ignoble competition of coarse shopkeepers but, on the other hand, he does not convulse the kingdom in trying to impose his order on a phase of history no longer his own. He recognizes that it is Telemachus who will fulfill the duty of an aristocrat in time of transition, "by slow prudence to make mild / A rugged people, and through soft degrees / Subdue them to the useful and the good," however dull the task.

Identifying with both the hero class and the people, Tennyson "is" neither Ulysses nor Telemachus. Therefore (in the temper of historical irony), he feels both the grievous loss of heroic nobility and the sympathy needed for those that carry on. If we must choose, the poet is certainly Telemachus. Tennyson's two celebrated statements about the poem support the idea that he was thinking vaguely of himself as left behind. "Ulysses," he said, was "written soon after Arthur Hallam's death, and gave my feelings about the need of going forward, and braving the struggle of life perhaps more simply than anything in 'In Memoriam'" (*Memoir*, 1:196). He said to Knowles that it "was written under the sense of loss and that all had gone by, but that still life must be fought out to the end."[13] Tennyson is always cast as Bedivere to Hallam's Arthur. So, given the delicate association of Hallam with the departure of a heroic ruling class, the statements do not confute the idea that Tennyson must go forward as the poet of the life that exists, even if it is bereft of heroic splendor.

The splendor is undeniably all with Ulysses. We can admire him and the protagonists of all four of these poems for the extraordinary will they excercise in reaching the outer limits of experience and in lifting history up with them, but Tennyson indicates that from the present perspective they are not without culpability in having done so. Ulysses's inordinate aspiration is Christian pride, Greek hubris, and that exacerbating "excitement" condemned by so many thinkers in the nineteenth century. Tithon says he was cursed by his desire "To vary from his kind, or beat the roads / Of life, beyond the goal of ordinance / Where all should pause, as is most meet for all"; he went beyond and

---

[12] See chapter 1, note 2.
[13] James Knowles, "Aspects of Tennyson," p. 182.

now withers "at the quiet limit of the world." Tiresias falls into this Faustian company, "wandering all the lands . . . With some strange hope to see the nearer God"; Pallas Athene tells him plainly "thou hast seen too much." A culpable Arthur inhabits the sketches and scenarios Tennyson made for the *Idylls* 1833–34 (see chapter 7).

This notion of a "limit"—a kind of utmost extension of self—with which all these mighty aspirers close, occurs in an interchange of lines and sentiments in early drafts of the four poems found in the Trinity notebooks. A comparison of these early drafts indicates the identity of the four protagonists in Tennyson's mind. Thus, the line "Beyond the utmost bound of human thought," so familiar in "Ulysses," appears in an alternate draft (watermarked 1832) of "Tiresias":

> I wish I were as in the days of old,
> Ere my smooth cheek darkened with youthful down,
> While yet the blessed daylight made itself
> Ruddy within the caves of sight, before
> I looked upon divinity unveiled
> And wisdom naked—when my mind was set
> To follow knowledge like a sinking star,
> Beyond the utmost bound of human thought.

In another notebook, the essential idea is attributed to Arthur and evokes the "all experience is an arch" passage of "Ulysses":

> Then spake King Arthur to Sir Bedivere
> 'Well said old Merlin ere his time was come'
> "Experience never closes all-in-all
> But there is always something to be learned
> Even in the gate of death."[14]

This interchange suggests how central to his understanding of all four protagonists was Tennyson's feeling about their consummation with the ultimate: something beyond human knowledge and experience, a divinity unveiled, wisdom naked.

This "ultimate" in Tennyson's thinking resembles what Jaspers calls the *Grenzsituation*, the "limit-situation." Surrounded by "suffering and death, flux and extinction," with the apparent failure of all ideals, all

[14]Trinity Notebooks 0.15.15 and 0.15.17.

knowledge of divinity, man is bound by existential limits. He can break these bounds only by recognizing in a tragic "readiness" a special kind of composure that involves the idea that "breakdown and failure reveal the true nature of things." In this "general shipwreck," as Jaspers's translators render *Weisen des Scheitern* (the breakdown of all certainty about man's essence, about historical meaning, about divinity), man is left with only his will and his tragic courage before an "inexorable limit. At this limit, he finds no guarantee of general salvation. Rather, it is in acting out his own personality, in realizing his selfhood even unto death, that he finds redemption and deliverance." "By 'selfhood'," explains Reiche, "Jaspers means individual consciousness and conscious inner activity—the process as its own product."[15]

Germanic and Apostolic thought, of course, was devout. Hardly of an existential persuasion, it postulated the Christian God. Yet, in the Judaic-Christian tradition, history is a record of shipwreck, for man's nature is fallen. In a general breakdown of all certainty and with no other recourse, heroes engage the limit and find their selfhood in failure and breakdown: blasted and blinded by encounter with godhead in the presence of historical convulsion. Theirs is a tragic victory. Perhaps for this reason there resound over the four poems those tragic echoes that are, in the case of "Ulysses" at least, "unusually insistent" (as Pettigrew puts it). Pettigrew terms Hamlet, Macbeth, Shakespeare's Ulysses, Milton's Satan, Count Cenci, and Byron's Napoleon all restless, Faustian men.[16] "Tiresias" is couched in the materials of Greek tragedy. The Malory matter is heavy with tragic import.

There is a critical tendency to deny tragic vision to Tennyson. "There is no Tennyson tragedy," Carr writes; "The themes of frustration can scarcely amount to that, and the tragic order of values is lacking."[17] But the question rests on our understanding of tragedy, especially if we see Tennyson's work at this time as falling into the tragic forms set up by modern theory. Apostolic thinking about the ultimates, especially in regard to the Neoplatonic reverence for myth, was centered upon the unfathomable mystery of the inner light and its symbolic projections, as well as upon the inscrutable, if terrible, superintendence of divine

---

[15] Karl Jaspers, *Tragedy Is Not Enough*, pp. 41–42, notes on p. 117, and p. 116 notes 1a and 3. The highest level of awareness is what Jaspers calls *Existenz*, which "lies in an intentional tending to something else: to Transcendence" (Kurt Hoffman, "The Basic Concepts of Jaspers' Philosophy," p. 99).

[16] John Pettigrew, "Tennyson 'Ulysses'," pp. 43–45.

[17] Arthur J. Carr, "Tennyson as a Modern Poet," p. 64. Jacob Korg asserts that Tennyson fails to write "genuine tragedy" ("The Pattern of Fatality in Tennyson's Poetry," p. 11).

justice in history. Such thinking is not unrelated to what Hathorn characterizes as the "revelation of mystery" in tragedy, wherein the protagonist as the "observer of the pattern is part of the pattern himself." His "tragic courage adds to the perception of the pattern the acceptance of its rightness, even as it involves oneself: 'a terrible beauty is born'."[18] Sewall describes the tragic hero as moving through three stages. He begins in anarchic individualism and pride, with a sense of the "terrible disrelations" of life; he "tests all norms" even "what society knows as a crime." He then makes a "pact with the world that is unremitting and sealed" and enters the "passion" where he discovers the unexpected evil at the heart of things. Finally, he moves into "perception," an enlightenment that is more than resignation: "At its most luminous it is Lear's and Oedipus' hard-won humility and new understanding."[19] Considering the total shape of tragic form, such as that of the Greek trilogies or that wherein Shakespeare moved out of tragedy into dark comedy, it can be said (in the words that make up the title of Jaspers's book) that tragedy is, finally, not enough. But at this stage and in this part of his mind, Tennyson has only the mystery and the tragic dislocation.

These four Tennyson poems find their energy in the terrible mystery of God's justice, and the protagonists are an integral part of the resulting historical pattern even as they reject all limits. The anarchic individualism of these heroes comes from the extension of the prophetic faculty. "In that hour," says the poet of his encounter with the Angel Mind of "Armageddon," "I could have fallen down/ Before my own strong soul and worshipped it," that is, worshipped the God of the inner light. In the disastrous shipwreck of "The Lotos-Eaters" and the four poems just considered, the protagonists also worship their own strong souls, albeit darkly, working out their individual salvations at the limit and outermost bound of their historical condition.

Tennyson was, then, not so much of two minds as able to carry in his thinking a providential pattern with two results: mankind engaging the divine potentials of active providence and heroes encountering the deadly stasis of ordinary providence. The nation is in gradual, meliorative transition, its heroes in apocalyptic disjunction. Freedom is broadening slowly downward and heroic powers of divination are being frustrated. Such ideas may and do exist in Tennyson as a kind of

[18] Richmond Y. Hathorn, *Tragedy, Myth, and Mystery*, pp. 223, 30, 221-22.
[19] Richard B. Sewall, "The Tragic Form," pp. 355-57.

opposing tension. That he was comfortable in such thinking may be suggested by his use of dialectic in "The Two Voices" (begun, apparently, about mid-June of 1833) or in the paired 1830 poems "Nothing Will Die" and "All Things Will Die." Dialectic is an oscillation rising from a sense of relativity and Tennyson seemed to convey this plainly in the 1830 "All thoughts, all creeds":

> All thoughts, all creeds, all dreams are true,
>   All visions wild and strange;
> Man is the measure of all truth
>   Unto himself. All truth is change . . .
> There is no rest, no calm, no pause,
>   Nor good nor ill . . .

The 1830 poem "The Kraken" is filled with dialectical ambiguities that can be synthesized from an historical perspective. Paden is persuasive in noting that Tennyson probably got from Faber's study of ancient mythologies the notion of a sea serpent representing the deluge or millennium.[20] We have here, then, a type of apocalypse. Yet this is a kind of progress poem too, not unrelated to "Armageddon" insofar as the evil principle is destroyed at the end of time. But in the way that the glorious apocalypse of "Armageddon" turned in Tennyson's hands to a dismaying vision of historical death in "Timbuctoo," the seemingly cheerful message of the death of evil in "The Kraken" is qualified by a context of secret sleeps in other poems of this period. Ricks observes that "the Kraken is like the Lady of Shalott in that he too will awake only to death."[21] However, if the Kraken represents an ineffectual state of sleep and dreams, in hidden places like palaces and mystic isles, then in rising into sight of "man and angels" he enacts an engagement with the world of active history. The Kraken's death may represent the same sort of failure that the protagonists of "The Lotos-Eaters" and "Ulysses" do: an inability to fuse inner powers with those prevailing on the surface world. On the personal level, Tennyson also may have regarded as beyond the limits of man's ordinary conditions his own vatic power, which is becoming questionably "heroic," perhaps inordinately aspiring, maybe useless in the coming age.

Certainly, a morbid drift seems to have been present in Tennyson from early days. No doubt, it was exploited at first for poetic purposes.

---

[20] Paden, p. 155.
[21] Christopher Ricks, *Tennyson*, p. 45.

The youth who wrote the 1827 "Remorse" can hardly be the speaker glancing "Back on the gloom of mis-spent years" and asking that "The vices of my life arise." The poem seems rather an exercise in the sense of original sin ("I was cursed from my birth") and in the inability to repent and be saved. In the 1830 "Supposed Confessions of a Second-rate Sensitive Mind" the speaker wants a sign, a "bolt of fire" to reenact a time "When angels spake to men aloud!" He wants to revivify the "human pride," the "unsunned freshness of my strength,/When I went forth in quest of truth," truth (specifically) in a shape certainly resembling the great Angel Mind of "Timbuctoo": "An image with profulgent brows,/And perfect limbs." The "doubts" that sprinkle the poem are doubts about that very faculty that makes gifted spirits able to communicate with divine purpose, the keystone idea of Tennyson's philosophy of history.

The 1830 "Perdidi Diem," one of Tennyson's finest poems, lays the doubts and difficulties in an even more perturbing context:

> You tell me that to me a Power is given,
> An effluence of serenest fire from Heaven,
> Pure, vapourless, and white,
> As God himself in kind, a spirit-guiding light,
> Fed from each self-originating spring
> Of most inviolate Godhead, issuing
> From underneath the shuddering stairs which climb
> The throne . . . the heart of God's great life.

This power is almost explicitly the Angel Mind of "Timbuctoo," who inspires mankind in history "step by step to scale that mighty stair/Whose landing-place is wrapt about with clouds," save that now the stairs are dubiously "shuddering" and the whole proposition placed in question by the "You tell me." If true, the alleged gift is almost malicious, a light

> Making a "darkness visible"
> Of that which without thee we had not felt
> As darkness, dark ourselves and loving night,
> Night-bats into the filtering crevices
> Hooked, clinging, darkness-fed, at ease.

Faith and doubt suffer tense counterpoise, with no resolution. In the remainder of these lines, the "malignant light" and the "loved mother" are contradictions held, nonetheless, as simultaneously true in a racking dialectic:

> I must needs pore upon the mysteries
> Of my own infinite Nature and torment
> My spirit with a fruitless discontent:
> As in the malignant light
> Of a dim, dripping, moon-enfolding night,
> Young ravens fallen from their cherishing nest
> On the elm-summit, flutter in agony
> With a continual cry
> About its roots, and fluttering trail and spoil
> Their new plumes on the misty soil,
> But not the more for this
> Shall the loved mother minister
> Aerial food, and to their wonted rest
> With them upon the topmost branch in air
> With sleep-compelling down of her most glossy breast.

In fact, salvation is first rescue from the fall from the summit of a kind of World Tree and then sleep, perhaps a lotos sleep: oblivion from malignant vision.

Though Tennyson is quite ready to grant that there is progress in history and a general melioration in the lot of common men, the problem is that he feels himself a poet and, therefore, possessed of uncommon divinatory qualities. In this he identifies with the heroic orders, but he does so guiltily in light of the very inordinateness of aspiration. The base of the elm in "Perdidi Diem" is like the beach morbid with mariners in lotos-land. As such it symbolizes an inability to adapt to common aspirations (indeed, it would be a contradiction in terms were these heroes able to adapt.) "The Two Voices" contains this dialectic as well. On the one hand, the speaker is quite aware that "The years with change advance," that "men, through novel spheres of thought / Still moving after truth long sought, / Will learn new things when I am not," and that "all the years invent; / Each month is various to present / The world with some development." On the other hand, there is no emotional affirmation. The speaker is "so full of misery." We can hardly doubt the personal nature of this poem. His son reports Tennyson as saying, "When I wrote 'The Two Voices' I was so utterly miserable, a burden to myself and to my family, that I said, 'Is life worth anything?'"

(*Memoir*, 1:193). The basic issue seems to be that the speaker is one of those "swift souls that yearn for light . . . Though watching from a ruined tower," who *must* engage transcendence. The still small voice bores in through this chink with "Thou hast not gained a real height,/ Nor art thou nearer to the light,/Because the scale is infinite." The malaise of Milton's Satan ("To be weak is miserable") is hubris, for he aspired to an ultimate for which he was not intended. So the speaker in "The Two Voices" remains "weak" (l. 95) because his pride demands "through thick veils to apprehend/A labour working to an end." This is "the fatal gift of eyes," as he says. Ricks identifies the speaker's blessing of the common lot at the poem's end with the Ancient Mariner's "release from guilt when he 'blessed them unaware/The self-same moment I could pray'."[22] But this redemption is oblique and ambiguous, for the speaker clearly continues to make "choice/To commune with that barren voice,/Than him that said, 'Rejoice! Rejoice!'"

This dialectic of the divinatory spirit, moving between empty prophetic heights and a common-day world that does not seem to need him, informs some other poems of this period. In "The Palace of Art," written 1831–32, Tennyson's godlike soul, the anthropomorphic projection of a God unrealizable any other way, is a feminine anima dwelling like the Lucretian gods of "The Lotos-Eaters" in "God-like isolation" among her treasures. Like the mariners and their gods, she, "Communing with herself," gazes on swinish mankind as "In filthy sloughs they roll a prurient skin" and so, just like the mariners, she sees only "dreadful time, dreadful eternity." Being also the soul of the natural aristocracy in personal if not social redemption, she finds her social conscience in the plight of the people (starved "corpses three-months-old" in her quarters) and descends to a "cottage in the vale" to "mourn and pray" and purge her "guilt." But her resolution is a weak one characterized by only vague ideas about bringing others some day to her palace, a veritable Hesperidian headland, a "huge crag-platform" with "ranged ramparts bright" that "scaled the light."

"The Lady of Shalott," written about May of 1832, is another anima (Jungian) that, as Stevenson says, is a personified image of the "unconscious" of a poet "futile in the face of the utilitarian Victorian age."[23] She dwells on a sacred headland in water, like one of the Hesperides, and in a castle like that of the soul in "The Palace of Art" but so high that she must "look down to Camelot." She has a curse but

[22] Ricks, ed., *Poems of Tennyson*, p. 540.
[23] Lionel Stevenson, "The 'High-born Maiden' Symbol in Tennyson," p. 136.

one that is only pending. She is safe as long as she weaves; only if she stops will the curse be upon her: "a curse is on her if she stay / To look down to Camelot." But, like the soul in "The Palace of Art," she finds that the equivalent of social conscience or "love" makes her tenure of the heights impossible. She follows Lancelot into Camelot but expires among men who fail to recognize the "supernatural," "crossed themselves for fear," closed their eyes with holy dread before the inspired visionary.

Seen in this progression, a poem like the 1830 "Mariana" also reflects the paralysis of an unresolvable dialectic. The symbols seem familiar. Mariana's moated grange is like a cottage in the vale to which a soul might descend to mourn, a kind of fallen headland or beach: a palace of moss, rusted nails, and broken sheds on "glooming flats." Like the ruin of an older heroic time, it too has fallen into vacant disuse and is haunted by ancient presences: "Old faces glimmered through the doors, / Old footsteps trod the upper floors, / Old voices called her from without." In being "thin, as voices from the grave" (to use the words of "The Lotos-Eaters"), these ancestral voices prophesy not war but obsolescence. Their song is not Hesperidian nor even the self-contained singing of the mariners of "The Lotos-Eaters" but only animal noise on the plane of ordinary providence: a blue fly that "sung in the pane," a mouse that "Behind the mouldering wainscot shrieked."

In this phase of the cycle, Mariana's dry season is in a mouldering moated grange that could well enact the role Eliot assigned to the "decaying house" in his "Gerontion" with its history of "many cunning passages." Mariana is stifling in uselessness and frustration. The soul, in brief, has nothing to do. "With time as vacancy," Ricks writes of this poem, "movement dwindles and petrifies."[24] The tree, like a projection of her consciousness, seems a central symbol of the disjunction between what should be and what is: "The shadow of the poplar fell / Upon her bed, across her brow." Gunter sees it as a "cosmic life force" (though specifically a "phallic symbol"),[25] yet if it is a "permeating life which courseth through . . . intricate and labyrinthine veins" (in the words of "Timbuctoo") it may well be a variant of Timbuctoo's "great vine of Fable." But Mariana cannot engage a cosmic life force, an active providence. Instead she experiences the desolation of a vegetating condition not unlike that of "The Lotos-Eaters." The tree mocks a promise of fecundity and knowledge (bed and brow) and is, as

[24] Ricks, *Tennyson*, p. 47.
[25] G. O. Gunter, "Life and Death Symbols in Tennyson's 'Mariana,'" p. 65.

Kincaid points out, a "teasing symbol of the growth and promise that are denied her."[26]

In this period, Tennyson wants not only a hero but an heroic poet. The divinity trickling down into the affairs of the nation is abstract and amorphous, the traditional titans of history are beached or embraced by various symbolic obsolescences, and a vatic poet is neither here nor there but shuttled irresolutely in the dialectic of two perspectives. Yet resolutions would come in the years to follow.

[26]James R. Kincaid, *Tennyson's Major Poems,* pp. 22-23.

IV The English Idyls and *The Princess*

IN THE PERIOD 1835-38, Tennyson worked in a broad variety of poetic veins. Presumably he experienced the aggravations of "Locksley Hall" and the "serene" temper of the English Idyls at the same time. He also dwelt in Wordsworthian simplicity in "Dora," in colloquial humor in "Will Waterproof's Lyrical Monologue," and in satiated cynicism in "The Vision of Sin." He wrote ballads and moral allegory. In this professional heterogeneity, however, we may see developing a synthesis of the dialectic discussed in the previous chapter. Faith in the providential intent in history and doubt about the role of the hero in the process come together in a resolution that works its way through the English Idyls and finally into *The Princess* of 1847. Active providence for Tennyson had descended from ancient divinatory heights to "mingle with the human race" ("Love thou thy land"); as a result, the historical process had become noumenal with the providential presence. Secular progress and eternal form intersect to produce a Great House paradigm, successive objectifications of which constitute the process of history. But heroes and prophets stuck at rarified heights cannot "plow the Present like a field" ("Mechanophilus"). So if Tennyson shows the divinatory faculty at all in poems of this resolution it is as a vestigial state of "weird seizures" of which the prince of *The Princess* is cured when he and Ida are ready to inhabit the Great House. Since God's presence, then, is to be deduced from history itself (and not from the

53

divinations of the hero), man encounters the providential intent in the record of the past even to the present moment.

The basic problem in such an understanding is how to distinguish between genuine and spurious manifestations of divinity in history. In Tennyson's 1839 "The Golden Year" James (Carlyle, now a potent influence on Tennyson) says the seedsman must "plunge/His hand into the bag" to bring forth a golden, utopian form which "is ever at the doors." Yet why does the moneybag of the family in "Locksley Hall" constitute one of those "sickly forms that err from honest Nature's rule"? The "gold that gilds the straitened forehead of the fool" may be presumed to have been gotten with a rigor equal to that of the seedsman. The solution to this dilemma is at the heart of the resolution being pursued here, namely, the state (quoting again from Tennyson's "I loving Freedom for herself") has "in the seed,/The model of her future form." The genuine "new" must be an outgrowth of the old by virtue of the nation being an "organic" whole.[1] Thus the present must be measured against the past if we are to understand the intent of providential dispensations. The rights and powers of the new commercial and industrial classes must be understood, for example, in juxtaposition to the ancient prerogatives of the landed aristocracy. Only by "collapsing" history in this way into a paradigm of society can the virtue of any particular event be determined. It follows that to understand what should be happening in the present, one must understand the past, realize how seeds planted in the beginning are developing further according to providential directives. Put in this way, the whole matter is one of the "medieval ideal" that all commentators see as animating the age.

But the past is infinite in terms both of data and of the meanings that may be drawn from these data. So, to understand the past, the imperatives of the present must be understood, that is, they must be understood if one is to know what to look for. The past, therefore, must be examined by a unique faculty of divination—the very faculty discussed in chapter 2 as characteristic of Niebuhr, the Liberal Anglican historians, the Apostolic circle, and Tennyson himself. The historian must be a mystic medium between the past and the present. The work of "mere" historians is useless in this endeavor, for chroniclers only compile data. Their eyes are too much on the past and not at all on the present. "Antiquarians and men calling themselves historians have

---

[1] See chapter 3, note 4 and discussion.

written so uninstructively of the ancient world," Arnold asserted, "for they did not understand the world around them."[2] Carlyle's *Past and Present*, published in 1843 or some four years before Tennyson's *The Princess*, scorns Dryadust's "mountains of dead ashes, wreck and burnt bones" that "assiduous Pedantry dig[s] up from the Past Time." That is, Jocelin's chronicle must be read "with ancient yet with modern eyes"; and also, Jocelin himself writes only about "what *he* finds interesting!" (II.2, 14, 1). As Arnold put it further, the "Past is reflected by the Present; so far as we see and understand the present, so far can we see and understand the Past, but no further."[3]

To mediate the imperatives of the Victorian present and those of a medieval time when the national genius began its work, Tennyson developed the idylic mode. Theocritus was his favorite classical poet, Tennyson wrote the "English Idyls," *The Princess* is usually seen as a complex idyl, and his major work he called the *Idylls of the King*. Being this important, the nature of the idyl has, of course, been noted in Tennyson studies. Its historical dimension has been stressed insufficiently, however, especially insofar as it is a natural vehicle for the medievalism of the period because of the way its "picturesque" quality implies an amalgam of past and present. This quality lies at the heart of the Gothic revival, in terms of landscape gardening, architecture, painting, but even more pertinently in a poetry that seeks a paradigm of social relationships.

The term *idyl* is protean, yet one quality all critics seem to agree upon is a certain sensuous pictorialism or picturesqueness. Stedman called the Theocritan idyls "*eidullia*,—little pictures of real life,"[4] and Mackail termed them "cabinet-pictures . . . each holding its tiny convex mirror up to nature."[5] But what is "real life" and what is "nature"? Rosenmeyer points out that "nature" in idyl may mean almost anything: "in one branch of the pastoral, not the main branch by any means, there is an attempt to capture the earthy feel of the countryside" but more typically, there lies in idyl what Herder recognized as a "'geistiges Arkadien,' a paradise of our hopes and wishes, a country that never was and never will be."[6] That is, idyl holds an ideal coming from the beginning of time.

---

[2] Quoted by Duncan Forbes, *Liberal Anglican Idea of History*, p. 88.
[3] Quoted by Forbes, p. 88.
[4] Edmund Clarence Stedman, *Victorian Poets*, p. 207.
[5] J. W. Mackail, *Lectures on Greek Poetry*, p. 219.
[6] Thomas G. Rosenmeyer, *The Green Cabinet*, p. 18.

In this picturesqueness, present real and past ideal meet. In his 1831 review of Tennyson's 1830 *Poems*, Hallam diagnosed the need to reinvigorate contemporary poetry through a kind of medieval ideal and noted how Tennyson would do this. He would "bring our over-civilized condition of thought into union with the fresh productive spirit that brightened the morning of our literature" by being a poet of "sensation rather than reflection," a successor to Keats and Shelley, who "absorb their whole being into the energy of sense ... they are picturesque."[7] Tennyson's poetry would mediate a spiritual "paradise" of primal beginnings and an overcivilized, commercial present where the spiritual elect are in danger of obsolescence.

Long ago Stedman discussed the idyl in terms of an extensive parallel between Theocritus's Alexandria and Tennyson's England. He noted the "luxurious, speculative, bustling, news-devouring hurly-burly of that strangely modern Alexandrian time" which, "if not that of a decadence, was reflective, critical, scholarly, rather than creative." So, to reinvigorate the dried-up fancy, Theocritus "flung himself right upon nature" for "common, everyday life."[8] Mackail agreed that Alexandrian poetry "had to find new patterns, had to attach itself as it could to a life that lay, swarming and monotonous, flat amid immense horizons, in the endless aimless afternoon." Therefore, Theocritus reinterpreted the "life of a past world" by a "return to nature" and the "common things of life," which was a "sustained attempt to translate the old motives, the traditional subjects."[9] Such remarks are addressed to the question of poetic purpose, yet it is difficult not to extend to the social plane as well this ability of idyl to merge past and present.

This sensuous picturesqueness, after all, invests more than poetry. Chandler observes that the very origins of the Gothic revival are "in the picturesque." She cites such houses as Walpole's Strawberry Hill as symbols of England's past in its quest for tradition and dynasty.[10] Malins notes that the term *picturesque* comes into Tennyson's time through the landscape and architecture of the eighteenth century and that it means precisely a "mixture of historical and pictorial," with particular reference to "mossy cells, old castles on cliffs and gloomy pines ... a ruin, ivy-clad and mouldering": all that is especially "capable of being illustrated in painting."[11] Carlyle introduces *Past and Present*

[7] Given in *Tennyson: The Critical Heritage*, p. 40.
[8] Stedman, pp. 205-7.
[9] Mackail, pp. 218, 212-13.
[10] Alice Chandler, *Dream of Order*, pp. 184-86.
[11] Edward Malins, *English Landscaping and Literature*, pp. 142-46.

with the "vast grim venerable ruins" of Saint Edmundsbury Abbey
(II.2) as a seed bed of correct religious and social value. It is significant
that the Houses of Parliament were rebuilt after the great fire of 1834 in
the form of a vast Gothic cathedral designed to evoke, as in idyl, the
medieval past.

What concerns us specifically, however, is the relationship of idyl to
the English Great House in the period. Such houses were being built in
great numbers (as money accumulated) either about the real ruins of the
early house, "ivy-clad and mouldering," or, if lacking these, about fake
ones. This architectural imperative is based on the desire to create a
symbol of social order by the merger of past and present, of feudal order
and growing modern "freedom." The estate that the Great House
represents is a burgeoning symbol of the form whose seed lay in
medieval time. It is new but it is also an outgrowth of the old, and its
virtue lies precisely in its having grown through historical time. The
"hierarchical scheme of which it is a product," writes Molesworth, is a
symbol of the "uses and value of history." The "paradigmatic nature of
the country" is "a mirror of the State itself" and, further, that of the
"eternal city, the dwelling free from changes and the ravages of
time."[12] Gill asserts that the Great House is a "symbol of humane order
and true community."[13] It is to this eternal city that man ascends in
this period of Tennyson's development, striving within the process of
history itself "step by step to scale that mighty stair," to use the words
of "Timbuctoo" once more.

But the road to Vivien place, the Great House of *The Princess*, is a
rocky one. Heroes must remove themselves from their ancient vantage
and wed with common interests, literally, if they are to continue the
dynastic line with children. Sir Edward Head of the 1837–38 English
idyl "Walking to the Mail," however, is no holy medium for the new
providence. He is descended, rather, from Tennyson's Ulysses, for he
was

> Vexed with a morbid devil in his blood
> That veiled the world with jaundice, hid his face
> From all men, and commercing with himself,
> He lost the sense that handles daily life—
> That keeps us all in order more or less—
> And sick of home went overseas for change,

[12] Charles Molesworth, "Property and Virtue," pp. 151, 142, 148, 152.
[13] Richard Gill, *Happy Rural Seat*, p. 227.

driven away specifically by the Reform Bill, "this bill that past,/And fear of change at home." His Penelope is a "woman like a butt, and harsh as crabs," the other half of an impossible marriage, for she "was the daughter of a cottager,/Out of her sphere." The transcendence of this degenerate Tithon is a tawdry "devil": a "jolly ghost, that shook/The curtains, whined in lobbies, tapt at doors,/And rummaged like a rat."

In fact, heroes have a hard time with the love union needed to seed the Great House. In descending from their heights they overdo the egalitarianism. As early as 1833–34, Tennyson had written "The Lord of Burleigh," a poem wherein a scion of ancient family weds a village maiden who thought he was but a painter. He took her, all unknowing, through a gateway with armorial bearings to a Great House that he suddenly announced was hers. This union of aristocrat and commoner immediately was blasted. The wife "drooped and drooped" and, after three children, died, apparently unable spiritually to ventilate at these social heights. Great lords may not wither at the summit now but they do carry some sort of corrosive afflatus from prior interchange with malignant divinities that is manifestly unsuitable to the lower orders. Not that they all have descended. The protagonist of the 1834 "Sir Galahad" is still on "lonely mountain-meres" but does not wither, even though he hears a transcendent "noise of hymns" in glowing forests and a "voice" in "some secret shrine." He is saved by the heroic medium of holy war. His "good blade carves the casques of men" and he pursues the holy grail endlessly. Unfortunately for the Great House model, he "never felt the kiss of love,/Nor maiden's hand in mine." "So pass I hostel, hall, and grange . . . I climb the height." Both depths and heights are unproductive in this mingling of hero and human race.

On the distaff side, the 1835 Lady Clara Vere de Vere is the "daughter of a hundred Earls" and a "great enchantress" but cold as the "lion on your old stone gates." No great love union is here—no plowing of the present, no children—for her lover Laurence (of "modest worth") has cut his throat. And she, though "in flowing health, with boundless wealth," is "sickening of a vague disease" and will never marry. From her Great House she will not minister to the "beggars at your gate," the "poor about your lands." Lord Ronald of the 1835 poem "Lady Clare" has been tricked out of his inheritance by the nursemaid who substituted her own baby for the real heiress (who died). Even after discovering this, he happily marries the same nurse's daughter. But the effect of this class fusion is muted by the necessary laundering of commonalty through a manor breeding.

Sir Robert of another English idyl from this period, "Audley Court" (1838), is dead, apparently a kind and scholarly man but dead nonetheless and unable to usher in the new age by way of proper heirs. At least his Great House hangs benignly (if vacantly) over the young men singing at their picnic and wondering "who would rent the Hall." In the 1839 poem "Edwin Morris," people move in but it is clear they are not yet the heroes of the future. The ancient heights and the low-lying acquisitions of the *noveaux riches* are juxtaposed at the start of the poem. Above are

> ruins of a castle, built
> When men knew how to build, upon a rock
> With turrets lichen-gilded like a rock:
> And here, new-comers in an ancient hold,
> New-comers from the Mersey, millionaires.

"Sir Robert with his watery smile / And educated whisker" with "sixty thousand pounds" and "lands in Kent and messuages in York" is patently no figure in whom past and present meet, in whom the medieval ideal may be embodied.

About this time (1839), however, Tennyson began work on *The Princess,* which he published in 1847. Thus, the poem appeared in the heyday of the Gothic revival, and the medieval ideal it embodied was not lost on the reviewers. Kingsley, for example, wrote that Tennyson "reached the ideal by the only true method,—by bringing the middle age forward to the Present one, and not by ignoring the Present to fall back on a cold and galvanized Mediaevalism; and thus he makes his 'Medley' a mirror of the nineteenth century."[14] Nor were the reviewers unaware that the poem was a kind of idyl. Among the earliest, Kingsley remarked its "idyllic manner"[15] and Stedman its "idyllic or composite order."[16] Modern critics certainly concur, calling it an "idyll protracted," a "series of idylls," and its prologue "virtually another 'English idyl'."[17]

The idylic picturesque is overtly a characteristic of the architecture

---

[14] Given in *Tennyson: The Critical Heritage,* p. 180.
[15] Given in *Tennyson: The Critical Heritage,* p. 180.
[16] Stedman, pp. 219–20.
[17] Respectively, T. S. Eliot, *Selected Essays,* p. 289; Clyde de L. Ryals, *From the Great Deep,* p. 23; and Jerome Hamilton Buckley, *Growth of a Poet,* p. 96.

of the poem's Great Houses. The Park House of *The Princess*'s outer shell is much like the Park Place of Walpole's cousin General Conway, which was an "enlarged Strawberry Hill" with "such embellishments as forty-five prehistoric stones . . . a rustic bridge over no water, a lonely tomb where nobody was buried," and "steep beech woods dropping to the river."[18] The poem's Park House has at its core the "Carved stones of the Abbey-ruin in the park,/Huge Ammonites, and the first bones of Time." The Abbey ruin itself is "High-arched and ivy-claspt,/Of finest Gothic lighter than a fire": "one wide chasm of time and frost." In the inner shell of the poem, Ida's archeological expedition takes place in the Gothic picturesqueness "where the river sloped/To plunge in cataract, shattering on black blocks/A breadth of thunder." They travel "o'er a bridge of pine-wood crossing" to the "flowery levels underneath the crag."

Through the idyl's ability to fuse past and present, history becomes palimpsest. The past is never lost. Its remains exist physically and its archetypal forms continue to animate the present. But the present can grasp the meaningfulness of the past only through the perspectives that focus the historical memory. Thus the poem holds its medieval core within a frame of vital, living interests and this core in turn envelops other, more ancient time frames. These mirrorings are suggested by the "Laborious orient ivory sphere in sphere" on the tables of Vivien place ("A Gothic ruin and a Grecian House"), crowded with remains from "every clime and age/Jumbled together." The prince in the middle shell of the poem's time frame is, in the outer shell, the speaker of the poem, the seven-headed narrator, Sir Walter manqué, and the archetypal "great Sirs" of all England. Beyond this, in the circumambient "real" present, he is Edmund Lushington about to marry Cecilia Tennyson, he is Tennyson himself estranged from Emily Sellwood, and he is also those friends since Cambridge days who often told such tandem stories. Receding into time, the prince is Sir Ralph and all the "knights,/Half-legend, half-historic, counts and kings/Who laid about them at their wills," won their ladies, and established their houses.

In the same vein, Ida is Lilia in the poem's outer time frame, yet Cecilia, Emily, Caroline Norton, Lucie Duff Gordon, and all enlightened women in the real world. In the inner frame, she is also that medieval "lady, one that armed/Her own fair head, and sallying through the gate,/Had beat her foes with slaughter from her walls," and, moving

---

[18]Malins, p. 120.

to the very center of the archetypal form, all the noble women from antiquity whom she enumerates at the beginning of book 2. The setting is the Great House, which also receives a multiple identity. In the outer frame, Ida's castle is Vivien place through which we see the Lushingtons' Park House and all the Gothic houses built in such profusion during Victorian times, perhaps especially Bayons Manor, the Great House of Tennyson's uncle Charles (now Tennyson d'Eyncourt). Inwardly, it is all castles and Great Houses. The formative encounter on the grounds of Ida's castle reflects the outer frame's gathering in the Abbey ruin and in the festival of the Maidstone Mechanics' Institution on the grounds of Park House, 6 July 1842 (the occasion of the poem—and a common occurrence in the Owenist movement of the time).[19] But it is also the image of social cohesion about castle and lord, one of those symbolic parties or picnics that Gill calls "ritual enactments of community" that bring "unity of past, present, and future," and are presided over by a majestic person, often the spirit of some "vital" woman.[20]

To actualize the ideal, the vital Ida and the prince must marry, but the problem is that, in her intense progressivism, she is immobilized in the future, facing away from the historically formative eternity ever at the doors. She is unable to work lastingly in the present because she "overlooks" it, rising "upon a wind of prophecy/Dilating on the future" with the "passion of the prophetess": a "Memnon smitten with the morning Sun." She stands "like a stately Pine/Set in a cataract on an island-crag," like a veritable Lady of Shalott tending to her transcendent knitting, uninvolved with the real. Ida's urge to "live, perforce, from thought to thought, and make/One act a phantom of succession" fixes her in the forward stages of discretely flowing time, ever in advance of the here and now. In this state she is, consequently, impatient with the medieval ideal. She is angered by the appeal to the enchantment of the "ungracious past" in the intercalary lyrics (that, indeed, seem to interpose static interruptions in the forward-flowing narrative). Tennyson said the "Tears, idle tears" lyric was inspired by "the yellowing autumn-tide at [the medieval] Tintern Abbey, full for me of its bygone memories" (*Memoir*, 1:253). The singer of the lyric, "thinking of the days that are no more," sings "with such passion that the tear,/She sang of, shook and fell, an erring pearl/Lost in her bosom." But Ida is disdainful that about "the mouldered lodges of the

---

[19] For topical interests, see Killham, *Tennyson and "The Princess."*
[20] Gill, pp. 12, 16, 13.

Past" may haunt "So sweet a voice and vague, fatal to men." So, "Well needs it we should cram our ears with wool/And so pace by . . . let old bygones be . . . let the past be past; let be/Their cancelled Babels." In brief, she rejects the medievalism the prince seems to stand for. She will march to a "trumpet in the distance pealing news/Of better . . . Not such as moans about the retrospect."

But the prince and Ida, however seemingly irreconcilable in representing retrospective past and progressive present, are united. They become one precisely through the brokerage of the chivalric code of the medieval ideal. The prince, the representative of rehabilitated traditionalism, begins by worshiping Ida in the courtly manner: "wore her picture by my heart,/And one dark tress; and all around them both/Sweet thoughts would swarm as bees about their queen." In the proper idylic setting, oft in the wild woods he "plucked her likeness out;/Laid it on flowers, and watched it lying bathed/In the green gleam of dewy-tasselled trees." Ida receives the news that the prince "worships your ideal" with the proper exclamations of liberated scorn: "barren verbiage, current among men,/Light coin, the tinsel clink of compliment." Yet Ida and her women succumb to the code. Lady Psyche clearly is attracted to "chivalry:/When some respect, however slight, was paid/To woman," and, most importantly, Ida, the chips down, relies on its conventions and accepts herself as prize: "Is not our cause pure? . . . fight; you failing, I abide/What end soever." Her brothers live by the code, crying "honour: every captain waits/Hungry for honour."

The prince cavils about "this wild wreath of air,/This flake of rainbow flying on the highest/Foam of men's deeds—this honour, if ye will," but agrees to fight for his lady. Arac bowls over Cyril, Florian, and the prince like ninepins, but the prince wins Ida by that inverse of the chivalric coin, the rights of weakness. Tennyson agreed with the judgment of Wallace, the editor of the 1891 edition of *The Princess*, that the prince's "too emotional temperament and susceptibility to cataleptic seizures . . . was probably intended to emphasize" that it was not his "physical or moral brilliance that won his lady."[21] The prince's very ineptitude arouses the spontaneous generosity of Ida's natural passions and, since it is from the most noble and strong that we expect altruism and noblesse oblige, Ida falls in love with the battered prince and nurses him back to health like an "infant." This is only turnabout fair play in a poet one of whose "main tests of manhood is 'the chivalrous reverence' for womanhood" (*Memoir*, 1:250).

---

[21] Quoted by Christopher Ricks, ed., *Poems of Tennyson*, p. 742.

The emotions now lavished on the prince by Ida had been turned on by a real "little child"—"the link thro' the parts" of the poem, as Tennyson said (*Memoir*, 1:254)—that Ida had taken "for an hour in mine own bed." Exercised from the first "About this losing of the child" in woman, Ida ironically finds a little child leading her to emotional floodgates, so that she too is reborn: "through her limbs a drooping languor wept" and "out of languour leapt a cry;/ Leapt fiery Passion," exactly as earlier the prince's heart had "beat thick with passion and with awe." "An emphasis on emotion," Chandler remarks, "the heart rather than the head—is always central to the medievalist tradition."[22] Ida finds, therefore, that "Love is of the valley" and she is redeemed by earthly love. She and the prince become the Janus-headed "conflux of two Eternities" (in Carlyle's phrase from *The French Revolution*, part 1, book 4, chapter 4), a "single pure and perfect animal" whose reproduction as a succession of unions and children will continue until the outer shell of the poem's time frame is reached.

A rebirth of medieval paradise (the very quality that Herder saw as the essence of idyl)[23] is, then, a recurring possibility. "Then comes the statelier Eden back to men:/Then reign the world's great bridals." The prince and Ida are a regenerated Adam and Eve, "side by side, full-summed in all their powers,/Dispensing harvest, sowing the To-be," like the seedsman of "The Golden Year" plunging "hand into the bag" to usher in the ritual millennium. On the mythic level, in fact, the ceremonies surrounding the establishment of their house, as Eliade says,

suspend the flow of profane time, of duration, and project the celebrant into a mythical time, *in illo tempore*. . . . However, the construction rites show us something beyond this: imitation, hence reactualization, of the cosmogony. A "new era" opens with the building of every house. Every construction is an absolute beginning; that is, tends to restore the initial instant, the plenitude of a present that contains no trace of history.[24]

In the poem's frame, Sir Walter presides over "This fine old world of ours" that "is but a child/Yet in the go-cart." The child, therefore, becomes a symbol for progressive history, yet (in the interests of temporal fusion) only through those parts of the poem that take place in the past. Those parts that occur in the present are presided over by

[22] Chandler, p. 153.
[23] See note 6 above.
[24] Mircea Eliade, *Myth of the Eternal Return*, p. 76.

the statue of Sir Ralph, symbol of the constancy of the medieval ideal. He appears in the festive present as "A broken statue propt against the wall,/As gay as any." Lilia "robed the shoulders in a rosy silk," literally coloring the past with latter-day thought and emotion. Ida had said that her champions would be "The sole men we shall prize in the after-time,/Your very armour hallowed, and your statues/Reared, sung to." Thus it is observed to her descendant and double, Lilia, that the "feudal warrior lady-clad"—there, "while they talked, above their heads"—"has got your colours." Lilia, "Half child" and palingenetic replication of the child that was a symbol of the future, unites with Sir Ralph, the palpable remains of the past, to become the Dioscuritic symbol of the poem's interpenetration of past and present. The costume drama even comes to a close as Lilia "Disrobed the glimmering statue of Sir Ralph," the "feudal knight in silken masquerade." In this inter-twining we see Tennyson's view that, as he said, "every human being is a vanful of human beings" (*Memoir,* 1:323 n.1). The ages are separate and yet joined. "The past and present and future should be linked together in a chain," Thomas Arnold observed, "that in every age the dead should still, in a manner be present among the living."[25]

The story told by the gathering in the Abbey ruin reflects the "realized" ideal of the scene in the poem's frame. On the grounds, the historically productive embodiment of concatenated generations is the "great broad-shouldered genial Englishman": Sir Walter. He is the apotheosis of the interpenetration between the ancient feudal rights and those of the Reform Bill that Tennyson had so welcomed. He enlists under the feudal nexus of the Great House the works of modern science and industry, the bounty of progressive farming, and the largesse of traditional hospitality:

> A lord of fat prize-oxen and of sheep,
> A raiser of huge melons and of pine,
> A patron of some thirty charities,
> A pamphleteer on guano and on grain,
> A quarter-sessions chairman, abler none.

He is in the forefront of "all the wonder that would be" (in the line from "Locksley Hall"), the enlightened patron, therefore, of Mechanics' Institution festivals, where the multitude is taught "with facts" yet in ways "that sport/Went hand in hand with Science." In this ideal order—

[25]Quoted by Forbes, p. 168.

the foundation of the medieval ideal—all together are a "nation yet, the rulers and the ruled," in "universal culture" under the aegis of the "great Sirs" that keep England free from the "Revolts, republics, revolutions" that rack France. The people hail Sir Walter with a "shout / More joyful than the city-roar that hails / Premier or king!" Such is, at his best, the "future man."

However (to anticipate the argument of the next chapter), certain things in the poem suggest this to be a somewhat uneasy resolution to troubled history. The celebrated "strange diagonal" of mode and manner takes its color from a certain diminution of the very medieval ideal that is being glorified. Peculiar "plants" in the idealized center of the poem cannot help reflecting upon the verity of the putatively real frame. Sir Walter indeed properly may embody the feudal element of the medieval ideal, but his progeny lounge picturesquely in the Gothic ruins and tell a story that, in its diminution and burlesque of this ideal, will invite later the wit of W. S. Gilbert in his adaptation, *Princess Ida.* The prince is a weak and feminized hero, a parody of the mighty son, with "lengths of yellow ringlet, like a girl." He and his friends depart "from the bastioned walls / Like threaded spiders" and arrive at Ida's castle in "female gear . . . maiden plumes." He reappears before his father like a "draggled mawkin . . . drenched with ooze, and torn with briers, / More crumpled than a poppy from the sheath, / And all one rag, disprinced from head to heel." His "weird seizures" are morbid, like a disease ("catalepsy"). In his opera, Gilbert named this character Hilarion.

The ranter king, the prince's father, is a mockery of the grave symbol of medieval authority. At news of Ida's repudiation of the marriage arrangements, he roars that he "Will crush her pretty maiden fancies dead / In iron gauntlets," then puts a foot through her tapestry. Throughout, he utters such sentiments as "Man is the hunter; woman is his game" and "Man to command and woman to obey." Ida's father Gama is a "little dry old man, without a star, / Not like a king." These are strange heroes. As to heroines, Ida's transformation from mighty prophetess to country housewife bears an aura of the absurd. She had from the start an air of inflamed egoism, ever since Lilia suggested she be "six feet high, / Grand, epic, homicidal." She makes an extravagant entrance with "two tame leopards couched beside her throne . . . liker to the inhabitant / Of some clear planet close upon the Sun, / Than our man's earth." Her later appearances are even more godlike as, facing her clamorous women (that "weight of destiny"), she hubristically "stretched her arms and called/Across the tumult and the tumult fell."

Nor is the Great House itself without this exaggerated, uncertain air. The medieval manors built in the time certainly had their critics, particularly poor relations like the Somersby Tennysons, who saw with some bitter amusement what their Uncle Charles was building with his inheritance. Everywhere, in the words of Tennyson's grandson, "were to be seen badges and coats-of-arms of the d'Eyncourts, Lovels, Beaumonts, Marmions, Greys, Plantagenets, Lancasters, Bardolphs and others, through whom Charles claimed descent," as Charles "endeavoured to give the impression of an ancient manor house, which had gradually evolved out of a feudal castle. Accordingly, the architecture was of many different medieval periods."[26] Such construction tends to become mere fashion in a sophisticated age; and fashion, as Emerson said in "Manners" (1844), is "virtue gone to seed: it is a kind of posthumous honor. It does not often caress the great, but the children of the great: it is a hall of the Past."

Neither Vivien place nor its social hierarchy inspires our whole admiration, neither the loungers within nor the "multitude, a thousand heads" and "happy faces" without. They play with gilded balls on waterspouts, a fired cannon, telescopes, electric shocks:

> round the lake
> A little clock-work steamer paddling plied
> And shook the lilies . . .
> A petty railway ran: a fire-baloon
> Rose gem-like up before the dusky groves
> And dropt a fairy parachute and past.

There is here the same questionable practice of *Past and Present*'s Quaker manufacturer, Friend Prudence, who "keeps a thousand workmen; has striven in all ways to attach them to him; has provided conversational soirées; playgrounds, bands of music for the young ones; went even 'the length of buying them a drum:' all which has turned out to be an excellent investment" (IV.5). Nor does the body of the poem shore up the frame's bemusement of the Great House paradigm. One suspects, in light of the ranter king's continuing vigor, that the prince and Ida will dispense the To-be as if by Gama's leave (in Gilbert's words from *Princess Ida*) in another comic-opera "Castle Adamant,/One of my many country houses."

[26] Sir Charles Tennyson, *Alfred Tennyson*, p. 159.

Tennyson is aware of the ambiguities in a strategy of multiple vision and his final concern is over the interpenetration, not only of past and present, but also of modes and genres. He says that the women are "realists" who demand "true-heroic—true-sublime." Their intercalary lyrics, which interrupt the flow of narrative, identify them with the prince's interest in the past. "Their silent influence . . . Had ever seemed to wrestle with burlesque," so that, even though the men are "mockers" and call for "mock-heroic gigantesque," the story ends in "quite a solemn close." The men, on the other hand, carrying the narrative forward and disdaining the past, become identified with Ida. In this complex interchange of roles, Tennyson himself "moved as in a strange diagonal,/And maybe neither pleased myself nor them."

The resulting medley has exercised critical description. Joseph, for instance, sets up a tension between the early Shakespearean comedies (characterized by mocking satire, burlesque, the male, narrative, comedy, and French revolutions), and the late dark Shakespearean comedies (characterized as near-tragic, female, elegiac, lyrical, heroic in their poetry, and stable in their social contexts).[27] Buckley suggests that the "diluted mock heroics" did not trouble a serious subject so much as an "admixture of solemnity" spoiled a potentially distinguished artificial comedy.[28] The mix is troubled. In that a new society seems to crystallize about a marriage, the poem falls into the mŷthos of New Comedy, but in that the medieval ideal that this marriage incarnates is mocked, the poem seems a type of Menippean satire. The burlesqued diminution of the elements in this ideal places it next to *The Rape of the Lock* as a mock-heroic poem, but the pathos of historical loss places it next to *Don Quixote*. Real, though idle, tears are asked for the poignant days that are no more, but real laughter is sought for the efforts to revive them. *The Princess* is, finally, a kind of historical pastoral or idyl, a strategy that rises directly out of its effort to detect ideal form in the juxtaposition of medieval past and Victorian present. The essence of the past can be caught only through the filter of the present, and so the fictive construct—a poem, a history—becomes like a drawing-room window on the pristine past, partially a mirror but one that reflects the observer as well.

Though Tennyson's diminution of the medieval ideal makes ambiguous this resolution of the problem of history, this is not to say that his penchant for the idylic mode rested on a desire for pastoral *otium*.

27 Gerhard Joseph, *Tennysonian Love*, pp. 78–88.
28 Buckley, *Growth of a Poet*, p. 97.

The point is that for one of his resolutions of life's contradictions he discovered an epistemology of history based on divinatory insight into the timelessness that appears in the long perspectives of the past. History's cycles are like superimposed rings through which by a kind of intellectual trompe l'oeil infinity is seen at point time. Gray sees an impaction of past and present in idyl "as a mode of differentiating and recombining effects on the basis of a new symbolism. . . . the poet of idyl utilizes his growing or changing awareness of relativity to give perspectives through the emerging mosaic of his poem. Idyl is nothing but open perspectives brought into focus."[29] Primal vigor, present temper, and even future expectations fuse by idyl into meaningful ways of thinking and feeling.

Such a strategy becomes useful especially because of the perspectives that come in an age of history. Chandler observes that in the Waverley Novels Scott utilizes four time frames to effect his enormous influence in the age.[30] Langbaum argues that the ambiguities of the dramatic monologue result from the fact that judgment had become "largely psychologized and historicized," that the "modern sense of the past involves, on the one hand, a sympathy for the past, a willingness to understand it in its own terms as different from the present; and on the other hand it involves a critical awareness of our own modernity."[31] This sense of expanding perspectives has as a natural dialectic the urge to focus them. Certainly, perspectives in *The Princess* are focused. The "sevenfold story" is intended to "kill/Time . . . The tyrant!" and to depict Ida's insight that "was, and is, and will be, are but is;/And all creation is one act at once."

This desire to focus perspectives, to bring past and present into fusion, is the basis for the Tennysonian predilection for "frames." The many framing devices Tennyson used in his poems have been commented upon so frequently that the proposition is not worth a lengthy review here. The mirrorings and framings of *The Princess* are intended to show that (in Carlyle's words) the "Ideal always has to grow in the Real, and to seek out its bed and board there" (*Past and Present*, II.4). "All things serve their time," Ida says, "Toward that great year," that "golden year" (VI.48). But that was before she married the prince. After, she knows with James (who is Carlyle) of "The Golden Year," that this ideal is "ever at the doors," in the light of common day.

[29] J. M. Gray, "A Study in Idyl," p. 114.
[30] Chandler, p. 31.
[31] Robert Langbaum, *Poetry of Experience*, pp. 107, 96.

In the streets of London one day in 1842, Tennyson made a remark to Fitzgerald that shows his belief at this time in an "informing spirit" in the ordinary world, realizable in the meeting of past and present. They had visited Saint Paul's and Tennyson noted that, "merely as an enclosed Space in a huge City this is very fine." After getting out into what Fitzgerald called the "central roar," Tennyson added, "*This* is the mind: *that*, a mood of it."[32] An unpublished poem of this period speaks to this interpenetration:

The breathing body of the Present drew
 This lifeblood from the dead heart of the Past
 So is not altogether old or new
Though all things in another mould are cast.
The informing spirit of the world exults
 In fruitful change and wide variety
And it is worth our while to live and see
 Old principles still working new results.
One thunderclap is loud: another dull.
 There is one law that sways the thunderstorms
And beauty never is unbeautiful
 Where beauty hath a million thousand forms.
Then wherefore gape you at the open door
It is the earth we live on evermore.[33]

---

[32] From Fitzgerald's annotated copy of Tennyson's 1842 *Poems*, vol. 1, p. 135 (Trinity Library, Cambridge listing Adv d/11/26; see also *Memoir*, 1:183, which has the material slightly misused). Note "roaring Temple-bar" in "Will Waterproof's Lyrical Monologue" (l. 69).
[33] Trinity notebook 0.15.23.

V In Memoriam

TENNYSON'S NEEDS FOR a divinity felt on the pulse and for a hero of magnified qualities were too great for *The Princess* to satisfy. Divinity is too suffused in the Great House paradigm of history, and the "great broad-shouldered genial Englishman" Sir Walter (and indeed, the cataleptic prince) is too mundane. The work's many strange diagonals suggest the limits of this resolution to history in Tennyson's mind. Tennyson's other resolution, to the problem of God and man in history, is seemingly far different, taking form within the individual mind. Tennyson comes to it by confronting the very shipwreck and sorrow of the human condition he found in the early thirties (see the concluding part of chapter 3). In this apocalyptic situation, God manifests a nature which, as an "other," is forever beyond man's understanding. History occurs in convulsive cycles, so there is in this resolution a stress on revolutionary disjunction instead of on peaceful gradualism. The hero is no longer an obsolete titan. He is a representative of the human race, and yet something more than a Sir Walter. His divinatory powers return to allow the apprehension of an anthropomorphic divinity once more. Now, however, it is the divinity within: the great Angel Mind in man. For Tennyson, as for Wordsworth, this now became "My haunt, and the main region of my song" (*The Recluse*). Not only is such a resolution a fusion of divinity, history, and mind characteristic for its time,[1] it also represents the mainstream of Tennyson's thinking. It works its way through "Locksley Hall" and into *In Memoriam*, and extends into *Maud* and the *Idylls*; but it also curves back to take in his youthful preoccupation with providence, historical disasters, and great heroes doing their duty in the mysterious meaningfulness of history.

"Locksley Hall" is a troublesome poem because it is at the juncture leading to these two resolutions. The hero vacillates between them, in fact, never sure whether he wants to be part of a wondrously evolving "Mother-Age" or to blow it up in revolution. The hero (call him Locksley) certainly identifies himself with a collective expansion of spirit and seems to carry forward the mood of Tennyson's earlier poems praising steady progress and mechanical wonders: "Men, my brothers, men the workers, ever reaping something new:/That which they have done but earnest of the things that they shall do." He is one with the "standards of the people," and embraces that "one increasing purpose" that runs through the ages (a phrase that Jowett once said was Hegel's *Philosophy of History* "buried under a heap of categories," *Memoir*, 1:425). But this purpose plainly does not include the medieval ideal's Great House, nor a Sir Walter hosting a Mechanics' Institution festival on the grounds. Locksley Hall is inhabited by a nasty gentry: a selfish uncle and Locksley's helpless cousin Amy. This landed aristocracy is characterized by "social wants . . . social lies . . . sickly forms . . . gold," and it is the *nouveaux riches* merchant princes who are glorified. Locksley's vision for the future has "heavens fill with commerce, argosies of magic sails./Pilots of the purple twilight, dropping down with costly bails." Seemingly, Tennyson's messiah is now Plugson purged of mammonism: "England's hope at present," as Carlyle says in *Past and Present* (III.12).

[1] Carlyle, for instance, under the impress of the same Germanic research and speculation that had helped shape the ideas of the Apostles, portrayed in the 1837 *The French Revolution* his central belief that historical "change appears not so much as organic growth but as disruptive action begetting a new world that is basically characterized by the fluidity of change" (Albert J. LaValley, *Carlyle and the Idea of the Modern*, p. 132). In this, for Carlyle (as for Hegel), "there is a 'cunning of reason' . . . working its will even while madness seems to be in command" (Philip Rosenberg, *The Seventh Hero*, p. 76). In the process, "Carlyle's great men and heroes [are] . . . instruments of God's will" (René Wellek, *Confrontations*, p. 100). Tennyson and Carlyle were, of course, friends, perhaps from 1834 but certainly from 1837 when Tennyson settled near London. By 1838 they were "members of that carefully chosen group of men who met for dinner together in London once a month to discuss literature and the world in general" (quoted words and probabilities for 1834 from William Darby Templeman, "Tennyson's *Locksley Hall* and Thomas Carlyle," pp. 39–41).

But this increasing purpose is disturbingly on a plane of catastrophic violence. Locksley longs "to perish, falling on the foeman's ground." His wondrous vision of the future includes air warfare complete with a "ghastly dew/From the nations' airy navies grappling in the central blue." One may speculate that this may be just commercial rivalry, but it is more likely a symbolic representation of the nature of the "one increasing purpose." In this imminent apocalypse, Locksley would find his ideal dying place where the "ranks are rolled in vapour, and the winds are laid with sound," as though in an updated version of what the great Angel Mind had shown the young poet in "Armageddon." The "heavens fill with shouting" in the "thunder-storm" through which the peoples rush in "Locksley Hall" is a scene comparable to "Armageddon"'s "gathering of nations . . . Of many thunders and confused noise,/Of bloody grapplings". Locksley's first word, *Comrades*, and his warlike predisposition both suggest a military role. His last pronouncement is a wish for a kind of universal apocalypse sweeping in from the great deep. He directs it toward (and it appears not restricted to) Locksley Hall: "Comes a vapour from the margin, blackening over heath and holt,/Cramming all the blast before it, in its breast a thunder bolt."

This fierce providential purpose is suffused through the people, yet it is quite different from the "Spirit of the years to come/Yearning to mix himself with Life" of the 1833–34 "Love thou thy land." Instead of English gradualism, in "Locksley Hall" we have the spirit of Carlyle's *The French Revolution* with its terrible fire sea, an abstract "fire-creation" that destroys an "old sick Society" (*Sartor*). The nature of the resultant historical process is more Carlyle's palingenetic fire birth than a progressive meliorism, in spite of such striking ideas as peace in our time (when the "war-drum throbbed no longer, and the battle flags were furled/In the Parliament of Man, the Federation of the world") and such images of linear progressivism as the world spinning "for ever down the ringing grooves of change." There is little in the poem that suggests a reconciliation of convulsive cyclicity and linear progressivism. Rather, the poem is torn by the dialectic. Yet something evolutionary seems to be taking place.

An analogy between natural evolution and historical development is not an unreasonable thing to expect in Tennyson, and his understanding of the former has been explored. Killham makes a case for Tennyson's sympathetic understanding of evolution and Saint-Simonism, augmented by his possible reading of an essay in the 1828 *Westminster Review* on

Tiedemann's discoveries about the "evolution" of the brain from simpler nervous systems. We know too that in 1836–37 Tennyson studied Lyell's *Geology*.[2] Killham concludes that in this period (from his Cambridge days to 1838 or so) Tennyson "was not unwilling to keep in his mind three mutually exclusive theories—the cataclysmic, the uniformitarian (Lyell's) and the quasi-evolutionary."[3] However, given Tennyson's (and all the Apostles's) disdain for the determinism of the Saint-Simonians, it may be doubted that Tiedemann's discoveries about the human brain developing organically through lower stages would persuade Tennyson of any inevitable progressivism in history. On the other hand, the cataclysmic explanation (Christian orthodoxy that species are the result of successive creations after a series of cataclysms) and Lyell's (that the apparent "development" of species was due to the gradual elimination of some by the struggle for existence after a simultaneous creation) would both suggest to Tennyson that major developments come about through warlike struggle and catastrophic upheavals in nature and history alike.

Insofar as such a line of thought would be a quest for "organic" form in both nature and history, Tennyson would be abandoning the gradualism of the resolution to history discussed in the previous chapter, although not letting go the idea that only through a fusion of past and present can the meaning of history obtain. Now, however, he inclines to the belief that the fusion must be a violent one in order to materialize true paradigmatic form for society. The idea of the phoenix death birth—which is a fair characterization of the historical process in "Locksley Hall"—is not new to Tennyson's thinking. Movement through radical but related stages was a natural cast of his mind, suggesting itself often by the image of the dragonfly emerging from a discarded chrysalis. It was used in "Timbuctoo" to convey the rise of thought to prophetic utterance and in "The Two Voices" for the process by which "Nature through five cycles ran,/And in the sixth she moulded Man." Ricks observes that the image was a traditional emblem for the renewal of life and was referred to in Bryant's *New System* (at Somersby).[4] The

---

[2] Hallam Tennyson says so (*Memoir*, 1:162) and an amusing, unpublished letter Tennyson wrote to Milnes in 1836 also mentions it. "Surely we are getting deep into the great Geological winter and inasmuch as a round belly is better than a white head, it were to be wished that we might wear down at the pole and grow up at the equator, that is, I would that our waste were greater at the pole and that we had an eye to it at the equator—(see Lyell Pr. Geol.)": Lord Houghton Letters at the University Library, Cambridge; Letter Cambr. 24[187].

[3] John Killham, *Tennyson and "The Princess,"* p. 250, and the entire chapter 11 about evolution.

[4] See Christopher Ricks, ed., *Poems of Tennyson*, p. 523.

image would suggest the supersession and convulsive sloughing off of antiquated form at the propitious moment, like the phoenix in stages of death and rebirth. The protagonist of "Semele" (printed by Tennyson's son as an 1835 fragment, although Ricks indicates it is found in a notebook with poems of 1833) out of a presumptuous desire to see the nearer god (like Tiresias) feels the "blast of Godhead," yet hails Dionysus: "son, who shalt be born/When I am ashes, to delight the world." This is much like the fire creation that destroys Carlyle's "old sick Society . . . in the faith that she is a Phoenix; and that a new heavenborn young one will rise out of her ashes."[5] Semele foresees the Dionysian energy "Moving on to victory," the victory of feeling over Apollonian knowledge, earthbound wisdom over Promethean aspiration.

The "blast . . . in its breast a thunderbolt" continues, then, but as a conventional imagery for the phoenix death birth of the society of "Locksley Hall." What kind of goodness will rise from this chrysalis is not clear, but the wave of Dionysian energy suggests that some kind will. The Apollonian mechanical wonders ride its crest. Such a confused mix of convulsive futurism and heroic agony augured hopelessness for many of the heroes and societies of earlier poems. There was no future for Arthur and Camelot, Tithon and Troy, Tiresias and Thebes, or Hanno and Carthage. But the death of Locksley in battle (if he gets his wish) and the blasting of Locksley Hall as the metonymic "Great House" representation of a sordid and soiled society apparently will bring about a revitalized future virtue. Finally, however, the poem is an irresolute and unsatisfactory effort at reconciling several themes that are at cross-purposes. The Dionysian-Apollonian dialectic poses one problem. The life-giving Dionysian energy requires the rite of consummation in the fire birth of new forms, but the Apollonian scientific and commercial progressivism requires a steady unfolding of the social fabric.

Locksley is no less a contradiction. He wishes to preside over both a fire birth and a society moving forward on ringing grooves of change. Presumptuously he seeks the heroic limit, and yet identifies with the workers and the merchants. He is racked by self-centered concerns about the loss of love, the inferiority of women, a permanently festering social order, and the determinism of "the individual withers, and the world is more and more." But on the other hand, he resists the temptation to withdraw into nature, the ordinary providence of

[5] See Jerome Hamilton Buckley's *Victorian Temper*, p. 97, for some imagery of the *Flammentod* in some literature of the period.

Lotos land (the "Paradise" of savagery), and embraces the progressive Christian purpose: "I count the gray barbarian lower than the Christian child"; in fact, "Better fifty years of Europe than a cycle of Cathay." The providential potentials must be developed. Hare, in *Guesses*, pointed to China immobilized in time, where providential "means and instruments" may "lie dormant and ineffective for centuries,"[6] and Thomas Arnold wrote of nations that never make the transition to manhood but go on "in protracted infancy."[7] Locksley embodies a strangely modern angst, inhabiting as he does a poem at the crossroads to *The Princess* and *In Memoriam*, and his purpose shuttles between the impulses of Ulysses and Telemachus. He avoids Cathay but his plans for Europe seem to include revolution and war. Progress is somehow a fire birth but Locksley cannot resolve the matter. He experiences the "damned vacillating state" of the hero of "The Two Voices"—not knowing, in effect, whether he wants to live or die.[8]

The protagonist of "The Vision of Sin" (apparently written about 1839) also wishes to "Hob-and-nob with brother Death" and seems a Locksley gone sour through a violent swing into radical progressivism with subsequent disillusionment. Locksley's wish for a social thunderbolt to blast forth a new age allies him with the revolutionary temperament, but the old epicurean of "The Vision of Sin" seems to have arrived at his bitter cynicism in large part precisely because of a failed French Revolution: "Freedom, gaily doth she tread;/In her right a civic wreath,/In her left a human head." And so, tyranny comes: "Drink to lofty hopes that cool—/Visions of a perfect State . . . /He that roars for liberty/Faster binds a tyrant's power." Having discovered such results to the phoenix death birth and failing, consequently, to see a hidden purpose in the world, he toasts ordinary providence with "Drink to Fortune, drink to Chance." He notes a dreadful paradigm of all human endeavor, "Every face, however full,/Padded round with flesh and fat,/Is but modelled on a skull." The correlative of the despair of this cloistered vice is the "vapour heavy, hueless, formless, cold" that detaches itself from the "still heights" where the power of God resides but as an abstract "awful rose of dawn." The "mystic mountain-range," the ancient divinatory height of Tennyson's earlier poems, is

---

[6][Julius Charles and Augustus William Hare], *Guesses*, p. 61.

[7]Quoted by Duncan Forbes, *Liberal Anglican Idea of History*, p. 27.

[8]Ricks sums up the critical awareness of psychological contradictions in Locksley which, given the biographical orientation, are characterized by such words as *evasion* and *secretive* (*Tennyson*, pp. 164-65).

inaccessible. At its base are "men and horses pierced with worms." One aspirer apparently makes it past this deadly foothill, for we hear "a voice upon the slope / Cry to the summit, 'Is there any hope?'"

> To which an answer pealed from that high land,
> But in a tongue no man could understand;
> And on the glimmering limit far withdrawn
> God made Himself an awful rose of dawn.

God is self-circumscribed, alien, and unavailable as active providence in human affairs. This most morbid of Tennyson's flawed heroes wishes to die, for life has no meaning: "All the windy ways of men / Are but dust that rises up, / And is lightly laid again."

Within a few years, however, the persona of *In Memoriam* moves from just such a despair to a luminous happiness precisely because he discovers that the whole history of man, characterized by violent disaster and death, has "meaning" after all. He not only wants to live but also develops a sophisticated frame of reference in support of doing so. He perceives the purpose in the dust and it thereby becomes living form: "life re-orient out of dust" (*In Memoriam*, 116). Tennyson had been at this long work since the time of Hallam's death in late 1833, and it seems to have come together about the same time *The Princess* did, in the mid forties. The Mechanics' Institution festival that inhabits the frame of *The Princess* and the marriage between Tennyson's sister and Edmund Lushington that is shown in the epithalamion at the end of *In Memoriam* took place near Maidstone in 1842, with Tennyson present at both. *The Princess* rehabilitated the landed aristocracy of "Locksley Hall," whose Great House became the aegis under which commerce and industrialism could flourish in a fusion of past and present. *In Memoriam* rehabilitates Locksley himself, whose feeling for catastrophic quantum jumps of spirit, the phoenix fire birth of new forms, becomes the resolution of the individual plane, wherein past and present also meet.

In Memoriam is a very difficult poem. Its excursions into individual, historical, and natural pasts suggest the comforts of progressivism by evoking the "end-determined" frame of reference ascribed both to Christian eschatology and to secular progressivism; and it is not readily seen how the idea of convulsive cycles underlies the poem. There are so many Christian pronouncements scattered through the work and such manifest allusions to some kind of progress that it is natural such a frame of reference should be claimed by the many studies of the poem. Early commentators assumed confidently that its "meaning" was basically Christian. In a review Kingsley referred to it simply as "the noblest Christian poem which England has produced for two centuries," with Tennyson "led, like Dante of old, by the guiding of a mighty spirit."[9] Tennyson did not discourage the notion by saying later that the poem was, indeed, a "sort of Divine Comedy."[10] Henry Sedgwick reflects the satisfactions of Christianity's secular eschatology in praising the "reconciliation of knowledge and faith in the introductory poem, and the hopeful trumpet-ring of the lines on the New Year—'Ring out the thousand wars of old,/Ring in the thousand years of peace,' and generally the *forward* movement of the thought" (*Memoir*, 1:302). In short, he lauds the apparent progressivism of "Locksley Hall"'s "Parliament of man, the Federation of the world."

Modern criticism is prone to credit the poem's "meaning" with a profane millenarianism: human perfectability as the "end" of social evolution based on natural law.[11] Yet (as the argument goes) the idea that the persona finds happiness within the framework of secular progress is as untenable as arguing that he finds it in a Christian ascent to a millennium. For the persona, the historical and natural worlds— causal, purposeful, and "organic" as they may be—are not "meaningful" in terms of either an inexorable, emotionally unverified "process" or the growth of "natural" form. It is true that certain sensibilities may find emotional satisfaction in sequential causality or in the fulfillment of teleologically induced form, but Tennyson was not one of these. If

[9] *Tennyson: The Critical Heritage,* pp. 173, 184.

[10] James Knowles, "Aspects of Tennyson," p. 182.

[11] Glossing the lines on the "one far-off divine event," Eliot accepts, however vaguely, the presence of an "end-determined" scheme in the poem by saying that the lines "show an interesting compromise between the religious attitude and, what is quite a different thing, the belief in human perfectability" (T. S. Eliot, *Selected Essays,* p. 293). Rosenberg concurs by noting that, for the synthesis of the poem, Tennyson "draws on two great myths, the myth of Progress and the Christian vision of the Kingdom of Heaven on Earth," with Tennyson "uniting evolutionary science and Christian faith," specifically in "the evolutionary argument of Section CXVIII (man thriving from clime to clime)" (John D. Rosenberg, "The Two Kingdoms of *In Memoriam*," pp. 235, 240, 236. Bishop addressed secular eschatology when he observes that "sympathy with Hallam's spirit" has shown the persona that "the cycles of nature and history are not 'seeming-random forms,/The seeming-prey of cyclic storms," but parts of a slowly spiraling ameliorative progress of which such individuals as Hallam are an inspiring prophecy" (Jonathan Bishop, "The Unity of *In Memoriam*," p. 13). And Pitt brings into play the issue of natural law and inevitable progress toward an "end" by saying that "the desire for, and the straining towards the vision of the perfect race of man living an idyllic life in bliss and concord was part of the romantic inheritance"; "it was only at this time that it begins to be linked to the laws of the physical and biological sciences" (Valerie Pitt, *Tennyson Laureat,* p. 116).

we equate "meaning" with God in the context of Tennyson's thought, we find him among the Apostles voting "no" on the question, "Is an intelligible First Cause deducible from the phenomena of the Universe" (*Memoir,* 1:44). His many political poems and his poems of mechanical progress may suggest pleasure in the phenomenon of a seemingly irresistible progress, but the notion of progress in "Locksley Hall" was basically exacerbating and in *The Princess* it was subsumed finally within the receding rings of perspective in the Great House paradigm. The persona of *In Memoriam* says plainly, "I found Him not in world or sun,/Or eagle's wing or insect's eye" (124). This is an explicit rejection of the "God from design" argument which, in the context of "organic" history, suggests that for the persona the past is not "meaningful" merely because there are patterns in it. As for Christian orthodoxy, Tennyson may have done little to disillusion such assessments of his work but the fact is that the introductory poem and many other such sentiments were added as late as 1849. At that time it appeared that Tennyson was about to convince Emily and her family that he was respectable enough religiously to become the head of a Victorian household. The orthodox "frame" is made additionally suspect by what is in the body of the work.

We cannot interpret properly a poem that is underlaid with a scheme of history without identifying both the framework of ideas and the convictions attending them. That is, a frame of reference is not meaningful unless the user is happy in it, nor is a mere euphoria meaningful if bereft of system. When the issues are as large as the power of God, the nature of the historical process, and the question of the hero's role in the scheme of things, Tennyson's resolution—given his temperament and his work to this point—must contain both rational understanding and emotional affirmations. The primary critical problem with *In Memoriam* today is that modern commentary separates system and conviction. In the schism, the poem's fundamental significance is lost. The poem's purportedly end-determined frames of reference—variations of the Christian scheme, secular versions, varieties of evolution, and systems of natural law—have been studied but with the assumption that whatever meaning the poem proffers arises automatically out of such a frame. Aside from questioning whether this does indeed follow, two critical assumptions cloud such explanations: that Tennyson's faith was a poor one and so he did not really believe in the Christian scheme, and that his thinking powers were not great (respectable, but not great) and so his secular system is somewhat of a muddle. As a result the poem is regarded as no meaningful explanation at all.[12]

On the other hand, there are persuasive studies of the persona's valuational transfiguration—religious, psychological, epistemological, esthetic. These usually focus on the mystical trance of section 95 as an archetypal "conversion."[13] In such studies, "meaning" is assumed to be essentially religious exaltation. Tennyson's system is recognized as a presence in the background, but it is not dealt with. Thus, the poem becomes a psychological or spiritual record rather than meaning in the full sense of this term. If the argument for Tennyson's cognitive equipment has been at all persuasive, if his poems do indeed reflect an intelligent and systematic groping for an understanding of the human condition, it is not likely that his final answer would be irrationality and mystical faith. The upshot of this dichotomy of system and conviction is that the persona's peripeteia from despair to happiness remains unsatisfactorily explained. As a recent critic notes, "With all the commentaries, analyses, and keys which have appeared since 1850 the poem still eludes consensus."[14]

The poem shows the persona moving into happiness not through perceptions of design nor through mystical trances, but rather through his developing consciousness, his willed construction of "meaning" in the disastrous past, and his faith in a God that is totally unknown

[12] "No longer does it serve," writes Marshall, "the purpose of bolstering faith in the meaning of life" (George O. Marshall, Jr., *Tennyson Handbook*, p. 122).

[13] Hough, although discussing the influences of science and Coleridge, finds the basis of the poem to be "Tennyson's own religious intuitions, based ultimately on an unanalysable but completely cogent mystical experience" (Graham Hough, "The Natural Theology of *In Memoriam*," p. 256). Buckley notes that "concern with the mode of perception and the reality of the perceiving self turns the essential 'action' of *In Memoriam* toward the inner experience," with the climax of the trance in section 95 bringing "renewed purpose and composure"; "the 'I' of the poem finds in his mystical insight the surest warrant for spiritual recovery" (Jerome Hamilton Buckley, *Growth of a Poet,* pp. 122, 123). Moore argues that the "trance-like experience of Section XCV marks the climax of the poet's efforts to commune with the spirit of Hallam; it provides a nexus between the disparate elements of doubt and faith" (Carlisle Moore, "Faith, Doubt, and Mystical Experience in *In Memoriam*," p. 158). Langbaum characterizes the poem as "epistemological sophistication. For *In Memoriam* is organized to show that after the poet has undergone a total transformation of perception, all the old facts and problems are transvaluated and absorbed into the affirmative movement that dominates the poem from Section XCV on"; the "real turning point" is "where in a mystical trance the poet has the epiphany that transforms and trancends all the problems" (Robert Langbaum, "The Dynamic Unity of *In Memoriam*," pp. 69, 65). Shaw terms this celebrated trance "truly a turning-point or conversion in Tennyson's spiritual history," behind which lie "concepts like God, eternity, or immortality, theological ideas": for example, the breeze of section 95 "is a Romantic equivalent of the Holy Spirit" (W. David Shaw, "*In Memoriam* and the Rhetoric of Confession," pp. 80, 90, 102).

[14] Carlisle Moore, p. 155.

except through this consciousness and this past. Tennyson builds a frame of reference that is not "end-determined" but "open-ended." The free will, in complex interaction with the potentials of the world, does not advance in the determinism associated with evolutionary or teleological "ends," but expands in convulsive cycles in an apocalyptic present: the eternity that James in "The Golden Year" says is "ever at the doors." Such quantum jumps of spirit—fiery rebirths, the "shattered stalks" of section 82—occur out of disaster and death, so that the conviction that attends this frame is an affirmation, not of faith in a Heavenly Father the author of all things, but of the sorrow of the free human condition. The persona, representing both individual and collective memory, perceives "meaning" as a fusion of self and past in certain master images, organic and mechanical, that carry the burden of both the system and the conviction.

The persona fails to find a supernatural "God" because all avenues to the divine are closed, so that he is, in effect, thrown upon his own resources. The poem specifically rejects mysticism, scriptures, and prophecy. What Tennyson understands about God is brought about by that "extreme subtlety and curious elaborateness of thought" that Matthew Arnold noted in "On Translating Homer: Last Words,"[15] namely, that divination which Tennyson called his "state of transcendent wonder, associated with absolute clearness of mind." This is that condition described in chapter 2 as Neoplatonic "reason," intelligence in its most excited state, the deity (as Plotinus wrote) "shining and unfolding himself in intelligible light."[16] Tennyson was, indeed, almost painfully cerebral, curious, and not at all tender-minded in regard to the ultimates. Most of his remarks on his understanding of "God" reveal the notion of the unavoidable humanness of divinity. His list of the three "Eternal Truths," for instance, includes belief in "an Omnipotent, Omnipresent and All-loving God, Who has revealed Himself through the *human* attribute of the highest self-sacrificing love; in the freedom of the *human* will; and in the immortality of the soul" (my italics). If these attributes are taken literally, Tennyson would see God revealing himself in human consciousness, and so it is that God is "unknowable" save that "our highest view of God must be more or less anthropomorphic" (*Memoir*, 1:311): that is, the God "within."

Tennyson added that "'Personality,' as far as our intelligence goes, is the widest definition and includes 'Mind,' 'Self-consciousness,' 'Will,'

---

[15] Given in *Tennyson: The Critical Heritage*, p. 267.
[16] See chapter 2, note 18 and discussion.

'Love'." The idea of God as mind, moreover, suggests Tennyson's participation in that thought of the age that saw God manifesting himself in the movement of collective mind in history. Tennyson was amused once, said Jowett, "at someone who said of him that he had versified Hegelianism" (*Memoir,* 1:312), but in many ways this is a valid observation. Tennyson said specifically that the persona of *In Memoriam* is the "human race":[17] collective mind. Any justification of the suffering past of the persona is, thus, extended to history as a whole, particularly if it is only through such "meaning" that God is revealed. Hegel said that his *Philosophy of History* was to be a "justification of the ways of God," that in universal history "Spirit displays itself in its most concrete reality," and that "Spirit is *self-contained existence* . . . self-consciousness—consciousness of one's own being."[18] The consciousness that can apprehend the "meaning" of the past intuits God; thus, both in Tennyson and Hegel, there is a virtual identity of God, history, and human mind.

In Memoriam begins by showing the rupture between this perceiving consciousness and the whole past on the levels of the traditional microcosmic and macrocosmic correspondences. The persona is in upheaval, his utterances accordingly "wild and wandering" (Prologue). All he sees is without form: the "bald street," the "blank day"; he hears only the "noise of life" (7). In his role as "human race," he experiences the crumbling of social form as "more and more the people throng/ The chairs and thrones of civil power" (21) in social revolution.[19] Nature is correspondingly fragmented: "The forest cracked, the waters curled" (15). Hallam—the apotheosis of disastrous convulsion in the past—is unavailingly "formless in the fold" (22), the focal point for developing consciousness throughout the poem.

In the general disorder, the collapse of an "end-determined" frame of reference is almost explicit as the persona falls "Upon the great world's altar-stairs/That slope through darkness up to God," able only to "stretch lame hands of faith, and grope,/And gather dust and chaff" (55). If the "end" is no reference point, the origins of rectilinear perspectives are also frustrated. The poet thinks how, when he and Hallam had been together, "all the lavish hills would hum/The murmur of a happy Pan" in a prelapsarian Eden, "And all we met was fair and

---

[17] *Memoir,* 1:305, and Knowles, p. 182.

[18] Georg Wilhelm Friedrich Hegel, *The Philosophy of History,* pp. 15-17.

[19] See the notes in Ricks, ed., *Poems of Tennyson,* p. 883, for a justification of the revolutionary referents.

good,/And all was good that Time could bring" (23). But this past is unreliable: "If all was good and fair we met,/This earth had been the Paradise/It never looked to human eyes" (24). The deepest desolation lies, in fact, in this epistemological confusion:

> is it that the haze of grief
> Makes former gladness loom so great?
> The lowness of the present state,
> That sets the past in this relief?

> Or that the past will always win
> A glory from its being far;
> And orb into the perfect star
> We saw not, when we moved therein? (24)

It may seem paradoxical in light of the critical view that Tennyson found most congenial, an art of "distancing" the world in an isolation of "ideal form,"[20] but the persona appears to reject perspectives in this "eternal landscape of the past" (46) as a distorting mode.

The "end-determined" frame breaks down because its divine author has become inaccessible as the underpinning of conviction. It is commonly urged that the lack of divinity must result in meaninglessness in history. To the problem of how, in the effective absence of God, there could be a justification of the disastrous past, Tennyson responds in a radically religious fashion. Recasting Eliot's observation about the poem in the spirit of modern theology, *In Memoriam* is religious not because of the quality of its doubt, but because of the quality of its disbelief.[21] Noteworthy is the lack of the "supernatural excitation" that assured the prone supplicant before the great Angel Mind in Tennyson's earlier poem "Timbuctoo." To be sure, the Prologue and the Epilogue of *In Memoriam* speak of the "Strong Son of God" and the "God, which ever lives and loves," but these "brackets" were placed late about the poem and render the orthodoxy dubious for the reasons given at the start of this discussion. Besides, as noted above, Tennyson characterized God as "unknowable." He said in addition, "It's too hopeful, this poem, more than I am myself."[22]   A God there may be, but a "web is

---

[20] As given, for instance, by John Dixon Hunt: "He needed an art that isolated, distanced and preserved even the immediate and contemporary within its own world of precision and ideal form" ("The Poetry of Distance," pp. 89–90).

[21] Paul Tillich, for example, says that "he who seriously denies God, affirms him . . . Being religious is being unconditionally concerned, whether this concern expresses itself in secular or (in the narrower sense) religious forms" (*The Protestant Era*, p. xi).

[22] Knowles, p. 182.

woven across the sky" (3). God and immortality are just human desiderata, mirrors:

> What find I in the highest place,
>   But mine own phantom chanting hymns?
>   And on the depths of death there swims
> The reflex of a human face, (108)

the persona's own. No prophets speak. In a suppressed passage, Tennyson wrote,

> Hope at awful distance set
>   Oft whispers of a kindlier plan
>   Though never prophet came to man
> Of such a revelation yet.[23]

The dead—Lazarus from his "charnel-cave"—give "no record of reply" (31). As for the alleged spirit contact with "The living soul"— uncertainly first "his" and then glossed by Tennyson as "perchance of the Deity"[24]—the spell is "cancelled, stricken through with doubt" (95).

Nor can the "immortality of the soul," the third of Tennyson's Eternal Truths, support an "end-determined" epistemology. The persona's imaginings about Hallam's afterlife appear never to be proffered literally:

> So hold I commerce with the dead;
>   Or so methinks the dead would say;
>   Or so shall grief with symbols play (85)

Hallam, finally, is a force in the persona's individual and collective memory, which is immortality of a sort but hardly of the orthodox kind.[25] "What art thou then?" asks the persona at the end of the poem, "I cannot guess . . . I seem in star and flower / To feel thee some diffusive power" (130). The persona appears hopeful for some stages of individuation after death but, ultimately, there seems to be oblivion in "light": "Remerging in the general Soul, / Is faith as vague as all unsweet," but there is only,

---

[23] Deleted portion of stanza 54, in Trinity notebook 0.15.13.

[24] Knowles, p. 186.

[25] Modern criticism indeed tends to view Hallam's immortality in this way. Bishop notes that, "so far as Hallam is the object of his surviving friend's contemplations, or the tenor for which these objects are vehicles, he is alive; he cannot, in fact, ever die, for the act of contemplating, itself a living action, becomes immortal by turning it into poetry" (p. 12).

> Upon the last and sharpest height,
>   Before the spirits fade away,
>   Some landing-place, to clasp and say,
> "Farewell! We lose ourselves in light." (47)

Tennyson's utterances were ambiguous on this point. He spoke *ex cathedra of* individuality after death, expressing to Knowles an apparently passionately held view of personal immortality.[26] But, as Bradley rightfully concluded, "an *ultimate* 'absorption into the divine' was not, like the idea of an immediate absorption, repugnant to him."[27] With the cutting away of ends and beginnings, of knowledge of God, and of immortality as this is generally understood, the persona at this point in the poem is

>   that delirious man
>   Whose fancy fuses old and new,
>   And flashes into false and true,
> And mingles all without a plan. (16)

The persona emerges from this slough of meaninglessness by engaging a past that is apocalyptically "open-ended." The world takes on "meaning" when it becomes informed with the anthropomorphism of the persona's creative imagination, which is, on this microcosmic level, an imitation of God. In reconstructing the suffering past, the persona epistemologically enacts an archetypal ritual. The effect of this ritual, in Eliade's words (applied previously to the resolution of history in *The Princess*), is to "suspend the flow of profane time, of duration, and project the celebrant into a mythical time, *in illo tempore*." Eliade notes further that the archaic ritual forms "grant suffering and historical events a 'normal meaning'" through the restoration of "mythical and primordial time, 'pure' time, the time of the 'instant' of the Creation"; similarly but beyond this, "Christianity translates the periodic regeneration of the world into a regeneration of the human individual."[28] This process is what Abrams calls the "psycho-historical parallelism" in Christain thought that results in a "theodicy of the

---

[26] Knowles, p. 169.

[27] A. C. Bradley, *A Commentary on Tennyson's "In Memoriam,"* p. 53. Yet Bradley underlays his analysis of the poem with an "end-determined" frame of reference by saying that we "must understand by 'immortality' simply the conscious and indefinitely prolonged life of the soul beyond death" (p. 54).

[28] See chapter 4, note 24, and further references in Mircea Eliade, *Myth of the Eternal Return*, pp. 100, 54.

private life." The individual, representing a collective reality, is able, "by consummating a holy marriage with the external universe, to create out of the world of all of us, in a quotidian and recurring miracle, a new world which is the equivalent of paradise."[29] The mind of the persona, then, mediates between the world and divinity, taking its form from both.

At first, however, because of his inert will, the persona cannot vitalize the past. The world is dominant and, therefore, empty of form and "meaning." "Sorrow" whispers to the persona that Nature is just her correlative, "A hollow echo of my own,—/A hollow form with empty hands" (3), for the persona is passive and anchored to despairing and mundane memory. This memory has for its symbol a cloud "That rises upward always higher,/And onward drags a labouring breast" and then, because it is merely natural, "topples round the dreary west" (15). The persona is suspended between the mirrors of inner and outer limits, the "deep self" as "some dead lake/That holds the shadow of a lark/Hung in the shadow of a heaven" (16). He is accordingly frozen in stasis, like the "deep vase of chilling tears,/That grief hath shaken into frost" (4) or the old yew—an appropriate symbol for the inextricable union of past and present—whose "fibres net the dreamless head" of Hallam, its "roots . . . wrapt about the bones" of a hidden, suffering past (2).

But the will (the second of Tennyson's Eternal Truths) becomes the catalyst in the revivifying fusion of self and human past. Being divine, a force of active providence, the will breaks the persona free of the "natural" correlatives of the plane of ordinary providence. The idea of "will" is, of course, dominant in *In Memoriam*, occurring overtly in eleven stanzas and, by suggestion, in many others. From the start, the persona laments his "helmless bark" and anticipates the wind of change: "With the morning wakes the will, and cries,/'Thou shalt not be the fool of loss'" (4). "Slowly forms the firmer mind," he says in section 18, and would "train/To riper growth the mind and will" (42). The poem is bracketed with the "Our wills are ours, we know not how;/Our wills are ours, to make them thine" of the Prologue and the "O living will that shalt endure" of section 131 (which Tennyson glossed as the "higher and enduring part of man," *Memoir*, 1:319). Finally, the persona has not merely perceived, he "faced the spectres of the mind/And laid them" (96).

[29] M. H. Abrams, *Natural Supernaturalism*, pp. 48, 95, 28.

This will is a kind of illative sense (what Newman called the will to believe) that brings new form into being from the interpenetration of past and present. The shadow lark materializes, as though a symbol for the poet's newly developing "scriptures": "Short swallow-flights of song, that dip/Their wings in tears, and skim away" (48). Later, in section 65 (which Bradley said was "perhaps the first section of *In Memoriam* that can be described as cheerful or happy"),[30] the bird breaks loose from the agonized chrysalis and becomes autonomous "meaning": a "thought" that somehow is now independent of both the disastrous past and a despairing solipsism. "Out of painful phases wrought/There flutters up a happy thought,/Self-balanced on a lightsome wing."[31] The seed and flower images also support the idea that the "produce of the common day" results from the complex interaction of present will and past vitality. The "thick noon, disastrous day" (72) of Hallam's death, with "Autumn laying here and there/A fiery finger on the leaves" (99), "sickened every living bloom" (72). But the potentials of the past—"expectant nature" (83), the "summer in the seed" (105)—meet the embrace of the creative will: "Now burgeons every maze of quick" and "in my breast Spring wakens too" (115).

This is not just a "natural" process. The "lower life that earth's embrace/May breed with" Hallam is a general "virtue out of earth," "transplanted human worth" that "Will bloom to profit, otherwhere" (82), i.e., in the memory of all men. "From his ashes may be made/The violet of his native land" (18), dispersed through the race. The yew may appear as a symbol for the individual persona, but is readily taken also for the previously discussed Nordic "cosmic life-tree" representing all of human time appearing in so many works in the period, and in such of Tennyson's poems as "Timbuctoo." In Carlyle's *Past and Present*, "the LIFE-TREE IGDRASIL, wide-waving, many toned, has its roots down deep in the Death-kingdoms, among the oldest dead dust of man. . . ." "Their crumbled dust makes up the soil our life-fruit grows on. . . . *Times*, Past, Present, Future, watering it from the sacred Well" (I.6; II.17).

What is apparent in this imagery is that the persona realizes he cannot be merely "overworn" (1) by forgetting, but must base "mean-

---

[30] Bradley, p. 159.

[31] Tennyson said that "man's Free-will is but a bird in a cage; he can stop at the lower perch, or he can mount to a higher. Then that which is and knows will enlarge his cage, give him a higher and a higher perch, and at last break off the top of his cage, and let him out to be one with the Free-will of the Universe" (*Memoir*, 1:318–19). This initial flutter is the first of the jumps of spirit that leads "open-endedly" to the God not found on the altar stairs of section 55.

ing" on the "old affection of the tomb," that "prime passion in the grave" (85). This flowering of spirit is "open-ended" but it is also a cyclic return upon itself: a reintegration of the past. The conviction that attends this system, then, is not evolutionary hope at the apogee of the cycle, but the sorrow at the epigee of death and disaster. Though both are part of the ritual reconstruction of time, it is past sorrow and not future hope that invests budding "meaning," just as the cross and not the open tomb of resurrection is the emblem of Christianity. The "Wild bird, whose warble, liquid sweet,/Rings Eden through the budded quicks," does so precisely because "in the midmost heart of grief/Thy passion clasps a secret joy" (88). Hallam's death accordingly invests almost every station of the persona's progress, just as Christ's death is the focus of the Christian "meaning" in history.

The ancient correspondences are invoked to suggest that Hallam is the apotheosis not only of individual but also of historical and natural destruction, and necessarily so if the epistemology of "meaning" is to be universal in the application. Hallam is the genius of such "revolution," for his face is made to "mix with hollow masks of night" and with:

> Cloud-towers by ghostly masons wrought,
>   A gulf that ever shuts and gapes,
>   A hand that points, and pallèd shapes
> In shadowy thoroughfares of thought;
>
> And crowds that stream from yawning doors,
>   And shoals of puckered faces . . . (70)

These lines generally are taken to attest to Tennyson's familiarity with Carlyle's *The French Revolution*. This historical terror is followed immediately by its equivalent, the terror of vanished natural species: "Dark bulks that tumble half alive,/And lazy lengths on boundless shores." Nature cries in section 56, "A thousand types are gone:/I care for nothing, all shall go." We seem to be given the historical equivalent in men "Who loved, who suffered countless ills,/Who battled for the True, the Just." Here, both extinct species and lost civilizations will be "blown about the desert dust,/Or sealed within the iron hills." Both nature and history, then, are "red in tooth and claw/With ravine" and it would appear that this is not sweet. Yet Hallam presides: "Looks thy fair face and makes it still" (70). How can this be?

Revolution and natural disaster are equated in section 127 as well.

Thou "O'erlook'st the tumult from afair," says the speaker to Hallam. Ancient institutions crumble as the "red fool-fury of the Seine" piles "her barricades with dead" and, as to nature:

> They tremble, the sustaining crags;
>   The spires of ice are toppled down,
>
> And molten up, and roar in flood;
>   The fortress crashes from on high,
>   The brute earth lightens to the sky,
> And the great Aeon sinks in blood.

Nothing in the poem suggests that these convulsive ways ever will change. Indeed, we are led to the somewhat startling but rigorously logical idea that these ways are, specifically, the

> Eternal process moving on,
>   From state to state the spirit walks;
>   And these are but the shattered stalks,
> Or ruined chrysalis of one. (82)

Hallam makes these disasters "still" or meaningful as eternal process because he is the seed core of "meaning" on both the microcosmic and these macrocosmic planes, the death center about which the new epistemology coalesces. On the personal level, Hallam's memory gradually becomes a salutary presence. The extraordinarily difficult section 116 reveals how sorrow is being refined and transcended. Here, the persona asks if it is sorrow alone that interacts with the sense of developing happiness (the seasonal images here are to be taken as correlatives of spirit):

> It is, then, regret for buried time
>   That keenlier in sweet April wakes,
>   And meets the year, and gives and takes
> The colours of the crescent prime?

The reply is that "regret" (a milder term than the earlier expressions of extreme distress) is not all there is to it; that, in fact, regret is less vital than what the persona himself has done:

> Not all: the songs, the stirring air,
>   The life re-orient out of dust,

Cry through the sense to hearten trust
In that which made the world so fair.

It may appear here that the persona is being consoled by natural process, but the songs are his and the "life re-orient out of dust" is, from many vantages, the result of his own imaginative re-creation. The phrase "that which made the world so fair" could be taken as a reference to a supernatural artificer, but it is taken as readily to refer to the human constructer himself. The "stirring air" seems to refer to wind, but "air" suggests the "correspondent breeze" of Romantic thought and is, also, song. In Tennyson's intricately wrought style, the word *re-orient* suggests both reorientation and the act of making something pearl-like. Life, like the poem itself, becomes a self-realized artifact of layered shells of time about a core of pain.

Thus, Hallam becomes the center about which historical "meaning" forms. The disasters are transfigured by his presence. In section 70, the persona hears a "wizard music roll,/And through a lattice on the soul/Looks thy fair face and makes it still." By section 127, the tone has become exalted. Hallam, "dear spirit, happy star,/O'erlook'st the tumult from afar,/And smilest, knowing all is well," because "Well roars the storm to those that hear/A deeper voice across the storm." The sorrows of revolution and natural catastrophe are affirmed as the means by which spirit ascends from ruined chrysalises, shattered stalks. These images suggest Carlyle's "clothes" philosophy of history, that movement occurs in a "Phoenix Death-Birth" when "fire-creation" destroys an "old sick Society . . . in the faith that she is a Phoenix; and that a heavenborn young one will rise out of her ashes" (*Sartor Resartus*, III.5). The conviction that attends the system of *Sartor* is also sorrow. Teufelsdroeckh's "Everlasting Yea" is uttered in a "Sanctuary of Sorrow," the "Divine Depth of Sorrow."[32]

As was observed above, Tennyson's readings during the period when he composed "Locksley Hall" included several works on different theories of natural change. Similarly, in the case of *In Memoriam*, both Christian orthodoxy about successive creations after cataclysms and Lyell's explanations for the stepped struggle in the development of the species may have suggested to Tennyson the imagery of apocalyptic

---

[32] *Sartor Resartus* (II.9). Carlisle Moore speaks of the fire and water imagery attending Tennyson's "conversion," which he compares to Teufelsdroeckh's (p. 158). Tennyson's celebrated phrase "Passion of the Past," in its use of *of* instead of *for* (as the phrase originally appears in a letter from Hallam to Tennyson), suggests redemptive historical suffering (*Memoir*, 1:81, 253; 2:319).

fire creations involving redemptive suffering.[33] Historical successions also bear this apocalyptic aspect, but the year metaphor that the historian uses for such change, particularly as it is scattered through the works of the Liberal Anglican historians, is not to be taken as mere natural process. Thomas Arnold's 1830 *Thucydides*, for instance, speaks of the autumn of the Greek city-states and the springtime of the Roman people, but the terms refer to conditions of moral being, i.e., a "will" to meaningful historical form.[34]

Sententiously put, man must suffer if he is to understand. He must contemplate the record of past suffering until he arrives at its "meaning." The line that follows the persona's immobilization on the "great world's altar-stairs"—that he would "faintly trust the larger hope"— means, said Tennyson, "that the whole human race would through, perhaps, ages of suffering, be at length purified and saved" (*Memoir*, 1:321–22). The persona gathers time about him to enact this redemption in his role as "human race" and, indeed, as hero of the central allegory of the Romantic poets, especially Wordsworth and Shelley. Abrams describes this central allegory as "the history of mankind as a circuitous journey back home":

> The protagonist is the collective mind or consciousness of men, and the story is that of its painful pilgrimage through difficulties, sufferings, and recurrent disasters in quest of a goal which, unwittingly, is the place it had left behind when it first set out and which, when reachieved, turns out to be even better than it had been at the beginning. Thus redemption, even after it has been translocated to history and translated into the self-education of the general mind of mankind, continues to be represented in the central Christian trope of life as a pilgrimage and quest.[35]

In *In Memoriam*, the quest is an inward one, a drama of the mind; and the persona, like Red Cross Knight, is both the individual and the human race finding salvation in an apocalyptic continuum available for everyman.[36]

---

[33] See note 3 above.

[34] Quoted by Forbes, pp. 20–21. Compare also the distinction by Stanley between the corporeal and moral analogy cited earlier (chapter 2, note 26).

[35] Abrams, p. 191.

[36] J. C. C. Mays writes "Tennyson solved the problem of form" in "the way closest to his own experience; he presents the drama of himself in the very process of discovering it, so that the continuity which underlies the whole poem's form is in the first place provided by himself in the role of hero" ("*In Memoriam*: An Aspect of Form," p. 26). Tennyson offered that in *In*

Because "meaning" is this type of willed human construct, the imagery in the latter part of the poem reveals a significant change from the organic to that of the fabricated artifact. The persona perceives that past disaster is the furnace in which historical man is transfigured. Where earlier, "Time" had been an artless "maniac scattering dust [not yet "re-orient"],/And Life, a Fury slinging flame" (50), with the realization that fire births are redemptive, the "flame" becomes purifying and transmuting. The fury turns into a "giant labouring in his youth" with the agonies of the revolutionary forge:

life is not as idle ore,

But iron dug from central gloom,
    And heated hot with burning fears,
    And dipt in baths of hissing tears,
And battered with the shocks of doom

To shape and use. (118)

With perfect form as a construct, like the pearl of section 116, we are given in section 117 the sundial and clock with "kiss of toothèd wheels" which the blacksmith might have made. But who is the blacksmith? The master craftsman is man himself, the anthropomorphic projection, as God and mind, of man's own nature as an ultimate. The smithy is at once the worker, the object, and the forge, insofar as he shapes and hardens his own spirit on the anvil of the world, with the "shocks" of disaster, through his own suffering.

"Out of darkness came the hands/That reach through nature, moulding men" (124). Tennyson's impacted language makes several readings possible. The "hands" are usually taken to be the hands of God, but Tennyson said that God was apprehensible only through human attributes. The fact that the hands "reach through nature" suggests that nature is the press within which man is worked; it is a variant, then, on the "shocks" that the anthropomorphic fabricator uses. Section 80 tells us that the persona senses the molding power of the past: "Unused example from the grave/Reach out dead hands to comfort me." On this collective level, the hands are the memory of the examples of previous heroic creators: statesmen, poets, the "legislators of mankind,"

Memoriam "the different moods of sorrow as in a drama are dramatically given" (*Memoir*, 1:304). C. F. G. Masterman long ago made the point that Tennyson affirms the "certain reality of the self ... the one and only thing of which by direct conviction we can assert reality" (*Tennyson As a Religious Teacher*, p. 61).

in Shelley's phrase. Some of Tennyson's other poems indicate the
context. In "Hail Briton!" for instance (and in the same stanzaic form),

> They wrought a work which time reveres,
>   A precedent to all the lands,
>   And an example reaching hands
> For ever into coming years. (ll. 81–84)

In "Tiresias," these creators are specifically those that dared

> For that sweet mother land which gave them birth
> Nobly to do, nobly to die . . .
>   their examples reach a hand
> Far through all years . . . (ll. 118–23)

This seems to imply the quality of Tennyson's first Eternal Truth, that
God "revealed Himself through the human attribute of the highest self-
sacrificing love" (*Memoir*, 1:311). These hands, then, are the divine
power of the formative past as the memory of sacrificial, heroic
spirit: those who (we were told in section 56) "suffered countless ills,/
Who battled for the True, the Just."

But the wine press of the world is not so much manned by
external forces (although they are there, as this formative memory
along with, of course, all the potentials of the world) as willed into
action by the apprehension of forces so available. Heroes may sacrifice
themselves by design or by chance (a free universe is by definition
chanceful). The "dark hand" that killed Hallam—"struck down through
time,/ And cancelled nature's best" (72)—performed a deed indifferently
providential and accidental. It is clear that, if the aspirant to "meaning"
wills himself to close with the apocalyptic nature of redemption, such
heroic examples become the dynamism of the human condition. Hallam
is the agent of the disastrous power by which man evolves, at once (like
Christ) both victim and God, for the persona feels "the pressure of thine
hand" (119) and "His being working in mine own" (85). The persona's
creative will meets this divine past and gives and takes in interchangeable
supremacy, not in redemptive determinism but in the freedom of the
human will.

The memory of Hallam—and of others like him—provides for the
persona, both as individual and as the human race, the vantage he lacked
in rectilinear, "end-determined" systems:

A pillar steadfast in the storm,

Should licensed boldness gather force,
Becoming, when the time has birth,
A lever to uplift the earth
And roll it in another course,

With thousand shocks that come and go,
With agonies, with energies,
With overthrowings, and with cries,
And undulations to and fro. (113)

Words like *pillar*, *force*, *lever*, and *shocks* reveal that here, again, the imagery is not organic but mechanical, appropriate to the fabricated nature of the embraced "meaning" of revolutionary change. Individual, society, and the very earth are thrust into another orbit through the energy of explosion that marks the "ruined chrysalis" of dead forms of consciousness, and so "men may rise on stepping stones / Of their dead selves to higher things" (1; a section written late). In Tennyson's style of multiple resonance, the "dead selves" refers to the molt of individual and collective spirit as well as to the memory of heroes like Hallam.

To apprehend the formative power of the past in this manner is to infuse the whole past with the historical imagination. From many vantages, *In Memoriam* is the "Way of the Historian," with "meaning" in the past a creative act: the past engaged with both passion and understanding in the classic problem of the historian who tries to write meaningful history. Section 128, in fact, can be seen as a list of the ways to interpret historical time, the "mysteries of good, / Wild Hours that fly with Hope and Fear." Their enumeration is a preparation for the celebrated conclusion of the section. The persona first wonders "If all your office had to do / With old results that look like new." This appears to refer to the drawing up of the "lessons" of history, an antiquated Enlightenment approach. The employment of history tendentiously, for religious polemicism, seems the purport of these lines:

If this were all your mission here,

To draw, to sheathe a useless sword,
To fool the crowd with glorious lies,
To cleave a creed in sects and cries,
To change the bearing of a word,

To shift an arbitrary power . . .

Further, merely to study the past, joylessly, and not to absorb its living power is "To cramp the student at his desk." Or, the past can be romanticized in the fashionable medievalism of the time (perhaps an unconscious reaction against his own *The Princess*): "To make old bareness picturesque/And tuft with grass a feudal tower." "Why then," the persona says to Time, if these are the uses of the past, "my scorn might well descend/On you and yours." But the culminating vision is that the historian must see as an artist: "I see in part/That all, as in some piece of art,/Is toil cooperant to an end."

Some commentary has gone into this "world as art" imagery, growing out of the critical tendency to aesthetic allegory. Johnson, for instance, rejects Bradley's quadripartite scheme of spiritual progress and its corresponding psychological progression to focus on Tennyson as craftsman: the journey is the "Way of the Poet" and the work a "poem of aesthetic quest."[37] This is so, but the issues here involve the art of the creative spirit at large and, more narrowly, the art of the historian. After all, Clio has been a muse for most all of her career. It is not likely that such a persona would find redemption in a literary artifact; he is after much bigger game. The "piece of art" is not some history "as it really is" that the persona suddenly has grasped, but rather the "meaning" he has constructed so laboriously in the welter of the past through both passionate conviction and rational system:

> The love that rose on stronger wings,
> > Unpalsied when he met with Death,
> > Is comrade of the lesser faith
> That sees the course of human things.

Conviction may be more important than system—for "I have felt" (95), as the persona says—but both are necessary if the historian is to find the "meaning" of the past.

To this historical art, Hallam can be seen as muse, attended by figures typologically significant. In section 37, the depressed persona is shamed by Urania for claiming only the "earthly" Melpomene and not aspiring to the higher, Miltonic inspiration. In section 58, Urania tells the persona to stay longer in the "cold crypts" where Hallam is buried, so that he can take a "nobler leave" rather than merely a sad farewell. In a variant reading, she tells him that a mere "speechless child can move the heart"—a qualification of the "I have felt" affirmation of

[37]E. D. H. Johnson, "The Way of the Poet," p. 148.

which critics have made too much—"But thine, my friend, is nobler Art."[38] As muse of "meaning" in section 103, Hallam is first merely a "statue veiled." But under the ministrations of both Clio and Urania— "one would sing the death of war,/And one would chant the history/ Of that great race, which is to be,/And one the shaping of a star"—he becomes a living presence on the "great ship" that moves on the deep of time. So inspired, the persona "felt the thews of Anakim,/The pulses of a Titan's heart." This is no supernatural frame of reference, however, for Tennyson quite plainly said that these figures represented "human powers": "all the great hopes of science and men."[39]

With "meaning" in the past a creative act out of human will and available in an apocalyptic present, this "great race, which is to be"— that "one far-off divine event" of the Epilogue—now can fall logically into an "open-ended" frame. Section 118, which contains the master smithy, has the clearest statement of the "meaning" of the whole past. Seemingly, the frame of reference is "end-determined" and this is the way in which it is usually taken. "They say," the persona offers,

The solid earth whereon we tread

In tracts of fluent heat began,
  And grew to seeming-random forms,
  The seeming prey of cyclic storms,
Till at the last arose the man;

Who throve and branched from clime to clime,
  The herald of a higher race.

But, he says further—leaving questionable this "evolutionary" process with the repeated *seeming*—man has the ever-present potential of realizing the higher state at any time:

And of himself in higher place,
If so he type this work of time

Within himself, from more to more;
  Or, crowned with attributes of woe
  Like glories, move his course.

It is a matter of the free, erected will facing the sorrowful past. In the Epilogue, the "one far-off divine event,/To which the whole creation

---

[38] See Ricks, ed., *Poems of Tennyson*, p. 913.
[39] Knowles, p. 186.

moves" (ll. 143–44) may appear to be an "end," but if man dwells in perpetual apocalypse this event is available in the here and now. This "event" is described specifically as "the crowning race/Or those that, eye to eye, shall look/On knowledge"—another qualifier on "I have felt"—"under whose command/Is Earth and Earth's, and in their hand/Is Nature like an open book" (ll. 128–32).

But Hallam had been such "a noble type/Appearing ere the times were ripe." Critics have given up trying to explain Hallam in an "end-determined" scheme, except as he is this type of a superior consciousness. Gibson argues that the message of section 118 is to "recapitulate Evolution within yourself and improve on it . . . To move upward working out the beast is to become virtually immortal, like the speaker who watched the solid lands shape themselves and go. It is to be not a man, but Man."[40] August observes that Tennyson believed that "evolution has shifted from a biological natural selection to a spiritual growth which is partly man-controlled. In man, evolution has become conscious of itself."[41] Yet if this increasing consciousness—a collective mind in history—wills its own "meaning," spiritual growth appears to be entirely man-controlled. Certainly Hallam attained it, and so may anyone in the eternal *kairos* realizable in the eternal now.

The poem closes appropriately with the epithalamion and the inception of the child, the latter a symbol of the fresh start struck into being with "star and system rolling past." The fetus gathers together in its development the history of the whole past, but clearly it goes to no "end" save as a flowering of the chrysalid form in the eternal present, free to fuse its own nature with such vestiges of the past. It is an "organic" symbol but, like the other organic imagery of the poem, should suggest neither biological determinism nor any other linkage in an evolutionary scheme, although critics have seen this symbol serving such a function. Rosenberg, for instance, asserts that the "foetus, recapitulating the 'lower phases' of evolution, will develop, as had Hallam, into a closer link with the crowning race of perfected mankind, whose advent had been 'heralded' in Section CXVIII."[42] Yet it is not clear how this physiological recapitulation advances the species, nor why this child should be more perfect than any other child, save as we postulate the very idea of evolution that we attempt to deduce from the poem.

[40] Walker Gibson, "Behind the Veil," pp. 65–66.
[41] Eugene R. August, "Tennyson and Teilhard," p. 221.
[42] Rosenberg, "Two Kingdoms," p. 240.

August observes that Tennyson accepted the notion of spiritual progress and that the poem's final idea contains the "process of Christogenesis, that is, an attempt to give birth to Christ again by evolving *AfterChrists*—to borrow Hopkins' word."[43] The child, then, could be a correlative of the "birth" that the persona by his reconstituted vision has come to represent, although the evolutionary emphasis should be resisted. Everything depends upon the strength of the human will. In the imagery of the epithalamion and the child, the persona attains a "holy marriage" between the human condition and and the cosmic nexus that (in Abrams' words once more) may "create out of the world of all of us, in a quotidian and recurring miracle, a new world which is the equivalent of paradise."[44] And this recurring paradise is precisely the final note struck in *The Princess* as well.[45] Both the resolution on the social plane, culminating in *The Princess*, and that on the individual plane, ending in *In Memoriam*, foretell a redemption. The modern theologian Bultmann describes such redemption in this manner: "Always in your present lies the meaning in history, and you cannot see it as a spectator, but only in your responsible decisions. In every moment slumbers the possibility of being the eschatological moment. You must awaken it."[46]

The poem worked. The eschatological moment was awakened with the publication of *In Memoriam*. Tennyson won Emily, the laureateship, and the recognition and stability he needed after forty-one years of life. He came to terms with an absentee God, the disasters of history, and the death and resurrection of heroes. For the time, he found social and personal redemption at work in the world. Carlyle had seen him in 1844 moving "through Chaos and the Bottomless and Pathless . . . carrying a bit of Chaos about him in short, which he is manufacturing into Cosmos!"[47] Manufacture it he did in *The Princess* and *In Memoriam*, but the optimism of this mid-century self-help, sorrowful as was its base, was not to last long. As he said of *In Memoriam*, "It's too hopeful, this poem, more than I am myself."[48]

---

[43] August, p. 224.
[44] Abrams, p. 28.
[45] See chapter 4, note 23.
[46] Rudolf Bultmann, *History and Eschatology*, p. 155.
[47] *The Correspondence of Thomas Carlyle and Ralph Waldo Emerson*, 2:66–67.
[48] Knowles, p. 182.

VI The Political Poems and *Maud*

IN THE PREVIOUS two chapters a case was made that *The Princess* and *In Memoriam* were informed by two resolutions to the problems of history. In the former, providential purpose is apprehended when past and present interpenetrate in the apocalyptic "point-time" of a medieval ideal to produce the Great House model of society under which the hero subsumes the nation's affairs, including commerce and industry: a Sir Walter (but a Prince too, winning his "Guinevere," establishing his Great House). In the latter, the persona (the spirit of the "human race") evokes active providence through a revolutionary fusion of present will and past heroic memory in an apocalyptic self-transfiguration, subsuming common emotions (sorrow, despair) under the aegis of an heroic self-discipline. The hero is returning but, whereas in the thirties he had been a furthest extension of "self" bereft of providential sanction, now he possesses the selflessness incumbent on one who effects in his person this providential intent for both the society and the individual. Such elements of Tennyson's philosophy of history inform the political poems and *Maud*.

Tennyson's political poems of the early fifties were occasioned by his concern that the nation was falling into anarchy on the plane of ordinary providence as a result of its failure to engage the historically formative power of active providence. More specifically, man microcosmically (unlike the persona of *In Memoriam*) was failing to make base passions (selfishness, sensuality, covetousness) subservient to the nobler conditions of selflessness, struggle, and sacrifice. Therefore, macrocosmically (unlike the society of *The Princess*), man was failing to enlist the forces of commerce and industry under the rule of the proper hero class. The result of this national fragmentation was weakness of will before the historical apocalypse ever at the doors, especially in the field of international affairs. Revolutions convulsed Europe in 1848 and Louis Napoleon's coup in 1851 once more mobilized England's traditional enemy under an unscrupulous dictator.

In 1851 the Tennysons were visited by Charles Kingsley, "then in the full fervour of his enthusiasm for F. D. Maurice and Christian Socialism," as Charles Tennyson says. In his 1850 novel *Alton Locke* and in his pamphlets and articles, Kingsley was attacking the "sweated labour and infamous housing and sanitation of our industrial cities." During the visit the Tennysons sympathetically listened to him "inveighing against the 'puling, quill-driving, soft-handed, effete and unbelieving age,' the only salvation for which, he maintained, lay in an alliance between the Church, the gentlemen and the workmen against the shopkeepers and the Manchester Radicals,"[1] notably Bright and Cobden, spokesmen for mercantile interests, and peace with France at any price. And sympathetically too, Tennyson must have read Carlyle's 1850 *Latter-Day Pamphlets*, in which the sage fulminated against the "Constituted Anarchy" caused by a "consecration of cupidity," wherein the sum of man's social obligations is but to "buy in the cheapest market, and sell in the dearest." England could be saved, Carlyle argued, only when it realized that "it is the everlasting privilege of the foolish to be governed by the wise," heroes who specifically are inspired by the "dust of our heroic ancestors" to introduce "God's Laws, instead of Mammon's."[2]

And mammon in England is in the minds of the "hogs, who can believe in nothing great,/Sneering bedridden in the down of Peace,/Over their scrips and shares," says Tennyson in "Suggested by Reading an Article in a Newspaper": "We drag so deep in our commercial mire . . ." This is a lotos peace of men dropping out of God's purpose: "Sweet Peace can no man blame,/But Peace of sloth or of avarice born,/Her olive is her shame" because "Tradesmen love her for gain" ("Rifle Clubs!!!"). In "The Penny-Wise," Tennyson castigates the ledger mentality: "The cheapest things are not the best." Rather, arm well.

[1] Sir Charles Tennyson, *Alfred Tennyson*, p. 260.
[2] Thomas Carlyle, *Works of Thomas Carlyle*, 13:287, 277, 281–82.

"O where is he, the simple fool/Who says that wars are over?" He is a member of the "babbling Peace Societies," but "if indeed ye long for peace,/Make ready to do battle—/To fight the battle of the world,/Of progress and humanity." (This is a veritable call to the apocalyptic "gathering of nations/Unto the mighty battle of the Lord" of the poet's early "Armageddon.")

In the 1852 "Ode on the Death of the Duke of Wellington" Tennyson indicates both the nature of active providence and the attributes of the "manlike God and Godlike men" needed to engage it in this hour of peril. Wellington is a military commander whose mystic "voices" come to him not from divine heights but from the mouths of cannon. "He with those deep voices wrought,/Guarding realms and kings from shame;/With those deep voices our dead captain taught/The tyrant" (the first Napoleon). Wellington is the earthly conduit that connects this power (the result of historical will and purpose) with future resolve. He, and men like him, constitute the heroic memory in the dust that will inspire later "voices" to speak as the cannon spoke:

> In full acclaim,
> A people's voice,
> The proof and echo of all human fame,
> A people's voice, when they rejoice
> At civic revel and pomp and game,
> Attest their great commander's claim
> With honour, honour, honour, honour to him
> Eternal honour to his name.

The journey of the funeral procession is to the "dome of the golden cross," Saint Paul's Cathedral, amid "streaming London's central roar," which is also to be identified with the voices of the cannon and of the people in civic conclave. Tennyson has faith in the "people" insofar as they are reverent toward Godlike men and toward those whom Wellington would "drill," certainly not the "brainless mobs and lawless Powers" who do not enlist in the "march of mind." Durham sees the cathedral as a "still and sacred point in a world which scarcely avoids chaos" and so renders this central roar a "profane confusion" since the nation "shapes itself around its religion."[3] But Tennyson made the

---

[3]Margery Stricker Durham, "Tennyson's Wellington Ode and the Cosmology of Love," pp. 281, 292.

distinction between central roar and Saint Paul's once before when he called this roar the "mind" and the latter merely a "mood of it."[4]

Religion, to be sure, but the strong identification of cannon with people with "streaming London's central roar" makes Wellington's type of agape very militant indeed. It is the spirit of a commander who would lead the people as Christian soldiers onward and upward toward the "toppling crags of Duty . . . close upon the shining tablelands/To which our God Himself is moon and sun." Though this "last great Englishman is low," the remembrance of "all his greatness in the Past" will bring about the desired explosive energy of national rebirth. This is the very formula of *In Memoriam*, where the persona, the "human race," is restructured by the "hands/That reach through nature, moulding men" (124) in the apocalyptic forge. As the argument was made in chapter 5, such hands are those of the heroes of the nation who (in the words of "Hail Briton!")

> . . . wrought a work which time reveres,
>   A precedent to all the lands,
>   And an example reaching hands
> For ever into coming years.

In *In Memoriam*, the focus of such a power was the dead Hallam but, in the larger perspective, it was all those who "suffered countless ills,/Who battled for the True, the Just" (56). This power of the formative past is evoked in the Wellington ode precisely. Men will remember "his greatness in the past" as that of a "Truth-teller" (an epithet that plays for historical perspective by coupling Wellington with King Alfred).[5] And by such historical memories, "men may rise on stepping stones/Of their dead selves to higher things" (in the words of *In Memoriam*, section 1).

Tennyson's poem "Will" apparently was intended for the Wellington ode but was not used.[6] The lines set up a distinction between the sacred heights of will and duty and the featurelessness of selfish passions, between an England as Tennyson wishes it to be and a France of the the "red fool-fury of the Seine" (*In Memoriam*, section 127).

---

[4] See chapter 4, note 32.

[5] John W. Hales observes that the epithet of "truth-teller" undoubtedly came to Tennyson from Sharon Turner's *The History of the Anglo-Saxons*, but that it was also "traditional" and had been applied to a long line of kings and nobles ("King Alfred 'The Truth-Teller'," p. 117). This may suggest the archetypal nature of Tennyson's evocation (Tennyson had Turner's history in his library in the 1807 edition).

[6] See Christopher Ricks, ed., *Poems of Tennyson*, p. 1017.

O well for him whose will is strong . . .
Who seems a promontory of rock,
That, compassed round with turbulent sound,
In middle ocean meets the surging shock,
Tempest-buffeted, citadel crowned.

This mighty fortress of our soul sits high, risen from the moiling deep, surrounded by oceanic vigor and violence (much as Britain is surrounded by "blown seas and storming showers," in the words from the Wellington ode). Over this violence, the soul can be dominant only by superior strength. So,

ill for him who, bettering not with time,
Corrupts the strength of heaven-descended Will . . .
He seems as one whose footsteps halt,
Toiling in immeasurable sand,
And o'er a weary sultry land,
Far beneath a blazing vault,
Sown in a wrinkle of the monstrous hill,
The city sparkles like a grain of salt.

The weariness suggests the dropping away from providential purpose in "The Lotos-Eaters": "Weary seemed the sea, weary the oar." Thus, the mariners decline to "war with evil" and become enchanted with indulgence of "self." In what appears to have been his father's own connectives, Hallam Tennyson suggests a relationship between the "awful rose of dawn" of the "Vision of Sin" and those who "better not with time" (*Memoir*, 1:322); in this poem, the rose of dawn is "Unheeded" because the protagonist is cynical and corrupt. As a result, the divine power reaches him as a "vapour heavy, hueless, formless, cold." This lack of form—as I should argue, historical form—is in the featureless landscape of sand and burning sky in "Will." The low-lying city is sterile in time, though "sparkling" with earthly heats (the "frantic city's flashing heats," as Tennyson describes Paris in "Hands All Round!").

By one of history's cunning passages, however, England in 1854 was allied with satanic France against godless Russia in the Crimean War. The blunder at Balaclava produced "The Charge of the Light Brigade," which contains familiar features. The quite common but "drilled" army men (it is Wellington's army) encounter a disastrous situation but tap some hidden power within themselves—certainly not the inspiration of their immediate commanders. It is as though they remember some "greatness in the past" (such as Wellington) or, more generally, the memory of a whole "trophied Past."[7] This power rises from the apocalyptic limit they face and it gives them the victory, although the company martyrs itself in the scheme of things. "When can their glory fade?" It cannot, for they themselves become part of the trophied past, available for the memory of those that come after them, both in battle and at home fighting the viler civil war of *Maud* (whose protagonist should mime their action shortly).

Maud is part of the frame of mind that produced both the political poems and the *Idylls*. Tennyson in fact had "begun work on a poem about the enchantment of Merlin," Charles Tennyson writes, "but he laid this aside for *Maud*, the composition of which occupied him during the last six months of 1854."[8] In July of 1855, *Maud* was ready for the printer; after this Tennyson returned to the Vivien idyll, which he wrote in February and March of 1856. The Vivien idyll prefigures the general decline of Camelot into imprisonment in the selfishness that would end in fratricidal civil war. The enchantment of Merlin (who may be considered a symbol for the "human race" that brought Camelot into being) is an adumbration of this destruction. Camelot's final descent is into the kind of primal anarchy that both precedes and succeeds the career of a mighty state. It is not unreasonable to suspect some connection in Tennyson's mind between the civil war that comes before and after Camelot and the Hobbesian anarchy that opens *Maud*, with its "Civil war, as I think, and that of a kind/The viler, as underhand, not openly bearing the sword" (I, 27–28). Nor is it unreasonable to look for some connection between what lifted Camelot from the anarchy of open field (or, what lifted the persona of *In Memoriam* from despair to happiness) and what is, at least potentially, the redemptive power for the society of *Maud*.

Briefly, the argument is that the hero of *Maud* represents his society as symbolic scapegoat, taking on its sinful, commercial, and murderous attributes. After this, like Merlin, he is enchanted into a ritual tomb through his "Vivien," the "disease, a hard mechanic ghost" (II, 82) that is not the spirit of Maud but (as in the case of Merlin)[9] the projection

---

[7] The phrase is from lines written at Somersby about the Russian soldiers' defeat of Napoleon (see chapter 1, note 27).

[8] Tennyson, *Alfred Tennyson*, p. 282.

[9] See chapter 8, note 2.

of his own "self," his base "anima." In the case of Merlin, this self was a world-weary sensuality. In the present instance, it is the private grief that finally must be exorcised (as was the case with the persona of *In Memoriam*) through a firming of the will and a resolve to historical involvement. The difference between the hero of *Maud* and Merlin is that the latter's imprisonment signals the irretrievable decline of Camelot, whereas the former's entombment—the ritual death of "self"—leads to resurrection into the disasters of the historical condition. Here the true Maud seemingly becomes the muse of apocalyptic fire birth (much the function Hallam served in *In Memoriam*).

The full argument about Camelot's career follows in the succeeding chapters, particularly the idea that civilization rises from and sustains its vital spirit by war against wicked states and base passions. Here I note merely that the pre-Arthurian stage was a time when (in the words of "The Coming of Arthur") "many a petty king" ruled and "ever waging war/Each upon the other, wasted all the land . . . Wherein the beast was ever more and more," with "wolf-like men,/Worse than the wolves." The "commercial mire . . . hogs . . . the thousand cankers of our state" (words from "Suggested by Reading an Article in a Newspaper") as described in *Maud* is much like this. The poem is replete with imagery of human nature red in tooth and claw in a nature "one with rapine," where the "Mayfly is torn by the swallow, the sparrow speared by the shrike" (I, 123, 124). We have the "heart of the citizen hissing in war on his own hearthstone" (I, 24) and the greater vampire—a "gray old wolf and a lean" (I, 471) in a "wilderness, full of wolves" (II, 292)—"that old man, now Lord of the broad estate and the Hall,/Dropt off gorged from a scheme that had left us flaccid and drained" (I, 19–20). All are as "venomous worms,/That sting each other here in the dust" (II, 46–47).

In this jungle state, people attack and kill each other in a type of civil war. The commercial combat has left the protagonist's father a suicide "Mangled, and flattened, and crushed" (I, 7). There is also the criminal equivalent; all are as pickpockets, "each hand lusting for all that is not its own . . . in the spirit of Cain" (I, 22). There is assault and murder in the family as in the larger brotherhood, where "only the ledger lives" and the tradesman's "cheating yardwand" serves to "Cheat and be cheated" (I, 35, 52, 32).

And the vitriol madness flushes up in the ruffian's head,
Till the filthy by-lane rings to the yell of the trampled wife,

And chalk and alum and plaster are sold to the poor for bread,
And the spirit of murder works in the very means of life . . .
. . . a Mammonite mother kills her babe for a burial fee,
And Timour-Mammon grins on a pile of children's bones. (I, 37–46)

The poisonous atmosphere, this "blighting influence of a recklessly speculative age," as Tennyson called it (*Memoir*, 1:396), extends to all parts of the nation and to all human relationships:

Below me, there, is the village, and looks how quiet and small!
And yet bubbles o'er like a city, with gossip, scandal, and spite;
And Jack on his ale-house bench has as many lies as a Czar.
(I, 108–10)

Even the hero's man and maid are "ever ready to slander and steal" (I, 120).

Like Merlin in regard to the growing sensuality and selfishness of the court, the hero of *Maud* is the carrier of every attribute of this commercial jungle. As such, he represents his age as scapegoat. "He is the heir of madness, an egoist with the makings of a cynic," Tennyson said, with a "suspicion that all the world is against him" (*Memoir*, 1:396). This certainly describes the mental condition of the inhabitants of this jungle, backed into their caves and hissing at fellow animals. The hero is suicidally inclined: "Must *I* too creep to the hollow and dash myself down and die" (I, 54)? He is "At war with myself and a wretched race" (I, 364), and his thought that Maud's brother is the "huge scapegoat of the race" bearing the "whole inherited sin" (I, 484–85) merely reflects back upon himself.

The hero of *Maud* equates "a time so sordid and mean,/ And myself so languid and base" (I, 178–79). *Languid* here refers to an egoistic retreat into a selfishness that makes him "like a stoic, or like/ A wiser epicurean" (I, 121–22), indifferent to mankind. He asks, "Shall I weep if a Poland fall? shall I shriek if a Hungary fail?" "*I* have not made the world," he adds sarcastically, "and He that made it will guide." "The drift of the Maker is dark" (I, 144–49), he says. His views of God are like the Epicurean views of the mariners in "The Lotos-Eaters," who will not "war with evil" and so see the gods "smile in secret, looking over wasted lands . . . careless of mankind." *Maud*'s protagonist thinks "We are puppets . . . moved by an unseen hand at a game" (I, 126–27), in

> A sad astrology, the boundless plan
> That makes you tyrants in your iron skies,
> Innumerable, pitiless, passionless eyes,
> Cold fires, yet with power to burn and brand
> His nothingness into man. (I, 634–38)

It is significant that he lives

> alone in an empty house,
> Here half-hid in the gleaming wood,
> Where I hear the dead at midday moan,
> And the shrieking rush of the wainscot mouse,
> And my own sad name in corners cried . . . (I, 257–61)

This is Mariana's house, part of an older, heroic time fallen into a vacant disuse and haunted by ancient presences (if the words of chapter 3 may be repeated regarding this poem). In "Mariana," the mouse

> Behind the mouldering wainscot shrieked,
> Or from the crevice peered about.
> Old faces glimmered through the doors,
> Old footsteps trod the upper floors,
> Old voices called her from without . . .

Tennyson uses this device again in *Maud* when he refers to the rat as "he lies and listens mute / In an ancient mansion's crannies and holes" (II, 298–99). The house here becomes a metonymic representation for the state of England, much as Tennyson used the symbol of the Great House to represent England's social order in *The Princess*. *Maud*'s hero hears the past calling but his will is too weak to respond properly. In his corrupt condition, the voice of the dead is too readily taken for, say, the voice of his dead father calling him to a "selfish grave" (I, 559), instead of being taken for the voices of the heroic past, those "hands / That reach through nature, moulding men," as in *In Memoriam* (124).

Such voices, however, reach the hero in the form of potentials with the coming of Maud and the battle song she sings:

> She is singing an air that is known to me,
> A passionate ballad gallant and gay,
> A martial song like a trumpet's call!

> Singing alone in the morning of life,
> In the happy morning of life and of May,
> Singing of men that in battle array,
> Ready in heart and ready in hand,
> March with banner and bugle and fife
> To the death, for their native land. (I, 164–72)

This "Singing of Death, and of Honour" (I, 177), this warbling a "chivalrous battle-song" (I, 383) is a somewhat startling type of expression for a "milkwhite fawn" so "meek . . . Pale . . . Passionless," as she is described but a few lines before (I, 158, 88–91). The passage testifies to Tennyson's determination to seed early the precise nature of the hero's final redemption. The hero falls in love with her in large part because of this song. He consoles himself with regard to his rival by the thought that, with such songs within her, "She would not do herself this great wrong,/To take . . . a lord, a captain, a padded shape,/A bought commission, a waxen face . . . For a man and leader of men," as her family wishes (I, 386–88, 358–59). This thought then leads into the potentially redemptive desire to emulate such warriors as the song glorifies:

> Ah God, for a man with heart, head, hand,
> Like some of the simple great ones gone
> For ever and ever by,
> One still strong man in a blatant land,
> Whatever they call him, what care I,
> Aristocrat, democrat, autocrat—one
> Who can rule and dare not lie.
>
> And ah for a man to arise in me,
> That the man I am may cease to be! (I, 389–97)

Tennyson puts it pluralistically, but there is no mistaking the hero's hope that somewhere out there a strong military ruler (like Arthur) is about to bring a tight order to the anarchy and civil war that presently characterize the nature of the state. With this love and this understanding, as the hero says, "*I have climbed nearer out of lonely Hell*." As he does so he constructs the same epistemology of "meaning" noted previously in the discussion of *In Memoriam*. He vitalizes the world by "consummating a holy marriage with the external universe" (in the words of Abrams).[10] This is the mark of a firming will imposing an interchangeable supremacy on the world. Consequently, the "sad astrology" now becomes "Beat, happy stars, timing with things below,/ Beat with my heart more blest than heart can tell" (I, 678-80). In brief, as Tennyson himself said, this song "awakens a love in the heart which revolutionizes and inspires the whole life" (Memoir, 1:397).

But, in a reversal that is also the fulfillment of the thematic purpose, the hero kills Maud's brother, in anger and pride and the "spirit of Cain." He becomes a criminal, losing his hold on the world and taking on as scapegoat the last and primal attribute of the society "one with rapine." Maud dies of grief and it may be said that he has killed her as well. Accordingly, Maud's role in the remainder of the poem is bifurcated. She serves first as a memory that becomes progressively meaner with the hero's despairing wanderings until that memory is exorcised in the ritual death of the madhouse tomb; and at the very end of the poem she becomes a memory that points the way to the apocalyptic limit in the Crimea. That the two are quite different is unmistakable, for when Maud "seemed to divide in a dream from a band of the blest . . . and pointed to Mars," the hero sees a certain "dreary phantom arise and fly/Far into the North, and battle, and seas of death" (III, 10-13, 36-37). Hellstrom makes a persuasive identification of this phantom with "the forces of evil."[11] Since this phantom is without doubt the "disease, a hard mechanic ghost" (II, 82) that has been accompanying the hero all through Part II, it follows that this presence has been inimical all along, insofar as she represents an obsession with self.

We cannot avoid the conclusion that what appears to be a progressive if painful improvement in the hero's spiritual condition in certain sections of Part II is really a declension of the "morbid poetic soul" Tennyson warned us was in play in the poem (Memoir, 1:396). The hero anticipates Maud's death when, seeing her house dark, "I shuddered and thought like a fool of the sleep of death" (I, 526). He holds strange morbid dialogues with himself on the subject of death. "Sullen-seeming Death may give/More life to Love than is or ever was/In our low world," he reflects; and he imagines that Maud responds, "The dusky strand of Death inwoven here/With dear Love's tie, makes Love himself more dear" (I, 644-59). The brother's death makes a mockery of the sentiment and instantly turns Maud into a "ghastly Wraith." The

---

[10] See chapter 5, note 29. Lowell called Maud the "antiphonal voice to 'In Memoriam'" (Memoir, 1:393).
[11] Ward Hellstrom, On the Poems of Tennyson, p. 86.

protagonist flees to land "on the Breton strand" (II, 32, 77), exactly where Merlin landed. Like Merlin, he becomes obsessed with a projection of his own selfish passion:

Plagued with a flitting to and fro,
A disease, a hard mechanic ghost
That never came from on high
Nor ever arose from below.

He diagnoses accurately the fact that, indeed, it comes from his madness, that it is "a juggle born of the brain" (II, 81-84, 90). Nor do his subsequent assessments of its nature allow any mitigation of its baseness: "abiding phantom cold," "deathlike type of pain," "the blot upon the brain," "shadow," "the maggot born in an empty head" (II, 195, 198, 200, 230, 276), and the madhouse utterance:

she is standing here at my head;
Not beautiful now, not even kind . . .
She comes from another stiller world of the dead,
Stiller, not fairer than mine. (II, 303-9)

Finally he is free of this Maud when he says in Part III, "It is time, O passionate heart and morbid eye,/That old hysterical mock-disease should die" (32-33). Early in Part II he appears to take inspiration from the "lovely shell,/Small and pure as a pearl" (49-50), which is

Frail, but of force to withstand,
Year upon year, the shock
Of cataract seas that snap
The three decker's oaken spine, (72-75)

but, if the shell is a symbol of his spiritual state, we are told plainly that "The tiny cell is forlorn,/Void of the little living will/That made it stir on the shore" (61-63). His resolve at this point is most unconvincing, especially given its necessary condition:

as long, O God, as she
Have a grain of love for me,
So long, no doubt, no doubt.
Shall I nurse in my dark heart,
However weary, a spark of will
Not to be trampled out. (II, 100-105)

Neither the mechanical ghost nor natural design provide the core of future redemption. Rather, the core is the memory of the "chivalrous battle-song" that Maud once sang. At first, "An old song vexes my ear," but then, in the midst of his "long grief and pain" (II, 95, 142), he has a dream (that always "essentially spiritual experience," as Charles Tennyson says):[12]

> 'Tis a morning pure and sweet,
> And a dewy splendour falls
> On the little flower that clings
> To the turrets and the walls. (II, 171–74)

This is reminiscent of "The splendour falls on castle walls / And snowy summits old in story." Like this song in *The Princess,* the passage evokes the "morning of life" (I, 168), the power of the feudal past to which an individual spirit, "the little flower," may cling securely. *Maud*'s hero hears in the dream "the ballad that she sings . . . in the meadow" (II, 183, 180), the same "passionate ballad" Maud had sung earlier "In the meadow" (I, 163–165). The ballad calls men to battle "To the death, for their native land" (I, 172). This call is what the true Maud stands for as an "inner psychic reality"[13] in Part III: "a hope for the world in the coming wars." This too "was but a dream, yet it yielded a dear delight." We may see here that Wellington's voices will speak once more: "the cobweb woven across the cannon's throat / Shall shake its threaded tears in the wind no more." The remembrance of all Wellington's "greatness in the Past" will be reaffirmed here epigonically in the "sudden making of splendid names, / And noble thought be freër," that is, freer to enlist all selfish passions under the banner of a selfless, cohesive "one desire" of the "higher aims."

"Consequently" (the logic is persuasive if Tennyson's premises are granted), the energy of commercial anarchy is transfigured by the overriding national purpose. "For I trust if an enemy's fleet came yonder round by the hill," said the protagonist early in the poem, "the smooth-faced snubnosed rogue would leap from his counter and till, / And strike" (I, 49–52) not his fellow predator but the common foe. So now "No more shall commerce be all in all." Farewell to a "peace that was full of wrongs and shames, / Horrible, hateful, monstrous, not to be told; / And hail once more to the banner of battle unrolled!" Within this

---

[12] See chapter 2, note 63.
[13] Dorothy M. Mermin, "Tennyson's *Maud*: A Thematic Analysis," p. 271.

fire birth, "From state to state the spirit walks" through "shattered stalks" (*In Memoriam*, 82) to effect the providential "purpose of God, and the doom assigned." Appropriately, the hero departs for the burgeoning "blood-red blossom of war with a heart of fire" on a "giant deck and mixed my breath/With a loyal people shouting a battle-cry." Insofar as the true Maud is the numenous presence,[14] the tableau resembles the redemptive dream of the reconstructed persona from *In Memoriam* joining the "great ship" of "shining sides" with Hallam as captain, and they move "From deep to deep" (103). Thus the hero of *Maud* is reconstructed, and he sails off to join the knighthood setting up a new social order, perhaps a Camelot.

[14]John Killham notes that Tennyson's theme is the "attainment through sexual love of a psychic balance, and that this must involve facing violence and death as part of the universal human lot" ("Tennyson's *Maud*—The Function of the Imagery," p. 228). Ricks points out an earlier use by Tennyson of a "war in a just cause as contrasted with despairing self-absorption" in "The Two Voices," lines 124–56 (*Poems of Tennyson*, p. 1091). The good Maud represents the one and the bad Maud the other.

VII   The Rise of Camelot

THE PREVIOUS CHAPTER described Tennyson's philosophy of history, coming into the fifties, as a convergence of the frames of reference from *The Princess* and *In Memoriam*: divinity is apprehended apocalyptically, historical form takes a hierarchical model, and heroes subordinate lower manifestations of self (and society) to the higher purpose. Such ideas and beliefs appeared in the political poems, the Wellington ode, and *Maud*. There they were depicted as an apocalyptic struggle between the heroic and base passions in society. In such a society anarchy results when commercial selfishness is not enlisted under the "manlike God and Godlike men" (words from the ode) who embody a militantly active providence. *Maud* and the Merlin idyll were conceived simultaneously and are complements. The former shows the fire birth of new historical form through the selfless hero's engagement of apocalypse; the latter portrays the lotos death of old historical form through its hero's withdrawal into self.

When Tennyson turned in earnest to the *Idylls* in 1856, he was looking for a key that would activate Camelot's rise and fall as an engagement with, and then a withdrawal from, the apocalypse ever at the doors. The poet had been groping for this for some time, as the record indicates. In the late forties he seemed to have settled on a metaphysically "allegorical or perhaps rather a parabolic drift in the poem" (*Memoir*, 2:127). In 1856–57, he read Hegel's *The Philosophy*

112

of History, and afterwards the *Idylls* came into place virtually as a whole, in spite of the fact that he wrote many of the individual idylls much later. For this reason, the *Idylls* is treated here fundamentally as a product of the fifties. Given the ideas and convictions Tennyson had, the Hegel work must have struck him as an almost familiar but unusually systematic explanation for the rise and fall of a civilization. This reading, I think, culminated the long record of Tennyson's work with the Arthurian matter and capped his studies in history and metaphysics during these years.

Tennyson from his earliest years had written out in prose various histories of Arthur. "The vision of Arthur as I have drawn him," Hallam Tennyson gives as one of his father's notes, "had come upon me when, little more than a boy, I first lighted upon Malory" (*Memoir*, 2:121, 128). But the statement is hardly faithful either to Malory, to the record of the figure's development in his mind, or to the changes in his conception of why Camelot fell. In the very earliest sketch, given by Hallam Tennyson as 1833, "dwelt the King in glory apart" in a kind of *fin de siècle* court while the Saxons "came nearer and nearer." There is a prophecy that Camelot "would topple into the abyss and be no more" (*Memoir*, 2:122–23). Here Arthur is not an ideal, nor is he one in a fragment in Tennyson's fine "early" hand (such as that in his Cambridge notebooks). In that fragment a speaker, presumably Modred, articulates Arthurian guilt along political lines as a crisis of pomp and malfeasance:

> Who that sees the court
> At full spring-tide of profligacy, who
> That looks upon the land, the husbandman
> Withdrawn from wholesome tillage of the soil
> To gape on pomps & shows — the whole long year
> Almost one holiday — so week by week
> Much treasure lavisht & the people drained —
> Who last, that contemplates our greatest grief
> The table round, two hundred knights, maintained
> At public charge — who by their vows are bound
> To deeds of honour, yet at license ride
> And pillage, wringing half the little left
> From worthier men — who sees all this can doubt
> But that the time is here?[1]

---

[1] Loose fragment (b Ms Eng 952.1 [97]) in the Tennyson papers of the Houghton Library, Harvard University.

In the 1833-34 "Morte d'Arthur" Camelot is in the grip of some kind of transcendent power, but the Malory matter is unaltered. It is to be assumed, therefore, that Arthur is culpable in fathering Modred and so in setting off the fatal chain of events. Arthur himself is broken, confused, not sure he is going to Avilion at all, and he looks on his efforts in fact "like one that feels a nightmare on his bed." An undertone of Arthurian guilt for the fall is present in the scenario for a musical masque in an 1833-40 notebook, for Arthur disobeys the Lady of the Lake who "endeavors to persuade him not to fight with Sir Mordred." The ladies abandon Arthur and "can return no more." Guinevere seems not to be an issue, although in the fourth act there is "discovery by Mordred and Nimue of Lancelot and Guinevere" (*Memoir*, 2:124-25).

In the last sketch we possess, however, there is a dramatic change in the conception both of Arthur and of the reason for Camelot's fall. This outline of a religious allegory was given by Tennyson to Knowles in 1869 as "between thirty and forty years old." It is placed by Wilson in 1839 because of its indebtedness to the Edwin Guest translation of *The Mabinogion*, the first part of which was published in 1838. Volume one of this work is in the Tennyson library, in Lincoln, but in the 1849 edition (and it appears on an 1850 Moxon billing).[2] Wilson also shows that the outline could be indebted to Edward Davie's *The Mythology and Rites of the British Druids.*[3] The latter was published first in 1809, but the edition in Tennyson's library is inscribed "To Alfred Tennyson from J. W. Bonchurch 19 June 1846," all of which suggests that the sketch was written in the late forties. Here, Arthur appears more helpless than guilty, though he has Guinevere, his first wife, "prim. Christianity," temporarily "put away" so he can take up with the second Guinevere, "Roman Catholicism." The first Guinevere returns but is "changed by lapse of Time." "Modred, the sceptical understanding" is allied with "Merlin Emrys, the enchanter, Science," who "marries his daughter to Modred." Both would be inimical to religion, though it is Modred who "pulls Guinevere, Arthur's latest wife, from the throne," the only direct cause for Camelot's fall that seems indicated.

[2] References to Moxon book-order billings (unpublished); various inscriptions, markings, and notes in the books in Tennyson's library; and transcriptions from Emily Tennyson's unpublished "Journal 1850-74" (except those portions published in the *Memoir*) refer to material in the Tennyson Research Centre. This material is used by kind permission of Lord Tennyson and the Lincolnshire Library Service, and is cited hereafter without further reference. Unless otherwise noted, the evidence for Tennyson's acquisitions, markings, and readings is from these sources. See also *Tennyson in Lincoln: A Catalog* for a list of the books on some of which my chapters 7 and 8 draw.

[3] Hugh H. Wilson, "Tennyson: Unscholarly Arthurian," p. 7.

The message appears to be that the state is built on moral foundations, weakened by time, and destroyed from within by secular tendencies (*Memoir*, 2:123).

This interest in religious allegory dovetails with Tennyson's theological readings in the fifties. He and Emily read Dunbar Heath's *The Future Kingdom of Christ*, E. W. Hengstenberg's *Christology of the Old Testament*, and a *Commentary on the Predictions of the Messiah by the Prophets* in 1852;[4] F. D. Maurice's *The Prophets and Kings of the Old Testament* (ordered from Moxon in 1853); and Maurice's *Theological Essays* (presented to Tennyson by Maurice in 1854). Tennyson also read Dr. Wordsworth's *Apocalypse* to Emily in early 1852 (*Memoir*, 1:355) and in 1852 he ordered from Moxon religious books with such titles as *The Apocalypse* by William (probably the 1852 *The Apocalypse, With Notes and Reflection* by the Reverend Isaac Williams), *The Eclipse of Faith; or, A Visit to a Religious Sceptic* (by Henry Rogers, 1852), and *Sketches of Modern Irreligion and Infidelity* by B. W. Wright.

On the other hand, this metaphysical interest is accompanied by a desire to understand the actual history of Arthur's time. Tennyson ordered from Moxon in 1850 Algernon Herbert's *Britannia After the Romans: An Attempt to Illustrate the Religious and Political Revolutions of that Province in the Fifth and Succeeding Centuries*, along with *The Mabinogion*. He already had in his library Sharon Turner's histories and the recent *On the English Conquest of the Severn Valley in the Sixth Century* (1842) by Edwin Guest. In the period 1850–59, he also added John Lingard's *The History of England, from the First Invasion by the Romans to the Accession of William and Mary in 1688*, William Barnes's *Notes on Ancient Britain and the Britons*, Henry Hart Milman's *History of Latin Christianity*, and George Robert Gleig's *English History and Sacred History*.

Out of these studies came the Vivien idyll in February–March and the Enid idyll in April–August of 1856. But as originally written, these two idylls have little to do with the mechanism of decline and fall either historically or metaphysically, for Merlin's loss seems to cause nothing, and after his wanderings Geraint returns to court as an exemplary knight. At this point, Francis T. Palgrave apparently gave Tennyson J. Sibree's 1857 translation of George Wilhelm Hegel's *The Philosophy of History*, the first English edition of this work. Tennyson might well

[4] *The Letters of Emily Lady Tennyson*, p. 63.

have read it sometime in 1857, although the first record of this interest is in Emily's journal for 25 February 1858, where she notes that they read "Deuteronomy, Hegel's *Philosophy of History*, Bede's *Ecclesiastical History* these evenings." Again, the journal entry of 14 April 1858 mentions that Tennyson "reads a little of Hegel to me."[5]

Too much, of course, can be made of Tennyson's debt to this reading. Yet Hegel's work is a philosophical embodiment of many ideas in the *Idylls*, and it is certainly true that the Guinevere and Elaine idylls, containing significant commentary on the causes of historical decline, followed hard upon this reading, as did the typical Tennysonian ruminations upon future idylls. The Guinevere idyll was written between July 1857 and March 1858 and the Elaine idyll between July 1858 and February 1859.[6] We know further that "on 28 June 1859, T. 'read Sir Pelleas and Ettarre [Malory, iv, 21–24] . . . with a view to a new poem'" and that "T. thought of writing 'a poem on Tristram and Isolt' in 1859."[7] Even the Grail theme was suggested to Tennyson by Macaulay in 1859, though he turned it down (*Memoir*, 1:456). Tennyson may well have found in Hegel what his own thinking was moving toward: a unified explanation, at once pragmatic and metaphysical, of the interplay of God, the historical process, and heroic man during a complete historical cycle.

The explanation must have struck sympathetic chords in Tennyson, given the concepts and beliefs I have been crediting him with throughout this study. Generally for Hegel, a "Providence (that of God) presides over the events of the World,"[8] the "State is the Idea of Spirit in the

[5] Sixteen years later, in a draft of a letter, Tennyson wrote that he had "hardly turned a page of Hegel, almost all that I know of him having come to me 'obiter' and obscurely thro' the talk of others; and I have never delivered myself to dialectics" (*Memoir*, 2:158), and now we know that the final letter (sent 1874 to an American philosopher named Blood) had it that he had "never" turned a page of Hegel and that he had merely not "vigorously" delivered himself to dialectic (David Staines, "Tennyson's Mysticism: A Personal Testimony," *Notes and Queries*, 24 [1977]: 405). Seemingly, Tennyson's 1858 readings of Hegel were not that important in his recollections. This may suggest, perhaps, that Hegel only reinforced what to Tennyson were ideas coming more forcefully from other areas.

[6] The dating of the four idylls published in 1859 comes from *Memoir* 1:414–28, and *Letters of Emily Lady Tennyson*, p. 131.

[7] From Hallam Lord Tennyson, *Materials for a Life of A. T.* (quoted by Christopher Ricks, ed., *Poems of Tennyson*, pp. 1687, 1705).

[8] Georg Wilhelm Friedrich Hegel, *Philosophy of History*, p. 13; further citations given parenthetically in text. Reference was made in chapter 2 to the consanguinity of the Hegelian "cunning of reason" to the Vichian notion of providence and, beyond this, to Mandeville's thesis and to Adam Smith's "invisible hand" (see footnotes 48 and 36). This concept is the root of the "irony" of history I trace in the *Idylls*. Tennyson could have been acquainted with some of Hegel's ideas while at Cambridge, although there is no evidence that the Apostles, through Hare and Thirlwall, were familiar with Hegel's lectures. The lectures were given first in

external manifestation of human Will and Its Freedom" (p. 47), and "World-historical men—the Heroes of an epoch" are those "whose vocation it was to be the agents of the World-Spirit" (pp. 30–31). These are precisely the three main notions of Tennyson's philosophy of history, held in one form or another since his Somersby days. According to Hegel, the state rises when, under "soul-leaders" (p. 31), worldly men activate its "vital principle . . . Morality" (p. 52) by enlisting the "self-will of caprice and passion" under "Law" (p. 41), which is orthodox Christian "freedom." Past and present interpenetrate in the state, for men know it consists both of "their deeds" and of "what their ancestors have produced" (p. 52). These are basic concepts to Tennyson as well; discipline under the higher principle and the power of heroic memory are the two primary ideas of both *In Memoriam* and *The Princess*.

Critics recognize that the *Idylls* contains "an allegory of the collapse of society," a "cyclic view of history," a "doctrine regarding history as an organic growth," and an idea of "evolution . . . tinged with Apocalypse."[9] Accordingly, the older moral-ethical explanation for Camelot's fall through the individual moral fault is no longer satisfactory, although no systematic historical explanation has been developed in its place. There is a tendency to recognize a multiplicity of reasons and to conclude that "there are no resounding causes for the fall."[10] But there is a central cause for a nation's decline, according to Hegel, and this cause lies in a certain irony of history (a drift in Tennyson I have been noting since the Somersby poems). The state is built on heroic spirit but, as the state develops, a point is reached when it eliminates external challenges and thereby reaches a deadly stasis of peace and rest. According to Hegel, the latter is a "mere *customary life*" that "brings on natural death. Custom is activity without opposition . . . a merely external sensuous existence which has ceased to throw itself

---

the winter of 1822–23 and later were published under the title *The Philosophy of History*. However, it would not be strange if the Apostles were familiar with these lectures. Hare was guardedly sympathetic to Hegel later: "Even by Hegel the historical process is regarded too much as a mere natural evolution, without due account of that fostering superintendence by which alone any real good is elicited" (*Guesses*, p. 335).

[9] Respectively, F. E. L. Priestley, "Tennyson's *Idylls*," p. 242; Jerome Hamilton Buckley, *Growth of a Poet*, p. 194; Clyde de L. Ryals, *From the Great Deep*, p. 102; and John D. Rosenberg, *Fall of Camelot*, p. 35. Ward Hellstrom surveys such critical commentary and, also, liberal Anglican historical thought in regard to the *Idylls*, pp. 29–33, 93–107; scattered references to Tennyson's historical thought are in J. Philip Eggers, *King Arthur's Laureate*.

[10] James R. Kincaid, *Tennyson's Major Poems*, p. 154; see also Priestley, "Tennyson's *Idylls*," p. 39, and Rosenberg, *Fall of Camelot*, p. 131.

enthusiastically into its object. Thus perish individuals, thus perish peoples by a natural death" through "political nullity and tedium" (pp. 74–75).

A summary of the *Idylls* will support this Hegelian explanation. Camelot rises in an apocalyptic condition of natural anarchy when oppositions are very real. Heroes enlist under Arthur as representative of world spirit bringing historical form and, microcosmically, they subordinate the "self-will of caprice and passion" to the higher faculty. Through the vows, they are reborn to be like Arthur, like their higher selves. Through this engagement with active providence, Camelot overcomes the Roman power and establishes its hegemony over various kingdoms, becoming a universal family with a wise and powerful head. Happiness is not pursued on the sensuous level, but rather as a joyous sacrifice and duty. This unity deteriorates when a time of golden rest and "custom" arrives, because external challenges have been eliminated (this is the necessary confrontation with active providence, as traced in Christian thought in chapter 2).[11] Heroic passions, being immutable (as was urged with regard to all Tennysonian heroes, Ulysses especially), begin to eat inwardly to produce an existence on the level of "self" (ordinary providence). Now, instead of knights like Gareth, "free" in perfect service, Geraint wanders self-imprisoned (although finally saved), Balin maddens and dies in fratricide, and Merlin immobilizes himself in Brittany. Dialectical variations from the spiritual mean appear in the form of Pellam and Vivien: asceticism and sensuality. The vows, also heroically immutable, are transferred to historically destructive objects: the Grail and women like Ettarre. Camelot produces its dialectical opposite in Pelleas's Round Table of the North. The contradictions in the historical condition can be held no longer and Camelot falls in apocalypse back into the natural anarchy from whence it arose.

Arthur appears at the start of the *Idylls* as agent of the fiery God of history. He embodies the state's vital principle, morality, and therefore, given man's mission in the "march of mind" (words from the Wellington ode), the strong sword arm. In Tennyson's sketch for a religious allegory in the *Idylls*, Excalibur is labeled *war* (*Memoir*, 2:123) and the Arthur who now wields it, while a leader of souls, is foremost a leader with intense passions for historically formative purposes. These include his own passions, although there is some critical tendency to deny that he has any. Yet his fury in battle is a prominent characteristic. Lancelot says,

---

[11] See chapter 2, notes 46–48 and discussion.

> I myself beheld the King
> Charge at the head of all his Table Round,
> And all his legions crying Christ and him,
> And break them; and I saw him, after, stand
> High on a heap of slain, from spur to plume
> Red as the rising sun with heathen blood,
> And seeing me, with a great voice he cried,
> "They are broken, they are broken!" (LE 302-309)

Arthur also patently has, early, a sensual passion for Guinevere. He "felt/Travail, and throes and agonies of the life,/Desiring to be joined with Guinevere" (CA 74-76) and, at the end, speaks of her "imperial-moulded form" and the "golden hair, with which I used to play" (G 544-45). He can become angered. When the evil King Mark offers Arthur a cloth of gold if he would be accepted in the company of the Round Table, "Arthur cried to rend the cloth, to rend/In pieces, and so cast it on the hearth" (GL 392-93). Arthur is "Ideal manhood closed in real man" (TQ 38) not because he is free of passions but because he subordinates the lower passions of battle lust, sensuality, and anger to the higher impulse that signifies the idea of Camelot. The "fire of God/Fills him," says Lancelot in reference to Arthur's prowess in battle (LE 314-15), but the celestial reference is equally appropriate in regard to any passion brought under the jurisdiction of the historically forma-tive ideal: Arthur cannot "work my work" without Guinevere (CA 87).

Nor can the knights work without their lower passions. The vows that bind the knights to Arthur in this labor too often are seen as a version of the Ten Commandments instead of as the working rules for great slaughters and, therefore, historical supremacy. They "serve as model for the mighty world," as Arthur says, and bring about the "fair beginning of a time" because they are quasi-military oaths for war against amoral heathen and immoral states: "To break the heathen" and "ride abroad redressing human wrongs." The warnings about adultery and slander are designed to "teach high thought, and amiable words/And courtliness, and the desire of fame,/And love of truth, and all that makes a man" (G 462-80). There is also a tenet of fitness: "utter hardihood" (GL 542). "To reverence the King, as if he were/Their conscience" (G 465-66) does not diminish the vows' military orientation in light of the "uttermost obedience" owed the king (GL 544) and the assignments given the knights by conscience through the course of Camelot's career. Arthur certainly stands for a religious principle but, as Hegel observes, "religion stands in the closest connection with the political principle," because "secular existence . . . receives its validity only in as far as the universal soul that pervades it—its principle —receives absolute validity" (p. 50). Arthur as universal soul asks for absolute obedience not in order to cloister the virtues but to make them active in military and political affairs.

At the coronation, as Arthur transubstantiates the knights through the vows, the wave and fire images carry implications of divine attendance. The Lady of the Lake, a divine anima who, "when the surface rolls,/Hath power to walk the waters like our Lord" (CA 292–93), is at his side. Even the keystone of Camelot's gate is "rippled like an ever-fleeting wave" (GL 211). These waves are symbols of form imposed over the formless deep, as Arthur himself came to bring historical form, moving "From the great deep to the great deep" (CA 410). At the time of Arthur's birth the waves were attended by divine light, and now, at the time of knightly "rebirth," pure sunlight (a wave form) prismatically breaks into color. Over Arthur's head, sunlight passes through the stained glass that depicts (in a foreshadowing of Arthur's final role) the Crucifixion. The white radiance of eternity materializes "Flame-colour, vert and azure, in three rays,/One falling upon each of three fair queens" (CA 274–75), queens "clothed with living light" (PA 454). Beyond this, the light falls upon the knights, themselves forms of Arthur the "stainless King," and Arthur is "broken" prismatically by the ceremony into versions of himself. During the ceremony, it was seen

> through all their Order flash
> A momentary likeness of the King . . .
> That when they rose, knighted from kneeling, some
> Were pale as at the passing of a ghost,
> Some flushed, and others dazed, as one who wakes
> Half blinded at the coming of a light. (CA 262–70)

Light is a common symbol for transcendence (*In Memoriam,* 47, equates light with the "general Soul"). Thus, in this tableau, the God of history himself materializes—through Arthur, through the knights—in various forms, "Fulfils himself in many ways" (PA 409). The world spirit passes through them all but the knights are affected differently— some paled, some flushed, variously according to their usefulness in the coming scheme of things.

Less symbolically, the ceremonial administration of the vows and the "realization" of Arthur also are rooted intellectually in works

Tennyson undoubtedly read. Maurice's *What is Revelation?* (1859) speaks of the realization of Christ, the earthly king of the heart, as "the unveiling of a Person" to the "Conscience, Heart, Will, Reason, which God has created to know Him and be like Him."[12] The Tennysons had both the first and second editions of Seeley's 1866 *Ecce Homo,* the first edition so marked and used that new covers were necessary. Emily's influence on Tennyson is suggested by the notation in her journal: "I look over *Ecce Homo* again and mark those passages which I want A. to see." In *Ecce Homo* we may see the administration of the vows in Seeley's comment that in religious commitment "some initiatory rite was necessary, some public formality in which the new volunteer might take, as it were, the military oath and confess his chief before man."[13] "The Coming of Arthur" was written in 1869.

As knights fall under Arthur's influence, they enlist the energies of their baser passions under their nobler passions, for historically formative purposes. Gareth, the perfect knight, emulates Arthur when he welcomes Lynette's spiteful hate, for as he says, "Fair words were best for him who fights for thee;/But truly foul are better, for they send/ That strength of anger through mine arms," anger by which he will overcome the time knights. After his mission is accomplished, Gareth adds a distinction between historically formative and individually "foolish" action, saying, "He scarce is knight . . . who lets/His heart be stirred with any foolish heat/At any gentle damsel's waywardness" (GL 924–26, 1147–50). Edyrn's dwarf strikes Geraint "with his whip, and cut his cheek" but Geraint "from his exceeding manfulness/And pure nobility of temperament,/Wroth to be wroth at such a worm, refrained/From even a word" (MG 207–14). Instead, he grimly resolves to avenge the insult to the queen (and by history's irony, saves Edyrn for Camelot's use in the process). The higher purpose controls the "instinctive hand," the baser passion. Clearly, the presence of "caitiffs and . . . wrongers of the world" (MG 96) whets this higher purpose through continual challenge and keeps resolve strong.

All the lower passions necessarily are directed by the soul in this formative time for, as Hegel says, "*Nothing great in the World* has been accomplished without *passion.*" Two elements comprise an investigation of history, "the first the Idea, the second the complex of human passions; the one the warp, the other the woof of the vast arras-web of Universal History" (p. 23). The former is active providence in the form

---

[12] John Frederick Denison Maurice, *What is Revelation?*, p. 54.
[13] [Sir John Robert Seeley], *Ecce Homo*, p. 84.

of Arthur and the vows, the latter is ordinary providence in the form of the passions. What follows from this proposition is the essential neutrality of the passions. Left uncontrolled, they are ahistorical because anarchically individual, and therefore (in this case) "evil" because not supportive of the providential scheme of world history. Voluntarily subjected to the higher impulse, however, the passions are formative historically and thus "good." Edyrn, for instance, is transmuted from vice to virtue through "good" violence. "There was I broken down," says he of his overthrow by Geraint, "there was I saved" (GE 850). Arthur, the vows, and the state are the embodiments of the moral life in this pristine time because they are felt collectively. They are projections of the universal higher self, the self to which Arthur merely leads man's "moral obligations, upon the Law which claims a free obedience," as Tennyson said, "and upon the pursuit of moral perfection (in imitation of the Divine) to which man is called" (*Memoir*, 1:317).

As the individual soul controls the passions, Arthur controls his knights, a condition which, in the Christian commonplace, is perfect freedom. Hegel articulates the idea when he observes, "Only that will which obeys law, is free; for it obeys itself. . . . The great point is, that Freedom in its Ideal conception has not subjective will and caprice for its principle, but the recognition of the universal will" (pp. 39, 48). In the kingdom of sense, there is also "freedom" but of an entirely different sort. Hegel continues: being "free" is a natural state "in which mankind at large are in the possession of their natural rights with the unconstrained exercise and enjoyment of their freedom." But, Hegel argues, such men "are marked by brutal passions and deeds of violence . . . untamed natural impulses, of inhuman deeds and feelings." Control of such passions, the philosopher asserts, "is a limitation of the mere brute emotions and rude instincts. . . . This kind of constraint is part of the instrumentality by which only, the consciousness of Freedom and the desire for its attainment, in its true—that is Rational and Ideal form —can be obtained" (pp. 40–41). Arthur does not tyrannize his knights because, in obeying Arthur, they obey themselves and are, therefore, for a spell, next to him in perfection and in freedom.

Tennyson's adherence to the idea of true freedom as perfect service to an ideal also might be inferred from corresponding statements in the writings of men whom he admired, especially the writings of F. D. Maurice,[14] the founder of the Apostles. Maurice's 1854 *Theological*

---

[14]Maurice's stature in Tennyson's circle may be suggested by Julius Hare (his brother-in-law) saying of him, "No such mind has been given to the world since Plato's" (quoted by Alan

Essays were dedicated to Tennyson, after Tennyson sought out Maurice to be godfather to his son Hallam. In this volume Maurice writes that the "righteous King of your heart . . . has taught you that you have been in chains. . . . To break them He must set you free. Self is your great prison-house. . . . The rod of the enchanter, who holds your will in bondage, must be broken by some diviner spell before the arms can be loosed, and the captive rise and move again."[15] The idea carried through Tennyson's whole life. The single book in Tennyson's library that was honored by passages marked with his approving "A" is Henri-Frédéric Amiel's *Journal* (published in England in 1885). In it Tennyson marked passages such as: "The religious consciousness of Jesus. The sacred sense of his Absolute Union with God through perfect love and self-surrender."[16] So, as Gareth says, "Who should be King save him who makes us free?" Gareth displays his perfect knighthood in submitting to his mother's wishes: I "yield me freely to thy will" (GL 136, 165). Tennyson himself said, "By King Arthur I always meant the soul, and by the Round Table the passions and capacities of a man,"[17] a statement that scarcely denigrates the passions. It merely states that they are to be put to the use of the moral idea.

The Round Table, then, is composed of strong, practical, and passionate men who, in proportion to their capacities, sense the potentials of historical circumstance and follow reverently a leader who represents active providence in the shape of their highest selves. In this, as Hegel puts it, the world spirit takes a "fresh step in history" through the "inmost soul of all individuals; but in a state of unconsciousness." The knights enlist their whole being under a person who represents consciousness (or conscience). The knights follow their soul leader for the same reason that Hegel says men follow all "World-Historical persons," because "they feel the irresistible power of their own inner Spirit thus embodied." Such heroes are the "clear-sighted ones; *their* deeds, *their*

Williard Brown, *The Metaphysical Society*, p. 117). Tennyson himself said, in reference to other members of the Metaphysical Society, that his "was probably 'the greatest mind of them all,' although often his thoughts were too deep to be easily understood" (*Memoir*, 2:168).

[15] John R. Reed cites this passage from the *Theological Essays* as an instance of a plain message: "To be free is to select voluntarily those rules worth following"; Reed finds in the *Idylls* a straightforward "moral design": "the conflict of faith and doubt in which pride struggles with humility" (*Perception and Design in Tennyson's "Idylls of the King*," pp. 204–5, 48–49).

[16] Henri-Frédéric Amiel, *Journal*, 2:45.

[17] James Knowles, "Aspects of Tennyson," 182. Tennyson also said to Allingham in 1867, "The King is the complete man, the Knights are the passions" (quoted by Christopher Ricks, ed., *Poems of Tennyson*, p. 1464).

words are the best of that time." They have an "insight into the require-
ments of the time—*what was ripe for development*" (pp. 30–31). In
Guesses, Hare says much the same thing: "Heroism is active genius. . . .
Many, yea, without number, are the sutlers and pioneers, the engineers
and artisans, who attend the march of intellect [Mind]. . . . At length
however, when the appointed hour is arrived and everything is ready,
the master-mind leaps into the seat . . . and the chariot advances further
and further, until it has reacht its goal, and stands as an inviting beacon
on the top of some distant mountain."[18] Ripeness is all, given two
things: this soul leader (who, just because he is extraordinary, tends to
some remoteness on his moral mountaintop) and the collective will of
the people to recognize him as an embodiment of their own "divine and
heroic faith," as Grote defined the mythic hero.[19]

As soul subdues and controls the passions and Arthur his knights, so
Camelot subdues and controls the centers of mere subjective will and
caprice surrounding it, forging a nation as it does so. First, it forces
"Rome,/The slowly-fading mistress of the world," off the historical
stage, for she was "grown too weak and old/To drive the heathen"
from the Roman wall (CA 503–11). In Browne's words, cited in chapter
1, "the glory of one State depends upon the ruine of another."[20] This
is practical politics, that is, precise historical thinking.[21] But implicit in
the lines is the commonplace of Roman corruption through sensuality
and later through asceticism, the very characteristics that eventually will
bring down Camelot. The loss of Roman authority had brought a condition much like what was observed in the previous chapter as the setting
of *Maud*, an anarchical civil war with each individual preying on the
other. "When the Roman left . . . their law/Relaxed its hold upon us"
(G 453–54) and so

> many a petty king . . . ever waging war
> Each upon other, wasted all the land;
> And still from time to time the heathen host
> Swarmed overseas, and harried what was left.
> And so there grew great tracts of wilderness,
> Wherein the beast was ever more and more,
> And man was less and less, till Arthur came. (CA 5–12)

[18] [Hare], *Guesses*, pp. 302–3.
[19] See chapter 2, note 41.
[20] See chapter 1, note 22.
[21] J. M. Gray, *Man and Myth in Victorian England*, pp. 17–18, observes that "The Coming
of Arthur" has a political "frame" of a "miniature history."

"King Leodogran/Groaned for the Roman legions here again,/And Caesar's eagle" (CA 33-35), but practically (though reluctantly) he settles for an alliance of marriage with Arthur's growing power, enlisting his forces, such as they be, under Camelot's hegemony. Leodogran is swayed both by Merlin's "craft" in maneuvering Arthur into the crown ("while the people clamoured for a king" and the barons milled about in furious confusion, CA 230-34) and by the tales of Arthur's supernatural origins (and, incidentally, by his own dreams, something not unlikely in such historical times).

The willful, anarchical barons are overcome by the voice of moral and, of course, military authority; they fall "before a voice/As dreadful as the shout of one who sees/To one who sins, and deems himself alone" (CA 115-17). Then they lie inert, like repressed base passions whose energies nonetheless come to Camelot in one shape or another. Arthur gave Lot "back his territory," and now Lot "lies there," as Bellicent humorously says, "A yet-warm corpse, and yet unburiable,/No more; nor sees, nor hears, nor speaks, nor knows" (GL 77-80). Lot's kingdom is a haunting symbol for the possibilities inherent in the historical condition. His sons collectively are a calculus of good and bad: Gareth the perfect knight, Gawain a mix, Modred a latent evil. Gareth is flawless. Gawain, though a profligate, is of decided use; his shield is "blazoned rich and bright" (GL 408-9). Modred has a shield "blank as death," yet presumably he is of some use or else he should not have been admitted to the Round Table (as Mark was not). The knights are not separated impractically by Arthur into perfect and imperfect and the latter eradicated as useless. The knights are as the passions. All of them are put to service. The boorish Sir Kay and the ambiguous Percivale are part of the scheme of things. So are the courts of Mark and Pellam; they are good for tribute if nothing else and are to be controlled by force if need be. At the periphery are the centers of brutal passions, like the kingdoms of Limours and Doorm, to be destroyed if they cannot be redeemed, as the occasion warrants.

In this way, Camelot expands into a national identity through a war-like and aggressive predisposition. The lesser identities are held together, like the Kingdom of Heaven, as a family with a wise and powerful head. Emily records in her journal for 1869, "A. reads me some of Maurice's *Social Morals*. A noble book: it seems to me as A. calls it." This 1869 work, *Social Morality*, traces the transition from family to nation to universal history as the movement from sin and determinism to freedom through obedience to a "gracious Ruler" within the "Universal

Family."[22] The same point is made by Seeley in *Ecce Homo*, wherein Emily marked for repeated meditation special passages, such as: "The first propelling power, the indispensable condition of progress, is the personal relation of loyal vassalage of the citizen to the Prince of the Theocracy. The test of this loyalty lay . . . in the mere fact that a man was prepared to attach himself to Christ's person and obey his commands. . . . a disinterested surrender is implied in the very notion of a political community."[23]

"The History of the World," Hegel writes, "is not the theatre of happiness" (p. 26). At this stage Camelot pursues not happiness as such but duty, self-discipline, and a disinterested surrender to the universal will, i.e., self-sacrifice that is, ironically, the source of true "happiness." Tennyson's copy of Maurice's 1854 *Doctrine of Sacrifice* is much marked, especially all of the following passages. "Self-sacrifice" is "the true ground of all action." "We should see that life and productiveness are the effects of even and regular submission."

> Confess by sacrifice that the earth can exist only by submission to a loving and gracious Ruler. . . . God calls nations out of a chaos of turbulent, warring elements. They find that sacrifice must keep them from relapsing into endless war. Individuals discover that all right-doing has its ground in sacrifice.

When they do, "they become free in their spirits, and they have the self-restraint, the obedience of man." And we are given the equivalent of the solid Victorian family: "Heads of families find that sacrifice is the only bond which can keep father and children, husbands and wives, brothers and sisters, at one."[24] Similarly, in *Ecce Homo* Seeley wrote, "Men are expected to sacrifice not a part of their happiness, but all of it, for the state."[25]

The idea of sacrifice—joyous sacrifice—occurs no less in the historians and metaphysicians. Tennyson's friend J. A. Froude wrote, "That which especially distinguishes a high order of man from a low order of man . . . is self-forgetfulness—it is self-sacrifice."[26] Charles Tennyson

---

[22] John Frederick Denison Maurice, *Social Morality*, pp. 434, 445.

[23] [Seeley], pp. 84, 121.

[24] John Frederick Denison Maurice, *Doctrine of Sacrifice*, pp. 65, 111, 112, 296.

[25] [Seeley], p. 121.

[26] James Anthony Froude, *Short Studies on Great Subjects*, pp. 15–16. This work (originally 1864 lectures) undertook to refute the scientific historian Buckle (and all such effrontery, including Comte).

comments on his grandfather's reading in Hinton,[27] and Lecky too remarked that "the writings of James Hinton especially came home to him in a way which I could not share, or indeed understand" (*Memoir*, 2:206). In the *Mystery of Pain* (1866), Hinton writes, "The individual must be sacrificed and suffer loss." "Human history, when it is closely scanned, confirms the thought. Dark and unmeaning as it looks, this at least is visible in it, that without sacrifice no permanent satisfaction or truly good result is suffered to be attained." But "man is framed for joy in sacrifice," yet "until it can be made his joy, sacrifice must be his torment."[28]

Accordingly, the first movement of the *Idylls* takes place in a mood of sacrifice, grievous hardship—and joy. The agony of the field is over. "Like a painted battle the war stood/Silenced, the living quiet as the dead,/And in the heart of Arthur joy was lord./He laughed upon his warrior [Lancelot] whom he loved" (CA 121-24). Watching the dangerous and bone-breaking jousts, Gareth "Was half beyond himself for ecstasy." To the struggle against the Astral knights, he "past with joy." Weary with the fighting against them, Gareth mistakenly is thrown by Lancelot and "laughed." Before the prickling horror of the Night, Lynette asks that he give the struggle to Lancelot, who is fresh: "Said Gareth laughing, 'An he fight for this'." The idyll ends in "dance/And revel and song . . . So large mirth lived" (GL 514, 686, 1195, 1311, 1387-91). Thus, by virtue of subservient passions and joy in sacrifice, we have the "fair beginnings of a nobler time" when Arthur and his knights "for a space/Were all one will" (CA 456, 514-15).

[27] Sir Charles Tennyson, *Alfred Tennyson*, p. 368.

[28] [James Hinton], *Mystery of Pain*, pp. 64, 65, 66. Hinton's 1859 *Man and His Dwelling Place* contains much the same message.

VIII   The Decline and Fall of Camelot

THE UNITY OF Camelot covered in the previous chapter begins to deteriorate, first as a fault (although one that closes) in the Geraint idylls and then as a widening breach in the Balin and Balan and the Merlin idylls that follow. The central cause for this growing disintegration is that real external opposition to Camelot's growth has been overcome. The will to continue an indefinite expansion has vanished, as has the disposition to take as significant the relatively minor disturbances within the empire. Accordingly, the knights no longer surrender themselves wholly to Arthur's purpose, and the passions (now without an object) become more and more difficult to control. Sacrifice begins to become painful. There is a rough progression in these five idylls. Soul's increasing inability to control sense is shown by Geraint's mendacious detachment from Arthur and by his purposeless wandering in the wilderness, by Balin's anarchical departure from court into the forest, and by Merlin's self-authorized journey into paralysis in Brittany. Internally, "maudlin and introspective morbidities," as Tennyson characterized irresponsibility (*Memoir*, 1:317), are gaining ascendency over the nobler passions involving historical purpose.

Geraint "made this pretext," that his territory was menaced by bandits and outlaws allowed to exist "till the King himself should please / To cleanse this common sewer of all his realm." The excuse (for there is no indication that his lands are menaced) allows Geraint to take

Enid away from the sumptuous court, but in his own kingdom he mimes Camelot's malaise by being "forgetful of his promise . . . of the falcon and the hunt . . . of the tilt and tournament" (MG 33–52). Pellam retreats into a "bushed . . . gloom" and fails to send his tribute. Arthur sends his "treasurer" to demand an accounting, but he returns with word that Pellam is withholding his taxes properly because there is peace. "Thy realm/Hath prospered," Pellam claims to Arthur (BB 92, 5, 95–96). There is no indication, after Balin's and Balan's fumbled quest fails, that Pellam ever is made to resume his payments. Vivien arrives at court explicitly "at a time of golden rest . . . While all the heathen lay at Arthur's feet,/And no quest came, but all was joust and play" (MV 140–43, lines added in 1875). As Percivale says later, these are mere "Vainglories, rivalries,/And earthly heats that spring and sparkle out/Among us in the jousts, while women watch" (HG 32–34). Hegel says of such a condition in a state, "The essential, supreme interest" has "vanished from its life, for interest is present only where there is opposition" (p. 74).

The wave and fire imagery in the *Idylls* (in the paragraph above, "cleanse the common sewer" and "heats that spring and sparkle") actually compose carefully controlled patterns that carry the burden of Camelot's complex peripeteia. Seemingly there is a critical problem, for waves bring both Arthur and inundating barbarism, while fire symbolizes both Arthur and Vivien: the ideal and the real. However, the wave imagery shows a cyclic development that suggests the rise and fall of spiritual effort. The Arthurian wave sweeps over the world and cleanses it but in the process loses its vitality, becomes polluted, and finally flattens and dissipates formlessly—and a new wave gathers power to bring another historical cycle. But fire invests all phases of the cycle with equal power. Fire represents the ever-present balance between the higher and lower passions, those held in use by conscience and those let loose, through a slackening of the will, as eros—and worse. First in historical form, then in formlessness, this energy comes with equal measure as God fulfils himself in many ways.

Arthur had come on the crest of a ninth wave "gathering half the deep," attended by divine shapes detaching themselves from the arching wave. "In the flame was borne/A naked babe." Picked up by Merlin, the "child and he were clothed in fire" (CA 379, 382–89) while the "white mermaiden swam,/And strong man-breasted things stood from the sea" bathed in "wild sea-light." From the shore could be seen in welcome "headland after headland flame/Far on into the rich heart of the West." A "flickering fairy-circle wheeled and broke/Flying, and linked again." Both the regularity of waves and the circling dance imply the coming of cyclic form invested with divine fire. "A wreath of airy dancers hand-in-hand/Swung round the lighted lantern of the hall" (G 240–60). The power of active providence is channeled into history; accordingly, throughout the *Idylls* Arthur is the "fire of God" (CA 127), the "great Sun of Glory" (GL 22), the "Sun in heaven" (LE 123), and so unbroken sunlight, perfect. He is a "stainless King" and "stainless gentleman" (MV 54, 790). Logically, his sword Excalibur, the primal symbol of historical form, was forged while "lightnings played about it" (GL 67) and was given to Arthur off the surface of the deep.

During this time of pristine beginnings, Gareth addresses a pine swept away by a cataract as a "false knight/Or evil king." He wishes himself a "knight of Arthur, working out his will,/To cleanse the world" (GL 5–25). Gareth imposes his will upon time by defeating the time knights: he throws Morning-Star cleanly; has greater difficulty coping with Noonday Sun who accidentally "slipt in the stream, the stream/Descended, and the Sun was washed away" (GL 1020–21); and has the greatest problem with Evening Star. Increasing obdurateness, clearly, inhabits the end of the historical cycle. The wave builds "To cleanse this common sewer" of Arthur's realm (MG 39; GE 894) and "all men's hearts became/Clean for a season" (HG 90–91). As the *Idylls* proceeds, however, we become aware of a weakening of the wave's power. In place of cataracts, torrents of pure water, and knights like Gareth, Geraint, and Edyrn acting historically, we find Balin and Balan ineffectual beside a "fountain-side" that "down,/From underneath a plume of lady-fern,/Sang, and the sand danced at the bottom of it" (BB 21–25). This loss of force is accompanied by gradually increasing pollution. Vivien is identified with "That old true filth, and bottom of the well" and is called by Merlin "false and foul/As the poached filth that floods the middle street" (MV 47, 795–96).

The attendant fire imagery undergoes a corresponding transformation. At the start, inspired by Arthur as the "fire of God," Gareth springs "Like flame from ashes" to make "deeds" (GL 536, 563) in the redemptive forge-and-work image pattern familiar from *In Memoriam* (118, for example: "life is not as idle ore" but "battered with the shocks of doom/To shape and use"). But in mid-*Idylls* the fire spreads formlessly or is put out entirely. Rumor and slander run like "Fire in dry stubble" (LE 730). Merlin's "fire for fame" is (as he withdraws from history) "quenched" by Vivien, who presages the stealthy process: "in an Ocean Cave/The blind wave feeling round his long sea-hall/In silence" (MV 415, 216, 229–31). As Arthur is represented by both wave and fire images, so Vivien is the apostle of "sun-worship" and "fiery flood" (BB 451, 448), but she bears a strange, inverse relationship to Arthur. He represents control of passion for the higher purpose, she the release of passion for the natural purpose. She sings:

> The fire of Heaven is on the dusty ways.
> The wayside blossoms open to the blaze.
> The whole wood-world is one full peal of praise.
> The fire of Heaven is not the flame of Hell,

and she calls all to follow her "through the fiery flood!" (BB 442–48). But Arthur had "felled/The forest, letting in the sun, and made/Broad pathways for the hunter and the knight" (CA 59–61) so that "all the land was full of life" (G 257), a life that civilized the wilderness. Vivien's paean is in the interests of savage nature and the sexual fires that animate it. Her prediction is quite accurate, for she speaks from strength, confident in the power of such passions:

> This old sun-worship . . . will rise again,
> And beat the cross to earth, and break the King
> And all his Table. (BB 451–53)

"A nation is moral—virtuous—vigorous," writes Hegel, "while it is engaged in realizing its grand objects, and defends its work against external violence during the process of giving to its purposes an objective existence." But with the challenges overcome, the state "realizes its potentiality—makes itself its own deed, its own work—and thus it becomes an object to itself." And so "Spirit is at war with itself; it has to overcome itself as its most formidable obstacle. That development which in the sphere of Nature is a peaceful growth, is in that of spirit, a severe, a mighty conflict with itself . . . a stern reluctant working against itself" (pp. 74, 73, 55). In Freudian terms, we may see Arthur as the reality principle warring against Vivien as the pleasure principle. Those wholly committed to the one or to the other do not display a schizophrenic agony, but those in whom spirit is struggling in further development are in conflict with themselves. Tennyson suggests this struggle as the Doppelgänger motif noted so often in these idylls.

Geraint falls into a despondent "uxoriousness" because he loves Enid "passionately" and becomes "forgetful of his princedom and its cares": two aspects of the same problem. "His passion masters him" (MG 54, 60; GE 10, 43). He is saved by the historically significant bloodletting in Doorm's castle and the arrival of Arthur to cap the redemption, his two idylls the two halves of his identity. Balin is more seriously beset; he moans of "My violences, my violences"—which are "fiends," as his brother says, that would "leap at thee to tear thee"— and despairs of attaining that courtesy that, earlier, had been the salvation of Edyrn. As Balin puts it, he kills his "brother and my better" (BB 429, 139, 52),[1] then dies himself, so that both brothers are lost to Arthur's purpose. Vivien is a projection of Merlin's base half: "There are two sides to Merlin," Kaplan notes, "and one of them is Vivien."[2] Concurrently, on the historical level, the emblematic "crown/ Of diamonds" that Arthur finds in a wilderness prefigures the end of this struggle with self: "two brothers, one a king . . . each had slain his brother at a blow." Later in the Elaine idyll, Lancelot's kin basely assault his disguised self in the tournament because of "fiery family passion" (LE 39–46, 475).

The Merlin idyll is the heart of the *Idylls*. It was the first idyll written and shows the self-engulfment of the most powerful figure in the kingdom. But it also required a "pendent," the Balin and Balan idyll, written as a "further introduction to 'Merlin and Vivien'" in 1872 (*Memoir*, 1:121). The two idylls together indicate the vitiation of the will to true freedom—self-surrender to the righteous King. They take the forms of certain developing forces that were present from the beginning but held in check by the will. In the course of this development, it is shown that the ideal is not a balanced opposite of the real and that the ideal is not transmuted into the real. Rather, the ideal is a controlling order for historical purpose that is lost gradually through the slackening of will that results when external opposition is eliminated. In this "time of golden rest" (MV 140), the first signs of asceticism and sensuality appear to indicate bifurcations of spirit. But from the start, a Pellam was incipient in the quest for purity and a Vivien in the sexual desire on which Arthur built the state. Each claims a freedom—one a cloistered virtue on the plane of active providence, the other a self-indulgence on the plane of ordinary providence. But each is destructive (opposing but mirroring malevolences) to the development of universal spirit, for the one represents historical formlessness and the other the

---

[1] "To interpret Tennyson's last idyll as a Doppelgänger resolves most of its difficulties" (J. M. Gray, "Fact, Form and Fiction in Tennyson's *Balin and Balan*," p. 105).

[2] Fred Kaplan, "Woven Paces and Waving Hands," p. 289.

forms of mere cyclic nature, the real. They go to the same end but repel each other. Pellam drives Vivien, and all women, from his gate "Lest he should be polluted," and Vivien is contemptuous of the "Old monk and nun" (BB 105, 439). Each is an example of the irony of history, that the state becomes torn by powers inherent in its inception, powers that gain dominance as a kind of unexpected precipitate. In Hegel's words, "in history an additional result is commonly produced by human actions beyond that which they aim at and obtain" (p. 27).

Merlin falls to Vivien, the more grievous fault. Later in the *Idylls*, the knighthood will fall to Pellam when the knights remove from court to chase the Grail. But of the two, the "sin" is worse, and Merlin embodies it. "The whole" of the *Idylls*, Tennyson said, "is the dream of man coming into practical life and ruined by one sin" (*Memoir*, 2:127). The sin first had reared its head (like a "worm within the rose," PE 390) in "The Marriage of Geraint" when Tennyson added the sin to *Mabinogion*, the source of the idyll. That "one sin" is the cause of Geraint's psychological collapse:

> when a rumor rose about the Queen,
> Touching her guilty love for Lancelot,
> Though yet there lived no proof, nor yet was heard
> The world's loud whisper breaking into storm,
> Not less Geraint believed it; and there fell
> A horror on him, lest his gentle wife,
> Through that great tenderness for Guinevere,
> Had suffered, or should suffer any taint
> In nature. (MG 24–32)

Why did Geraint believe it? The fault is a failure of will in a bad time, when the court is secure and opulent. Enid's humility and faded silk dress contrasts dangerously in Geraint's eyes with the prideful, gorgeous gowns in which Guinevere would dress her. Whether the sin is or is not yet real, Geraint allowed himself to believe it. "The allowed sin not only poisons the spring of life in the sinner," said Tennyson, "but spreads its poison through the whole community. . . . Tender natures sink under the blight, and that which is of the highest in them working their death" (*Memoir*, 2:131). Clearly Geraint should not have sunk; he did not do so later when, saved to Arthur's purpose, he presumably continued to see the sin in court more flagrant than ever. He died, in fact, uncorrupted further, the "fair death" at Arthur's side (GE 967).

In "Balin and Balan," the sin is obvious to anyone, like Balin, who wanders about the court. It is even common knowledge in remote castles like Pellam's. Neither the smell of the rose garden nor Lancelot's encounter with Guinevere are sweet to Balin. The court is languorous and its courtesy is becoming precious. No battle alarms ring. The sin causes the deaths of Balin and Balan, for Balin had made the queen's worship (instead of the king's) central to his value system. He maddens when Vivien lies about seeing Lancelot and Guinevere kiss. "Some loyal souls are wrought to madness" under the sin's blight, Tennyson commented (*Memoir*, 2:131). Tennyson had worked the sin well into the *Idylls'* fabric by the time of the Merlin idyll.

Kingmaker, empire builder, city engineer, Merlin was called "Science" in the religious allegory of the late forties; he was also the father-in-law of Modred (the "sceptical understanding"). Thus, it seems, he represents the champion of a secular relativism. Merlin "angered" Bellicent, who would believe in Arthur's mystic origins, by his riddling "truth is this to me, and that to thee" (CA 406). Nor does Merlin appear to take sides before Gareth on the question of whether the king is "real." Indeed, he offers that it "is a shame / A man should not be bound" by the vows, "yet the which / No man can keep" (GL 266–68). The statement is patently false, for many do keep the vows. Though Arthur calls those that stand with him at the end a "remnant" (G 440), a stalwart remnant it must be, for the final battle is a match, even with the heathen thrown in. From one vantage, such a sceptic might be considered the first who would fall away from an ideal. From another, Merlin is the "aged persona" that appeared last in poems written at the time of the 1833–34 "Morte d'Arthur." The case was made in chapter 3 that such personae represent historical obsolescence. Without meaning to push the comparisons overly, Merlin, like Ulysses, is morbid and suicidal; like Tiresias, he is cursed and blinded by an inimical divinity of his own discovery; and, like Tithon, he is withered and immobilized by a fiery Eos. All four are closing with or looking for death in a providential universe that implies their own obsolescence. In Camelot's case, the passions once had been beneficent (Arthur could not have worked his work without his passion for Guinevere), but they are now inimical. Merlin, like Lancelot and like many in Camelot, is hoisted with a sensual passion that, previously, was subjected to historical purpose. Though Merlin sees Vivien as "poached filth" (MV 796), he cannot resist engaging the primal inspiration: "The pale blood of the wizard at her touch / Took gayer colours, like an opal warmed" (MV 947–48). He is exhausted in a "storm, its burst of passion" (MV

959) the symbol for his own "sin." This is the final exertion with Duessa before Orgoglio's prison of self. Tennyson explained, "Some among the highest intellects, become the slaves of the evil which is at first half-disdained" (*Memoir*, 2:131). At the midpoint of the *Idylls*, a deadly languor is vitiating Camelot's control over the passions. Vivien is there to encourage them, Pellam serves as an example for those who would withdraw from the struggle, and the "sin" becomes a cancer that saps the vital impulse to perfectibility.

In the four idylls before the final debacle—"Lancelot and Elaine," "The Holy Grail," "Pelleas and Ettarre," and "The Last Tournament"—Arthur, the vows, and the state itself become progressively oppressive. As Hegel says, with external dangers eliminated, people begin to sense that, in this struggle, they were "fortifying a position for Right and Order *against themselves*" (p. 27). Arthur becomes something different at this point, an oppressive "other," rather than the embodiment of the universal self. As a result, the vows are transferred from him to the sensual and then to the ascetic object. At the beginning of the Elaine idyll, Guinevere is suffocating beneath her Arthur, "the faultless King,/ That passionate perfection," and under the "vows impossible." There is some critical tendency to admire the "woman" in such irrational complaints as, "He never had a glimpse of mine untruth,/He cares not for me" and "He is all fault who hath no fault at all" (LE 121–132), but given the metaphysical premises of the argument, Guinevere is as muddied as Balin. Lancelot is little better. He declines to participate in the tourney, his heart "Love-loyal to the least wish of the Queen," and is only "vext at having lied in vain" (LE 89, 102) for she is irritated at possible gossip. Lancelot's reverence for the least wish of the king is notoriously missing. The seamy tableau shows the transformation of the vows in the minds of Camelot's chief inhabitants. Later in the same idyll, Gawain resents the Arthurian mission that he deliver the prize to the unknown victor, "Nor often loyal to his word, and now/Wroth that the King's command . . . made him leave/The banquet." Gawain is parted forever from soul with Arthur's "ye shall go no more/On quest of mine" (LE 557–60, 711–12).

The vows are being transferred from Arthur, the perfect mean of the soul-sense unity, to the extremes splitting off from such a mean. Lancelot's vows are clearly to Guinevere. Pelleas is equally entranced by Ettarre, specifically by the "beauty of her flesh": "Behold me, Lady,/A prisoner, and the vassal of thy will . . . for I have sworn my vows." Discovering the object of his worship false, Pelleas concludes that the king "Hath made us fools and liars, O noble vows!" (PE 74, 232–36, 470) and, as Red Knight, he fashions the alternative vows of straightforward vice. Contrariwise, the knighthood is enchanted by the insubstantial purity of the Grail and "sware a vow to follow it" (HG 282). Tristram diagnoses the malaise accurately as one of long standing, conceived in the very crushing of external opposition. He tells the crippled Dagonet—appropriately Arthur's "one true knight–/Sole follower of the vows"—that he, Tristram, "came late, the heathen wars were o'er,/The life had flown, we sware but by the shell . . . The vows!/ O ay—the wholesome madness of an hour" (LT 302–3, 269–70, 669–70).

Even "custom," the ossification of the vows, suffers a degenerate metamorphosis in the luxury-ridden court. The tournaments are what Emerson, in his 1844 essay "Manners," called "fashion": "virtue gone to seed: it is a kind of posthumous honor." Camelot's mental fix is here, like a fly in amber: the predisposition to warlike struggle that had brought historical success. That Tennyson felt this was a necessary predisposition is shown by numerous utterances. He "felt strongly that only under the inspiration of ideals, and with his 'sword bathed in heaven,' can a man combat the cynical indifference, the intellectual selfishness, the sloth of will, the utilitarian materialism of a transition age." Disturbed about Europe in 1870, he recommended that "we ought to have all boys at school drilled, so that we may be more ready for defensive war than now" (*Memoir*, 2:129, 101). The problem is in the effects of transition. In a time of peace and languor, the old ways no longer work, and what we see is that love, war, and tournament are being transformed through an irony of history. In his *Martyrdom of Man* (a volume that Charles Tennyson says "had a powerful effect" on Tennyson)[3] Reade explains the transformation this way: "Nature has raised us to what we are, not by fixed laws, but by provisional expedients, and that the principle which in one age effected the advancement of a nation, in the next age retarded the mental development, or even destroyed it altogether. War, despotism, slavery, and superstition, are now injurious to the progress of Europe, but they were once the agents by which progress was produced."[4]

As the tournaments run their irrelevent course, in the absence of

---

[3] Sir Charles Tennyson, *Alfred Tennyson*, p. 361.

[4] William Winwoode Reade, *Martyrdom of Man*, p. 502. Charles Tennyson says that Tennyson first met Reade in 1865 (*Alfred Tennyson*, p. 361). Reade's book was published first in 1872. The 1887 edition is in the Tennyson Research Centre.

real opposition, Camelot makes war on its own inner principle. It does so, in Byron's words about another World-Historical figure, Napoleon, "Even as a flame unfed which runs to waste / With its own flickering, or a sword laid by, / Which eats into itself and rusts ingloriously" (*Childe Harold's Pilgrimage*, Canto III, Section XLIV). In "The Last Tournament," Lancelot's kin disregard knightly fair play. Oddly, Arthur makes no demurral to this broken courtesy save to call Lancelot "fantastical" and to regret that "His kith and kin, not knowing, set upon him" (LE 591, 596). During the horrid Tournament of the Dead Innocence, Lancelot, presiding, "saw the laws that ruled the tournament / Broken, but spake not," even though a "knight cast down / Before his throne of arbitration cursed / The dead babe and the follies of the King" (LT 160–63). Arthur's own actions are equally strange at that very moment, for he is "swording right and left / Men, women" (and children?) of the Round Table of the North in "massacre", while his men "trampled" the head of the Red Knight into the mire. This ferocious disregard for rules of war (LT 469–76) suggests a furious self-recognition in this mirror image of Camelot. Earlier, Arthur ambiguously had "withheld / His older and his mightier from the lists, / That Pelleas might obtain his lady's love" and, of course, the prize (PE 152–54), an event that leads directly to Pelleas's transformation into Red Knight. Arthur's only ignoble actions in the *Idylls* come, thus, in his role as tourney and battle leader, the very petard by which a warlike spirit is hoist in time of peace.

The continuing transformation of the water and fire imagery carries the burden of the argument. The flattening, polluted wave diminishes even further. Pelleas sits befuddled in the lush, moonlit gardens as "one rivulet from a tiny cave / Came lightening downward, and so spilt itself / Among the roses, and was lost again" (PE 416–18). The malice in the heart of Modred "Rankled in him and ruffled all his heart, / As the sharp wind that ruffles all day long / A little bitter pool about a stone / On the bare coast" (G 49–52). Guinevere calls herself "one pollution" (G 614). Everything ends in the stagnant swamp of "The Last Tournament," when Arthur lets the Red Knight

> heavily to the swamp
> Fall, as the crest of some slow-arching wave,
> Heard in dead night along that table-shore,
> Drop flat, and after the great waters break
> Whitening for half a league, and thin themselves,

Far over sands marbled with moon and cloud,
From less and less to nothing.

The degenerate knights trampled the Red Knight in the mire "and slimed themselves" (LT 460-70).

God's fire is now only "earthly heats that spring and sparkle out/ Among us in the jousts" (HG 33-34). Where once each knight had seen "That pure severity of perfect light" (G 641), now Pelleas sees as the "light" the damsels errant who go (in a clearly sexual image) "to tilt against the knights" (PE 58, 62). In the last tournament Lancelot "gazes on a faded fire" (LT 157). As these fires find an outlet in the flesh, they turn ruinous in history. Early in the *Idylls* we were given an image of Camelot as a "city all on fire/With sun and cloth of gold" (CA 478-79), but the Grail vision, instigated by the insubstantial nun for whom human love had been "rudely blunted," arrives in destructive formlessness as lightning: a "cracking and a riving of the roofs,/And rending, and a blast, and overhead/Thunder" (HG 75, 183-85).

The Grail vision's effect on Camelot seems to augur the curse of the sexually frustrated Pelleas: "The crack of earthquake shivering to your base/Split you, and Hell burst up your harlot roofs" (PE 456-57). The questers perform no useful historical tasks but "follow wandering fires/ Lost in the quagmire," in "A mocking fire," in "A dying fire of madness" (HG 319-20, 667, 765). The fires possess no historically viable form; it is only Arthur's statue that seems to "flame/At sunrise." Percivale and Galahad climb a dreadful hill where "dry old trunks about us, dead,/Yea, rotten with a hundred years of death,/Sprang into fire" (HG 242-43, 495-97). At the end, in a complex image, a "ghastly something" flies at Guinevere from the setting sun; it

> touched her, and she turned—
> When lo! her own [shadow], that broadening from her feet,
> And blackening, swallowed all the land, and in it
> Far cities burnt. (G 78-82)

Now she is the prism through which light acts, but to burn instead of build. Quite properly, then, the queens that had been with Arthur as prism "Flame-colour, vert and azure" (CA 274) are now "Black-stoled, black-hooded" as Arthur passes onto the "level lake" (PA 359-65).

Arthur and the sea creatures had risen from the cresting historic wave in a nimbus of fire; now in the flat trough at the end of the wave new shapes burn. Pelleas sees Ettarre and her women "Strange as to some old prophet might have seemed / A vision hovering on a sea of fire, / Damsels in divers colours" (PE 49–51) in "the fiery flood" called for by Vivien (BB, 448). Arthur had been the "word" acting, and the vows had been the forms for controlling historic chaos. Now, in the last stages of decline, the knights, says Dagonet, play "at ducks and drakes / With Arthur's vows on the great lake of fire" (LT 344–45). Arthur's vows, once symbolized by the Lady of the Lake walking on and "controlling" the water, are now stones skipping over the flat surface, "free," imminently to sink and disappear. Arthur moves as soul "From the great deep to the great deep" (CA 410) on a sea journey that can be taken as spiritually purposeful.[5] But, at the end of the "wave," Merlin's Breton voyage "across the deeps" in pursuit of his sensual object (MV 199) and Lancelot's seven-day sail "along the dreary deep" (HG 805) in pursuit of the Grail are journeys into degeneracy.[6]

Amidst morbid languors, the sacrifices required in tourney and field grow increasingly painful. Even existence is pain, at least for those who retain some memory of the inceptive purity of the state. Joyous self-sacrifice characterized the first two idylls. Gareth's "large mirth" (GL 1391) was the "joy of life in steepness overcome, And victories of ascent," as Tennyson said of this idyll (*Memoir*, 2:130). In descent, however, Lancelot presides "Sighing weariedly" in "languorous mood" as the "great umpire" over the Tournament of the Dead Innocence. Here too, "dame and damsel glittered at the feast / Variously gay" all in "the revels, and with mirth so loud," while a "swarthy one" (in Tennyson's crack about a growing racial impurity) "Laughed shrilly." But all is pain. After the tourney (and after several comments at her expense), Guinevere "slowly to her bower / Parted, and in her bosom pain was lord." Just as the Pelleas idyll was being written in the fall of 1869 (a year before "The Last Tournament"), the Tennysons read Lecky's *History of European Morals* admiringly and received its author at Faringford (*Memoir*, 2:200). Lecky wrote: "Sensuality is the vice of young men and of old nations. A languid epicurianism is the normal condition of nations which have attained a high intellectual or social civilization, but which, through political causes, have no adequate sphere for the exertion of their energies."[7] Indeed, with the Red Knight eliminated, "all the ways were safe from shore to shore, / But in the

---

[5] See George Roppen, "Ulysses' and Tennyson's Sea-Quest," pp. 77–90.

[6] Ryals notes the "ambiguous" and "ironic" effect in the use of river and water imagery in many of the idylls (*From the Great Deep*, pp. 60–63).

[7] W. E. H. Lecky, *History of European Morals*, 1:152.

heart of Arthur pain was lord" (LT 156–239, 484–85). Lancelot sacrifices for Guinevere and, like Balin, is driven into "wastes and solitudes/For agony," his mood "like a fiend" (LE 250–52). We can see that "man is framed for joy in sacrifice," as Hinton said, but "until it can be made his joy, sacrifice must be his torment."[8] The historical transition is the root reality in this psychological transformation.

There is some critical disinclination to allow Arthur—and Tennyson —the full primacy of the "sin" in this civic and psychological decline. "Came thy shameful sin with Lancelot," Arthur tells Guinevere at the end,

> Then came the sin of Tristram and Isolt;
> And others, following these my mightiest knights,
> And drawing foul ensample from fair names,
> Sinned also, till the loathsome opposite
> Of all my heart had destined did obtain.
> And all through thee! (G 484–90)

But, as indicated in the previous chapter, critics find a profusion of causes for Camelot's decline. Arthur, then, as Rosenberg notes, is "never more blind to this complexity than when he concludes his denunciation of Guinevere, 'And all through thee!'."[9] Yet, to deny the primacy of the "sin" is to deny the moral center in history. This center fails when there is a betrayal both of the "righteous King of your heart" (Maurice's words) and of the fealty due the head of state. The temptation to sin is a "test of this loyalty" (Seeley).[10] All follows from this. Passions and evil men can be controlled with will and self-sacrifice, but the slack in golden rest brings "the allowed sin," as Tennyson said, that "poisons the spring of life" (*Memoir*, 2:131). Civilization fails by a loss of nerve that spreads contagiously from the center of power.

It follows that sin is an ever-present negative potential whose appearance merely allows a transformation of things into their "loathsome opposite[s]." The relative powerlessness of evil in the *Idylls* has been noted often. Vivien tempts and she plants rumors but, like Mark or Modred, she offers no special threat to Camelot, except as a relaxed will permits it. In 1870 the Tennysons read Ker's *Sermons*, a book that depicts evil as an "identity," like all collective human enterprises, with

---

[8] See chapter 7, note 28.
[9] John D. Rosenberg, *Fall of Camelot*, p. 131.
[10] For Maurice's phrase, see chapter 7, note 15, and for Seeley's, Chapter 7, note 23.

the "power of tempting," which "is no more strange than that human spirits should possess it." But evil "can no more compel than they, and he gains in influence only as we yield him place."[11] About 1892, Tennyson said of Bruno, "His view of God is in some ways mine" (*Memoir*, 2:424), and he marked with vigorous lines passages such as this in the book about Bruno's thought given him by Walt Whitman: "Sin Bruno explains as something wholly negative, an incompleteness of God. . . . The Christian dogmatic notion of sin as a positive entity he rejected. In accord with him in this opinion are the noblest thinkers of our century, those great souls who look before and after, the mighty bards [and the enumeration, to be sure, could not have displeased Tennyson], Goethe, Browning, Tennyson, Whitman, and many another."[12] And in Amiel, Tennyson read, "The independence which is the condition of individuality is at the same time the eternal temptation of the individual."[13] Similarly, Hegel writes: "Individuals, to the extent of their freedom, are responsible for the depravation and enfeeblement of morals and religion. This is the seal of the absolute and sublime destiny of man—that he knows what is good and what is evil; that his Destiny *is* his very ability to will either good or evil—in one word, that he is the subject of moral imputation, imputation not only of evil, but of good" (p. 34). That man is free is a constant Tennysonian referent.

None of the evils that descend on Camelot are inevitable, then, even in the dangerous peace where no real challenges rise to test the will to moral perfectibility. Balin, Merlin, Tristram, Pelleas, and particularly Lancelot and Guinevere, all fall into the "sin" of their own choosing. In the general decline, as Merlin—and presumably Tennyson—tells us, Arthur continues the "blameless King and stainless man" (MV 777). Man was made, as Milton said, "Sufficient to have stood, though free to fall." The apple eating and the "sin" alike are acts symbolic of rebellion against this "righteous King of your heart." Guinevere may have fallen in love with Lancelot at first sight (MV 773-75), as Vivien did with Mark (MV 60-61), but no immutable consequences need have followed. In Lancelot's initial devotion to Guinevere and in Arthur's approval of it, presumably we have no condition other than the courtly love that fosters great deeds. Yielding to temptation changes this into the sin, but it need not have. Submission to the prince of the theocracy (in Seeley's phrase) requires that such impulses be controlled—sacrificed—

[11] John Ker, *Sermons*, p. 290.
[12] David Garrison Brinton and Thomas Davidson, *Giordano Bruno*, p. 34.
[13] Henri-Frédéric Amiel, *Journal*, 2:47.

in view of the higher moral purpose. The knights and ladies are free to choose.

Even after sinning, however, the situation is not irredeemable. Edyrn sinned with innumerable Guineveres and Viviens. The lady that accompanies him at his first appearance is hardly his squire. But, in the freedom of total submission to Arthur, Edyrn was able with "Both grace and will to pick the vicious quitch / Of blood and custom wholly out of him, / And make all clean, and plant himself afresh" (GE 902-4). Such "sins" may be the staple of the western love ethic and the rebel may be the great symbol of modern man, but the appeal of the situation and the vigor of representation should not seduce the critical reader. Neither Milton nor Tennyson would have us interpret either Satan or Lancelot and Guinevere as noble or admirable. Lancelot and Guinevere approach being so when they repent, but not while they are in damnable rebellion against God and Arthur. From such a theological vantage, the "sin" is disruptive of the cosmic order even more than of the individual microcosm. "There is in man an instinct of revolt," Amiel writes, "an enemy of all law, a rebel which will stoop to no yoke, not even that of reason, duty, and wisdom. This element is the root of all sin."[14] Men fall away from the good because of a flawed will, just as they rise to it through a strength of will.

"A paradox. Men do *not* like freedom. What is base in them likes base things. . . . Do we not see weak consciences every day lay down the burden of their freedom?" wrote Lushington in a work about the French plebiscite that gave Louis Napoleon dictatorial powers.[15] His friends, the Tennysons, read Lushington's essay with admiration in November of 1857.[16] The French action was a revolt against freedom because it was a revolt against laws mutually ascribed to: the "sin" in its historical dimension. Maurice made the same point in his 1869 *Social Morality*: Julius Caesar brought "the only kind of government in which the Will of the Majority would become faithfully embodied and enforced," but this was "where Society has through a series of self-seeking plots fallen to the depths." With the "coarse and bloody hands of Octavius . . . Law was now declared to proceed from the mouth of the Emperor."[17] But Arthur represents law and, therefore, freedom:

---

[14] Amiel, 2:47.

[15] Henry Lushington, *La Nation Boutiquière*, p. xxi.

[16] Emily Tennyson's journal for 21 November 1857: "A. reads me some of Harry Lushington's things La Nation Boutiquèri Inkermann & we agree that they are very noble." Lushington died in 1855.

[17] John Frederick Denison Maurice, *Social Morality*, pp. 251-54.

the freedom of perfect service under the higher purpose.[18] Weak consciences lay down the burden of freedom through a failure of will to find joy in sacrifice, to discover, as Reade put it in *Martyrdom of Man*, that the "Unknown God has ordained that mankind should be elevated by misfortune, and that happiness should grow out of misery and pain."[19] Through will, torment was transfigured into joy by the persona of *In Memoriam*. In a failure of will, the inhabitants of Camelot transcribe a reversed course, finding that unhappiness grows out of peace and luxury.

Thus, the *Idylls* speaks to a profound irony in human affairs, but there is a Christian heart to the mystery. Seeley wrote of the "paradox" (his word) that "no man is so happy as he who does not aim at happiness . . . men are expected to sacrifice not a part of their happiness, but all of it, for the state."[20] Yet all states pass inexorably into oblivion, through the very agencies that brought them into being. Tennyson's awareness of the baffling nature of history may be suggested by the stroking of his approving "A" across this passage from Amiel:

> Absurdity is interwoven with life: real beings are animated contradictions, absurdities brought into action. Harmony with self would mean peace, repose and perhaps immobility. By far the greater number of human beings can only conceive action, or practice it, under the form of war—war of competition at home, a bloody war of nations abroad, and finally war with self. So that life is a perpetual combat, it wills that which it wills not, and wills not that it wills. Hence what I call the law of irony—that is to say, the refutation of the self by itself, the concrete realization of the absurd.[21]

In this regard, Tennyson is gloomier than Hegel, who wrote, "Spirit—consuming the envelope of its existence—does not merely pass into another envelope, nor rise rejuvenescent from the ashes of its previous form; it comes forth exalted, glorified, a purer spirit" (p. 73). Hegel sees an abstract phoenix rebirth of the ideal, but Tennyson grasps these effects incarnate in the human breast and so ever hears the "creaking cords which wound and eat / Into my human heart, whene'er / Earth goes

---

[18] Ryals finds Arthur "guilty of violation of the freedom of others," and so their own "moral responsibility" is never allowed to develop (pp. 90–91).

[19] Reade, p. 543.

[20] [Sir John Robert Seeley], *Ecce Homo*, p. 121.

[21] Amiel, 2:220.

to earth, with grief, not fear,/With hopeful grief" ("Supposed Confessions"). There is, finally, only tragic courage: "To descend without murmuring the stream of destiny," as Amiel adds (again with Tennyson's "A" across the lines), "to pass without revolt through loss after loss, and diminution after diminution, with no other limit than zero before us,—that is what is demanded of us."[22] Universal spirit may be marching on, but the loss is grievous and the outcome uncertain.

The paradox of Camelot's diminution—the "*dialectical* nature of the Idea in general" (as Hegel put it), that "it assumes successive forms which it successively transcends" (p. 63)—is that this change is not so much a metabasis, a reversal of things from good to bad, as a peripeteia in the somewhat ambiguous Aristotelian sense of things becoming their opposites. A situation that seems to be developing in one direction suddenly develops in the reverse direction, through the very forces locked into the inceptive form. The condition of failure seems incipient in the condition of success; indeed, success is but failure in the initial state. Critics have noted transformations and dialectical oppositions in the *Idylls*, but generally they have failed to give credit to the historical faithfulness of the representation. Shaw finds that a "sort of Hegelian dialectic is at work" in the *Idylls* but a "dialectic of ideas": "All ideas both require and imply their opposites; most ideas are 'truths' whose opposites are also true."[23] The poem shows a "subsuming principle of order, disorder, and human re-creation," but Shaw finds that this is "not a commentary on the outside world at all"; there is no Tennysonian belief in a "cyclical theory of history." The poem consists of "narrative or imagistic paradoxes."[24] Solomon approaches the poem even more as artifact, finding "paradoxes which are in themselves meaningful; that is, instead of imposing ideas on the poem in order to enrich the texture, he develops his paradoxes so that the significance of the *Idylls* inheres in the narrative structure itself."[25]

However, such ironies and paradoxes as the *Idylls* contains are those that inhere in the historical condition. "Each of the parts is given an appropriate seasonal setting," Buckley observes, to "symbolize the moral condition of the realm."[26] But winter is a condition of spring. We always "see/Within the green the mouldered tree," as Tennyson says

---

[22] Amiel, 2:227.
[23] W. David Shaw, "*Idylls of the King*: A Dialectical Reading," pp. 187–88.
[24] W. David Shaw, "The Idealist's Dilemma in *Idylls of the King*," pp. 52–53, 48.
[25] Stanley J. Solomon, "Tennyson's Paradoxical King," p. 271.
[26] Jerome Hamilton Buckley, *Growth of a Poet*, p. 173.

in *In Memoriam* (26), and to these lines Tennyson joins the historical equivalent: "towers fallen as soon as built." The "circular progression" of the beast image, says Engelberg, shows the "surrender to the Passions."[27] But, as Arthur observes (with Hegel), nothing great in the world can be accomplished without passion, for Arthur cannot "work my work" without Guinevere. Lancelot's complaint of his own condition, that "the wholesome flower / And poisonous grew together, each as each, / Not to be plucked asunder" (HG 772–74), is only partially perceptive, for such is the whole state of man, with only the "work" as the directing idea that makes one or the other predominant.

In the lines added to the Merlin idyll in 1875, Tennyson has Vivien articulate the proposition:

My father died in battle against the King,
My mother on his corpse in open field;
She bore me there, for born from death was I
Among the dead and sown upon the wind.

She is as much a product of the idea as are the golden towers of Camelot, for where else has the idea ever been based except upon the carnage of the battlefield? This is, as she says, "That old true filth, and bottom of the well, / Where Truth is hidden" (MV 42–48). It is Tennyson's greatness to show that this is, indeed, so. The ideal must rest on the real. The water and the filth are inseparable. The trick is to draw the water unmuddied, to draw it both with use and with purpose and "for a space" (CA 514), until the water table drops (to carry the image to its logical conclusion). Vivien is this insidious process of the real that "Leavened" Arthur's hall, the "little rat that borest in the dyke / Thy hole by night to let the boundless deep / Down upon far-off cities while they dance" (MV 144, 110–12) in the forgetfulness spawned by lack of external dangers. The irony of history, civilization at harvest, is suggested by Vivien's song (the 1856 lines) as a "little rift within the lover's lute / Or little pitted speck in garnered fruit, / That rotting inward slowly moulders all." This is a call for a willed, total surrender—"Unfaith in aught is want of faith in all"—the very attitude toward Arthur and law that brought historical ascendency, but it is now elicited for the self (MV 387–93). In consummation with self, the supremely powerful Merlin is logically a casualty of the "time of golden rest" (MV 140), in that there is nothing left for him to do. With Vivien, Merlin subsides into the real.

[27] Edward Engelberg, "The Beast Image in Tennyson's *Idylls of the King*," p. 287.

Arthur as law and moral idea had held the contradictions of the human condition as a "balance or reconciliation of opposite or discordant qualities," in the words (from Chapter XIV of his *Biographia Literaria*) of one of the idols of the Cambridge Apostles, Samuel Taylor Coleridge. But with the attenuation of control brought about by the lack of challenges, the forces locked into Camelot's inception begin to oscillate in a destructive dialectic. There is first a movement to sensuousness and then a countermetamorphosis that turns the court from eroticism to asceticism. Pellam inaugurated it, in a foreshadowing of the Grail quest. Once as fiery a warrior "as ever dashed / Horse against horse," he took "to holy things" that would not be defiled "With earthly uses" (BB 94–97, 415–16). The Grail quest proper is inaugurated by the insubstantial nun, an unstable compound of real and ideal who had experienced a "fervent flame of human love, / Which being rudely blunted, glanced and shot / Only to holy things." Her brother Percivale turns into a Pellam, for after "noiseful arms, and acts of prowess done / In tournament or tilt," he passes "into the silent life" (HG 74–76, 1–4), like Merlin "lost to life and use and name and fame" (MV 968). For the most part, the quest is a case of hysterical religiosity. The nun's making of a sword case for Galahad out of her shorn hair is unsavory, even without the Freudian symbolism; and the "deathless passion in her eyes" and her "My knight, my love, my knight of heaven, / O thou, my love" all too clearly suggest an erotic asceticism. "Holy virgins in their ecstasies," Gawain says sourly. Arthur plainly diagnoses the quest as a "sign to maim this Order which I made" (HG 149–53, 864, 297), yet he rebukes Gawain for his remark and comments on the significance of the events attending the end of an historical cycle: "Blessèd are Bors, Lancelot and Percivale . . . God made music through them" (HG 870–74).

In fact, Tennyson invests spirit's transition with the deepest ambiguity. Certain emblematic friezes in the poem show the cyclic progress of soul and almost illustrate Hegel's remark about the "devouring agency of Time . . . the negative element in the sensuous world" (p. 77). In the 1868 "The Holy Grail," the "great zones of sculpture" that Merlin made for Arthur's hall show that

> in the lowest beasts are slaying men,
> And in the second men are slaying beasts,
> And on the third are warriors, perfect men,
> And on the fourth are men with growing wings. (HG 234–37)

The import of this succession is made clearer in the Gareth idyll, written in 1871–72. The pictures of the Time-knights on the walls of the "cavern" are an allegory of the "war of Time against the soul of man":

> five figures, armèd men,
> Slab after slab, their faces forward all,
> And running down the Soul, a Shape that fled
> With broken wings, torn raiment and loose hair,
> For help and shelter to the hermit's cave. (GL 1159–79)

Caves and caverns are dubious retreats. At the very moment the Grail appears in his hall, Arthur is rescuing from the "cavern" of a "bandit hold" an "outraged maiden" who looks much like soul:

> her shining hair
> Was smeared with earth . . . and all she wore
> Torn as a sail that leaves the rope is torn
> In tempest. (HG 207–13)

The image is appropriate, considering her divorce from use in history, a use fixed on the side of the goblet representing the Grail in Pellam's moldy retreat: "one side had sea / And ship and sail and angels blowing on it" (BB 359-60).

On the other hand, shortly hermit caves are all that will be left for soul, and there whatever continues must have its residence. Lancelot is healed in a chapel cave dug by a "knight / Not far from Camelot, now for forty years / A hermit, who had prayed, laboured and prayed." Clearly this is a holy man left over from a previous civilization, for, as Rosenberg points out, Camelot from first to last occupies twelve years.[28] The hermit's presence as a seed core for Camelot is as untenable as is the idea that Camelot's own holy remnants will have an effect on future civilizations. We have in the hermit merely the typology of the last stages of historical decline, an indication that Lancelot will "die a holy man." The latter event is foreshadowed rather grandiosely by his being wounded in the side with a spear (LE 399–401, 1418). The terrible ambiguity of such saving remnants as Lancelot, Guinevere, and Percivale is in Arthur's assessment of the nun: "Holier is none, my Percivale

[28] Rosenberg, *Fall of Camelot*, p. 56.

than she." As for the rest, all are as Arthur, a "hind/To whom a space of land is given to plow . . . being done,/Let visions of the night or of the day/Come, as they will" (HG 296, 902–7). At best, these visions remain in the hermit retreats as legend and as mythic form: "truth embodied in a tale" that "Shall enter in at lowly doors" in some future time, in the words of *In Memoriam* (36).

Arthur, too, dies a holy man, on the cross of the world. Like Christ, he says, "My God, thou hast forgotten me in my death" (PA 27; some loose manuscript lines in the Tennyson Research Centre have, "My God My God Thou hast forsaken me"). All of Camelot enacts what Reade describes history to be: "The Martyrdom of Man."[29] Something is working its way in the world, something that requires grievous suffering. Its nature is not to be known save in what Lancelot saw of the Grail: a "seventimes-heated furnace" that left him "Blasted and burnt, and blinded" (HG 840–41). This is just about the state in which spirit leaves Camelot finally. Yet out of every such phoenix conflagration something is saved; Arthur "passes and is healed and cannot die" (GL 493).

The Arthurian wave passes. At the end, Tristram sings of "A star in heaven, a star within the mere!" (LT 726). It is a reflected, cold, and distant fire within a mere flat, like the "dead lake" of *In Memoriam* (16) "That holds the shadow of a lark." On the banks of this "level lake" (PA 359) is the jetsam, like Dagonet, a "mock-knight," a "water-sodden log" (LT 2, 253). Vivien was part of a seemingly inexorable pattern: the "little rat that borest in the dyke/Thy hole by night to let the boundless deep/Down upon far-off cities while they dance." And all "heard and let her be" (MV 110–12, 144), freely let be the hole that, with vigilant inspection, could have been plugged. But a wind is rising, "the winds that move the mere" (LT 732). New waves are gathering upon the deep: "The heathen," that "ever-climbing wave,/Hurled back again so often in empty foam" (LT 92–93) by Arthur. Unchecked, however, the new wave inundates Camelot.[30] The growing savagery of the knights as they attack the unknown Lancelot in the Elaine idyll is given

---

[29] "I give to universal history a strange but true title—The *Martyrdom of Man*" (Reade, p. 543). Even the positivist Frederic Harrison wrote, "What a tale of patience, courage, sacrifice, and martyrdom is the history of human progress!" (*The Meaning of History*, p. 24). Tennyson knew Harrison through the Metaphysical Society whose meetings Tennyson attended sporadically in 1869–78. *The Meaning of History* was published first in 1862.

[30] Tennyson spoke in 1887 of the "mighty wave of evil passing over the world" (*Memoir*, 2:337).

> as a wild wave in the wide North-sea,
> Green-glimmering toward the summit, bears, with all
> Its stormy crests that smoke against the skies,
> Down on a bark, and overbears the bark,
> And him that helms it. (LE 480–84)

Tristram represents this new wave of barbarism, and a vigorous wave it is by the strength of the imagery. He repeats Vivien's song: "Free love— free field. . . . New leaf, new life—the days of frost are o'er:/New life, new love . . ." Tristram arrives to hear the tournament crowd, the "voice that billowed round the barriers roar/An ocean-sounding welcome" (LT 275–79, 167–68) to him—and to Camelot. And new fire comes as well, first the "long glories of the winter moon" (a mere reflection of fire) and then, weak and pale, but real, the "new sun rose bringing the new year" (PA, 360, 469).

Arthur's words after the final battle in Lyonnesse refer to the waves crashing on the shore as "this great voice that shakes the world,/ And wastes the narrow realm whereon we move" (PA 139–40).[31] Civilization waxes and wanes, but spirit continues, as Hegel says, "in a variety which is inexhaustible," for God is "Infinite Power . . . Infinite Form . . . Infinite Engery" (pp. 73, 9). Hegel's is a proposition Tennyson seemed to subscribe to in 1870 with his remark, "I don't find it difficult to believe in the Infinity of Worlds" (*Memoir*, 2:96). In this succession of historical forms Camelot becomes a martyred sacrifice by which an unknown God "fulfils himself in many ways," simply because "one good custom should corrupt the world."

---

[31] John R. Reed notes in the *Idylls* a declension of voices, language, names, cries, words, all suggesting that "signification is not an achievement, but a process that must forever be incomplete, for in the ever-changing circumstantial world the hundred names of the Nameless must be constantly renamed. The attributes which are at once the highest qualities in man and the attributes of the Nameless undergo a continuous transformation" (*Perception and Design in Tennyson's "Idylls,"* p. 183, and the whole section on "Language," pp. 146–85).

IX The Final Stage: Poems of the Sixties

IF CLIO IS THE muse of meaningful history (by the definitions of the Introduction), then the period of the sixties must be taken as her last residence in Tennyson's major poems. Philosophy of history deteriorates when understanding and emotional affirmation begin to separate and, specifically in Tennyson, affirmation withers when active providence disengages the historical process. History now unfolds on the plane of an ordinary providence characterized by the chanceful anarchy of natural field, as this is characterized by various aggressions and animal passions uncontrolled by a higher purpose. The suicidal heroes of "Enoch Arden," "Aylmer's Field," and "Lucretius" represent this decay of social order. But their actions are without the ironic sanction conferred by active providence settling elsewhere in the historical cycle. Enoch embodies the chanceful misfortune of the dog-eat-dog economic decline of his society, Aylmer is the murderous remnant of the Great House self-destructing into "open field," and Lucretius is a symbol of the human race overwhelmed by the same animalisms that destroyed Camelot. As Hare observed, the "ultimate tendency of civilization is toward barbarism."[1]

For Tennyson the decade began with political aggravations similar to those of the fifties. Europe once more was in apocalyptic turmoil

---

[1] See chapter 2, note 58.

and England again was fragmented and weak. Tennyson wrote political poems exhorting his country to arm for the defense of truth and liberty. He wrote "Riflemen Form!" and the unpublished "Jack Tar" whose first version had it that "the times are wild!" with animal passions amok, specifically those of the French "Bearded monkeys of lust and blood/Coming to violate woman and child!" Invasion, rape, and anarchic passions constitute the theme of the 1860 "Boädicea" wherein, under Roman flogging, raping, and plundering, the native Britons "Madly dashed the darts together, writing barbarous lineäments" as the heroine "Yelled and shrieked." In this barbarism, "Fell the colony, city, and citadel, London, Verulam, Cámulodúne." That the poem is a metaphor for contemporary times may be suggested by a fragment in this meter about politics: "Half a home of clashing systems, half of refluent barbarism,/While the peoples foamed together, multitudinous anarchy."[2]

The 1861–62 "Enoch Arden" may appear to have little to do with savage passions or an anarchic universe, but it is laid within a world of chance and fortune that is without pattern. It chanced that "Ten miles to northward of the narrow port/Opened a larger haven" and Enoch's economic fortunes shrink. He goes to work there but "clambering on a mast/In harbor, by mischance he slipt and fell." While recovering, he finds "Another hand crept . . . across his trade" in the stealthy aggression of the commercial anarchy of *Maud*. He decides to try the fiscal potentials of the deep and to make his fortune on a ship named "Good Fortune." The ship seems in outward passage to be moved by the "breath of heaven," but the deep is indifferently good and bad in the chanceful universe of ordinary providence. So, "Less lucky her home-voyage," with first calms "and then winds variable,/Then baffling, a long course of them; and last/Storm" and shipwreck on an isle "the loneliest in a lonely sea."

The isle certainly can be taken as a correlative for Enoch's personal economic venture. But beyond this, insofar as it "mirrors the basic topography of the bleak fishing village" from whence Enoch had departed, even to the cave where the children had played,[3] the isle seems also a symbol for the dead end into which his order (venturesome capitalism)[4] has fallen. Another isle served this role for the Lotos-Eaters

---

[2] See Christopher Ricks, ed., *Poems of Tennyson*, p. 1119.

[3] Douglas C. Fricke, "A Study of Myth and Archetype in 'Enoch Arden'," p. 109.

[4] Note in this context Enoch's resemblance to Robinson Crusoe insofar as Crusoe embodies the qualities of the unethical "capitalistic adventurer" (Max Weber, *The Protestant Ethic and*

in the passing of the heroic age. "The lawns/And winding glades," the "slender coco's drooping crown of plumes," suggest certain imagistic resemblances. In this state of nature Enoch becomes much like the mariners, "hardly human . . . Muttering and mumbling, idiotlike." The God of these isles comes in visions. Enoch speaks with "That, which being everywhere/Let's none, who speaks with Him, seem all alone." But regardless of "seem," the result is death and isolation; the boy suffers for five years and dies, another companion "fell/Sun-stricken," and Enoch himself lingers in "death-in-life" (line 561). Meanwhile Annie is interpreting a dream that Enoch is "sitting on a height,/Under a palm-tree, over him the Sun" as a sign that he is in paradise. She therefore feels free to marry Philip. Ricks refers to "the strange equivocation of providence" and cites Ruskin on this "*Vain* Providence, the Good Spirit becoming a Lying one."[5] Yet if the premise is granted, that Tennyson at this stage regards active providence to have withdrawn from the order of history of which Enoch seems somehow representative, then what Enoch and Annie engage is actually the voice of ordinary providence (that "other" voice of God). "Death-in-life" is its emblem and the paradise of nature, wherein the obsolete vegetate, its primary symbol. Ulysses and the mariners established an empathy with the Lucretian Gods on their isle; these projections of their own spirit, a spirit that at the same time symbolized the fate of their order, told them truly that the heroic order was being withdrawn from the historical process. Enoch and Annie get the same message in the case of the commercial order moving into the chanceful anarchy that Tennyson had shown previously in *Maud.*

Given the general "shipwreck," Ulysses really should not have come home again, yet he did. So does Enoch, saved by the same chance that wrecked him, by another ship "blown by baffling winds,/Like the Good Fortune, from her destined course." He returns to an emblematic tavern "propt, worm-eaten, ruinously old." He looks in on his Penelope, and then, like Ulysses, abandons her and his claims in a similar kind of suicidal life-weariness. He lives a year longer like a holy hermit in the "stinted commerce of those days." He dies and the village honors his renunciative act with an expensive funeral. The act and the funeral have exercised criticism since. The poem indicates Enoch to be a "strong

---

the Spirit of Capitalism, trans. Talcott Parsons [New York: Charles Scribner's Sons, Scribner Library Paperback, 1958], p. 20), and as this concept is developed by such critics as Ian Watt, "*Robinson Crusoe* as a Myth," *Essays in Criticism* 1 (1951): 95–119.

[5] Christopher Ricks, *Tennyson*, p. 280.

heroic soul" and Hallam, presumably with good reason, associates the poem with the "joy of my father in heroism" (*Memoir*, 2:6). Yet a contemporary review saw Enoch's conduct as "that of a dastard," mean and cowardly,[6] and Bagehot called Enoch's sacrifice the "dismal act of a squalid man."[7] Modern criticism is equally divided between thinking him ennobled by "self-sacrifice" in an act of "highest heroism"[8] and thinking him "masochistic ... suicidal ... neurotic" in an act of "martyrdom-suicide."[9]

The Ulyssean character too is seen as everything from noble and heroic to neurotic and suicidal. The resolution of this contradiction was suggested in chapter 3 as lying in a critical understanding of the irony of history. Ulysses is necessarily morbid and suicidal, for his heroism eats inwardly (the argument for Camelot's declining condition), yet he is heroic too in departing to realize his extended "selfhood," in his attempt to find an individual redemption at an apocalyptic "limit" in which God reveals something of his nature to man. This is a condition of "high" tragedy incumbent on an heroic perception of universal "shipwreck."[10] Enoch is in the same situation but he does not represent an heroic order nor, therefore, does he possess magnified qualities of "self." His is the obsolescence and tragedy of commercial man, symbol of a commercial age. Thus, Enoch must realize a "selfless-hood" (like the hero of *Maud*, faced with the same society) at the only "limit" available to him in a universe from which God has departed taking his external apocalypse with him: a "limit" at the utmost contraction of self. As Reed notes in regard to Enoch's renunciative act (and this could be said about *Maud*'s hero as well), "To escape the self is the means of salvation."[11] The village honors Enoch in his ritual death, as Ithaca presumably honored Ulysses. The crucial difference is that "Ulysses" is played out before a presiding providential purpose, active providence settling elsewhere in the national cycle; in *Maud*, this is also a possibility. This providential purpose gives "meaning" to affairs. Enoch, on the other hand, can enact only what Camelot enacted in its final stage: "The Martyrdom of Man."[12] Now spirit is available

---

[6] Quoted by Ricks, *Tennyson*, p. 282.

[7] *Tennyson: The Critical Heritage*, p. 291.

[8] Respectively, Winston Collins, "Enoch Arden, Tennyson's Heroic Fisherman," p. 50, and F. E. L. Priestley, *Language and Structure*, p. 79.

[9] Respectively, Martin Dodsworth, "Patterns of Morbidity," p. 14, and Ricks, *Tennyson*, p. 282.

[10] See chapter 3, note 15 and discussion.

[11] John R. Reed, *Perception and Design*, p. 93.

[12] See chapter 8, note 29 and discussion.

only to hermits and to holy ones withdrawn from history's pollutions.

The 1862–63 "Aylmer's Field" handles the theme of "self-sacrifice" in even more bitter a way. The deaths of the young people trigger a precipitous descent into animal anarchy. The intellectual center of the poem is Averill's sermon built about the verse "Behold,/Your house is left unto you desolate," Jesus's lament over Jerusalem from *Luke* xiii. The occasion is the death of the heirs to the lines of Aylmer and Averill and the self-destruction of the Great House paradigm of society (once, in *The Princess*, the chief hope of man). The sermon begins with references to the flood that rolled "o'er the palaces of the proud" but this produced only the worship of Baäl with its injunction "to thy worst self sacrifice thyself": "Gash thyself, priest." Christ came and was slain as a martyr sacrifice, but a still worse religion followed, one with a God "far diffused in noble groves/And princely halls, and farms, and flowing lawns,/And heaps of living gold that daily grow,/And title-scrolls and gorgeous heraldries." But "Thou wilt not gash thy flesh for *him*." Rather, this latter-day worshipper gashes others and so is "the more base idolater" and "Crueller: as not passing through the fire/Bodies, but souls—thy children's—through the smoke,/The blight of low desires." Edith has been sacrificed in Aylmer's plans for her money marriage, dying of abuse, depression, and fever; and Leolin follows in death by suicide (the first suicide in Tennyson since the frustrate swain in "Lady Clara Vere de Vere" of some three decades before).

Averill, an impassioned prophet in the line of the denunciators of Tennyson's Somersby poems, wishes his voice "A rushing tempest of the wrath of God/To blow these sacrifices through the world—/Sent like the twelve-divided concubine/To inflame the tribes," even if the "red fruit of an old idolatry" (the butchery of the French Revolution, which is the background of the poem) is the result. Averill almost arouses a peasant revolt in the congregation, sends Lady Aylmer "shrieking" in a swoon to the floor (to die within a month), and makes Aylmer "Imbecile" (and dead two years later). Past and present fuse in the poem to suggest the destruction of the aristocratic order. "That long-buried body of the king,/Found lying with his urns and ornaments,/Which at a touch of light, an air of heaven,/Slipt into ashes, and was found no more," presages at the start of the poem the demise at its end of "These old pheasant-lords,/These partridge-breeders of a thousand years,/Who had mildewed in their thousands, doing nothing." All heroic spirit dies out, Aylmers' and Averills' both, without the issue "Which else had linked their race with times to come." The total destruction of the Great House is enhanced by the impending eruption of the "central Hell" of the French Revolution that Averill invokes, a Revolution that sent the "heads of chiefs and princes" in "a river of blood to the sick sea" by "shores that darken with the gathering wolf."

The animal imagery at the close of the poem makes plain what is to follow, the movement onto the plane of nature: ordinary providence. "The great Hall was wholly broken down" and the "broad woodland parcelled into farms." The succession is to the hard peasants of Tennyson's 1865 "Northern Farmer: New Style," to owners who will think only of "proputty, proputty." The last five lines in "Aylmer's Field" stress an animal existence distressingly; hawks, moles, and hedgehogs live here now and the "rabbit fondles his own harmless face." The effect is chilling, given the overtones of the deadliness of sacrifice, of spiritual death, and of the predatory barbarism into which civilization is falling: "The slow-worm creeps, and the thin weasel there / Follows the mouse, and all is open field."

A couple of years later, in 1865, Tennyson began work on "Lucretius," a poem about another suicide. The poem was published in 1868. Classicists are content that the "spirit and tone of Lucretius are reproduced," along with the "poetic manner, the science, and the ethics."[13] Most interpreters see Lucretius's madness in relation to the Epicurean system as standing for Tennysonian distress about the ability of Victorian religion and imagination to sustain itself before the onslaughts of science and of general materialism.[14] There has been some critical interest in the historical dimension of "Lucretius." Bush sees that the "subject is 'historical' and not mythological" and that the "poem is a very powerful picture of a noble Roman patriot who feels himself breaking along with the old republic," but the republic's troubles are really "Victorian religious and ethical problems."[15] Buckley notes an important correspondence, that Lucretius experiences a

[13] Respectively, Wilfred P. Mustard, *Classical Echoes in Tennyson*, p. 80, and Ortha L. Wilner, "Tennyson and Lucretius," p. 348.

[14] Lucretius's madness is a "metaphor for the mood of introspective depression which throughout his life harried Tennyson's attempts to fix his faith, but which he tried increasingly to sublimate in his poetry" (E. D. H. Johnson, *Alien Vision*, p. 34). "In trying to judge religion and mythology by scientific laws, Lucretius . . . is destroying whatever imaginative adequacy religion may have"; here Tennyson is "groping toward some synthesizing form, a version of Arnold's 'imaginative reason' or Newman's 'illative sense'" (W. David Shaw, "Imagination and Intellect in Tennyson's 'Lucretius,'" pp. 137, 138).

[15] Douglas Bush, *Mythology and the Romantic Tradition*, p. 214.

"capacity for a passion parallel to the violence of the decadent republic" and feels the "bestiality that now seems the one law of a blind evolution," yet the threat is the "total destruction of the imagination and the intellect."[16]

In chapter 4, the parallelism between Alexandrian and Victorian times was noted in regard to *The Princess* and the English idyls. The influence of Theocritus on Tennyson was attributed partly to the Greek poet's position in an age of serenity and synthesis and to the idyl's ability to revivify traditional modes of thought by tapping Alexandria's heroic past, much as Tennyson himself did in the sanguine forties with England's medieval times. With Tennyson's growing pessimism about history during the sixties, it seems reasonable to suppose that the same habits of historical thought should bring to his mind a parallelism of declines of civilization, specifically between the Rome of Lucretius and the gloomy world Tennyson saw in these sixties.

Tennyson's unquestionable belief in historical cycles would make certain concatenations attractive. The Epicurus whose three hundred scrolls Lucretius is studying and "whom he held divine" was, about 270 B.C., the Roman contemporary of Theocritus in Alexandria. For Alexandria in the twilight of the Greek civilization, it was still a period of material prosperity, of expansion of empire, and of a hard, pragmatic materialism. But for rising Rome it was a time of heroic national triumph, somewhat like Camelot's insofar as Rome at this time established her hegemony over the entire peninsula. A time of origins is elicited by Tennyson when he has Lucretius mention Lucretia, from whom "sprang the Commonwealth"; Lucretius "bears one name with her," she the beginning, he the end of Rome. That Lucretius was the end can be seen by rehearsing some elementary dates concerning the time in which he lived. Lucretius was born about 99 B.C. and died in 55 B.C. Civil wars convulsed Rome and her territories 88–82 until Sulla, with immense bloodshed, established his tyranny in 82, the first such tyranny in 120 years. This tyranny lasted until 79, when Sulla went into retirement, dying the next year. What followed was a succession of disasters: war in Spain from 80 to 72, civil wars of various magnitudes, the revolt of the gladiators under Spartacus 73–71, the third Mithridatic War 74–64 (Tennyson had written "Mithridates Presenting Berenice with the Cup of Poison" at Somersby), and the conspiracy of Catiline 64–63. (This sustained fratricide and invasion is much like Camelot's end.)

[16] Jerome Hamilton Buckley, *Growth of a Poet*, pp. 166–67.

Tennyson could have read about Sulla in Clough's 1860 revision of Dryden's *Plutarch*, a copy of which was given by Clough to Emily Tennyson just before he died in 1861.[17] "Clough and Tennyson had many deep instincts and experiences in common," says Charles Tennyson, and "Tennyson felt deeply the death of the younger poet."[18] It is not unlikely that Tennyson should have examined this volume out of interest in Clough's work (and perhaps in his death as a sign of the times), but that he read Plutarch is certain. The phrase "mulberry-faced Dictator" has its origin in the putative words of an Athenian jester quoted by Plutarch: "Sylla is a mulberry sprinkled o'er with meal."[19] Plutarch also dwells on Sulla's bloody mindedness and voluptuousness. In Plutarch and elsewhere, of course, Tennyson would have read about certain features of the Rome at that time. Those features may have been distressingly familiar to anyone worried in 1865 about the impending Second Reform Bill. Lucretius's Rome was characterized by the breakdown of law and order, a great extension and adulteration of the franchise, a vast unemployed proletariat numbering perhaps 300,000, the corruption and ineffectuality of the senate, and the rise of demagogues.

In retrospect, comparing this Roman situation with that of England in 1865 appears intemperate indeed, but for the people debating the Reform Bill (which became law in 1867) the dangers were real and quite serious:

As early as January 1865 the Reform League had been formed to put forward the working-class demand for manhood suffrage, while in opposition to this a Reform Union had been established at Manchester on behalf of the middle-class demand for household suffrage. To the venom of class war there was added the distress consequent on an economic crisis. The 1865 harvest was bad, cholera had reappeared, and the Limited Liability Act of 1862 had encouraged a wave of speculation which was followed in May 1865 by the failure of one of the greatest financial houses in London, Overend and Gurney. This naturally involved the collapse of many other enterprises, and the prospect of unemployment stirred London crowds to make demonstrations. A great gathering marched from Trafalgar Square to Gladstone's house, crying "Gladstone and Liberty"; and

---

[17] See this information in item 3367, *Tennyson in Lincoln: A Catalogue*, p. 161.

[18] Sir Charles Tennyson, *Alfred Tennyson*, p. 334.

[19] John Dryden, trans., and Arthur Hugh Clough, rev., *Plutarch* (New York: Random House, Modern Library, n.d.), p. 546.

on 23 July, when Hyde Park was closed to a vast meeting scheduled to take place there, the crowd got out of hand and tore down 1,400 yards of the railings.

The Bill would almost double the size of the electorate and make demagogy on the ascendent. "There were many who watched the approach of this new age of the masses with alarm" (continuing the quotation): "'What I fear,' wrote Walter Bagehot . . . 'is that both our political parties will bid for the support of the working man; that both of them will promise to do as he likes, if he will only tell them what it is'."[20]

With Tennyson's susceptibility to the apocalyptic, his fears about spirit overwhelmed by passions in the historical arena could have been stimulated by these natural, fiscal, and political prodigies of mid-1865. In his mind they signaled perhaps the doom of the republic in the hands of a tyrant like Sulla, like Napoleon III, or like the czar. Such fears certainly had been with Tennyson since the scheme of the *Idylls* took shape in the fifties. At that time he had seen spirit splitting from an Arthurian mean into asceticism and sensuality. The result was a decline of Camelot in the self-destructiveness that characterized the inhabitants of mere natural field. In "Lucretius," the Roman people are destroying themselves in civil war and sensuality. Correspondingly, the Lucretian family unit destroys itself in a struggle between asceticism and sensuality. And Lucretius himself, in the role of the "human race" (in Tennyson's habit of using an historical symbolism, such as that in *In Memoriam*), represents the cloistered virtues overwhelmed by passion, after which he self-destructs with a dagger.

Though Lucretius loved his wife "none the less," he neglects the sensual emotions that made Arthur a whole (as the latter unity was argued in chapter 7). When she greeted Lucretius with a kiss, "the master took/Small notice, or austerely." Faithful to the prevailing mores, she finds this intolerable and tries to bring back his love with a witch's philtre in his drink. "This destroyed him" (the poem says plainly) because it "checked/His power to shape," that is, his power to think his proper way. It is, accordingly, somewhat unfair to believe that Lucretius is a "preacher of serenity whose creed has failed him"[21] or to conclude that here we are to see that "the unaided reason is not in

---

[20] Anthony Wood, *Nineteenth Century Britain: 1815–1914* (New York: David McKay, 1960), pp. 273, 276.
[21] Bush, p. 214.

itself strong or sure enough to discipline man's sensual nature."[22]
Lucretius was, after all, poisoned. This is where the critical stress should
lie: on the self-destructiveness of the family when passion either is
neglected or is elevated to the all-in-all. The dreams of the "brute
brain" then follow, during a stormy night when Lucretius saw lightning
strike the mountainside, out of which came "A riotous confluence of
watercourses / Blanching and billowing in a hollow of it, / Where all but
yester-eve was dusty-dry." The passage is quite ambiguous, but it seems
to suggest the ambivalent nature of passion: vivifying and destructive,
dependent on place and use (the same point made in the previous two
chapters with reference to the gist of the wave and fire imagery in the
Idylls).

The first dream picks up the image of this torrent to portray the
sudden and inexplicable sundering of all bonds. The dream also suggests
the chancefulness central to Lucretius's philosophy.

> A void was made in Nature; all her bonds
> Cracked; and I saw the flaring atom-streams
> And torrents of her myriad universe,
> Ruining along the illimitable inane,
> Fly on to clash together again, and make
> Another and another frame of things
> For ever.

The second dream connects with this one, however, and completes the
cyclic career of the torrent flying out of earth, into the sky, and down
again as rain:

> I thought that all the blood by Sylla shed
> Came driving rainlike down again on earth,
> And where it dashed the reddening meadow, sprang
> No dragon warriors from Cadmean teeth,
> For these I thought my dream would show to me,
> But girls, Hetairai, curious in their art,
> Hired animalisms, vile as those that made
> The mulberry-faced Dictator's orgies worse
> Than aught they fable of the quiet Gods. . . .

[22]Johnson, *Alien Vision*, p. 33.

Insofar as these two dreams are connected, two critical conclusions present themselves. First, there is the despairing idea that, at this end of Roman civilization, no renewal is to be anticipated: no warriors will fight to a remnant in civil war and found Thebes. This is much the same despair given near the end of the poem in the death of Lucretia, from whose suicide "sprang the Commonwealth, which breaks/As I am breaking now!" Only natural passions remain: the Hetairai that "yelled and round me drove/In narrowing circles" into the animalism of natural field. Second, if there is an historical dimension in the second dream, there should also be one in the first. We may see Lucretius's fiery torrent in Plutarch's description of the omen that announced Sulla as "entirely the creature of a superior power . . . Fortune." Specifically, "the earth near the Laverna opened, and a quantity of fire came rushing out of it, shooting up with a bright flame into the heavens. The soothsayers upon this foretold that a person of great qualities, and of a rare and singular aspect, should take the government in hand, and quiet the present troubles of the city." The event was also momentous, a revolutionary change in history. The Etruscan sages affirmed that such prodigies

> betokened the mutation of the age, and a general revolution in the world. For according to them there are in all eight ages, differing one from another in the lives and the characters of men, and to each of these God has allotted a certain measure of time, determined by the circuit of the great year. And when one age is run out, at the approach of another, there appears some wonderful sign from earth or heaven, such as makes it manifest at once to those who have made it their business to study such things, that there has succeeded in the world a new race of men, differing in customs and institutes of life, and more or less regarded by the gods than the preceding. . . . The diviners foreboded commotions and dissensions between the great landed proprietors and the common city populace.[23]

The third dream then completes the general idea:

> from utter gloom stood out the breasts,
> The breasts of Helen, and hoveringly a sword

---

[23]*Plutarch*, pp. 550, 551. Note also Plutarch's mention of Marius's having taken into alliance a villainous Sulpicius who gathered together "a company of young men of the equestrian class ready for all occasions, whom he styled his Anti-Senate" (pp. 551-52). Tennyson began thinking about both the Pelleas idyll and "The Last Tournament" (with its Round Table in the North, an anti-Camelot) in 1859. He finished the former idyll in 1869 and the latter in 1870. (For the dating, see Ricks, ed., *Poems of Tennyson*, pp. 1687, 1706.)

Now over and now under, now direct,
Pointed itself to pierce, but sank down shamed
At all that beauty; and as I stared, a fire,
The fire that left a roofless Ilion,
Shot out of them, and scorched me that I woke.

It is to be presumed that Tennyson would not have us admire the
fleshly beauty (say, of an Ettarre) that would destroy a civilization.
From this it follows that the sword (say, Pelleas's) is culpable in sinking
and not in piercing that deadly bosom. The analogy is a variant on the
"allowed sin" that destroys Camelot, on the disinclination to "war with
evil," as the Lotos-Eaters say.

Lucretius does, in fact, embody the spiritual schism of Camelot,
torn apart through asceticism and sensuality. He is on the one hand the
Pellam who, like Lucretius's gods, is removed from all the passions of
"envy, hate and pity, and spite and scorn" (passions that, as argued
previously, were used by knights like Gareth for historically formative
purposes). Thus, he dwells apart from historical struggle in the sinful
but to him "sacred everlasting calm." On the other hand, Lucretius is
like the Vivien who represents "myriad nakednesses,/And twisted
shapes of lust . . . animal heat." The combination is the erotic asceticism
embodied by the nun who started the Grail quest, one of those "holy
virgins in their ecstasies," as Gawain said. This unstable compound is
the basic flaw in Lucretius's philosophy, a flaw that finally finds its
center in the sensual chancefulness of nature,

The all-generating powers and genial heat
Of Nature, when she strikes through the thick blood
Of cattle, and light is large, and lambs are glad
Nosing the mother's udder [in] . . . the Italian field.

Lucretius's abstract system denies the anthropomorphism of the gods (a
tenet held strongly by Tennyson with regard to the Christian God). As a
result, Lucretius is unable to bring about that classic union of powers
evoked in his despairing plea in lines 80–84:

Nay, if thou canst, O Goddess, like ourselves
Touch, and be touched, then would I cry to thee
To kiss thy Mavors, roll thy tender arms
Round him, and keep him from the lust of blood
That makes a steaming slaughter-house of Rome.

This commonplace about harmony as the union of the "fierce and contentious" and the "generous and pleasing" is, in the traditional understanding, the kind of temperance and "chastity" that Arthur represents.[24] In the failure of the moral center, these powers fuse instead into the "Twy-natured" satyr who is "no nature," for, as Lucretius says, "him I proved impossible." And Lucretius is set soon to make himself impossible.

The idea of self-destruction is furthered by the contrast between

> .   Plato where he says,
> That men like soldiers may not quit the post
> Allotted by the Gods . . . [and] he that holds
> That Gods are careless, wherefore need he care
> Greatly for them, nor rather plunge at once,
> Being troubled, wholly out of sight.

This is the contrast between the Arthur of the *Idylls*, who

> must guard
> That which he rules, and is but as the kind
> To whom a space of land is given to plow.
> Who may not wander from the allotted field
> Before his work be done, (HG 901–5)

and the Lotos-Eaters' Lucretian gods, who are "careless of mankind" and "smile in secret," hearing from earth a "doleful song / Steaming up, a lamentation and an ancient tale of wrong." Lucretius's sun god too "sees not," though he hears absently a "wail of pain" from man. In this, Lucretius stands for the cloistered virtues, virtues that are without an historical role and therefore are readily brought down by the assault of passion.

That Lucretius is to be taken as the "human race" is suggested by the correspondence in the poem between Lucretius in his private agony and Rome in hers. Like Rome, Lucretius is oppressed by the Orgoglio-like "cloudy slough" of the cosmic Venus, a "mountain o'er a mountain,—ay, and within / All hollow as the hopes and fears of men." Beside the complex sexual resonances, this evokes the Mount of Arthur of the early sketch in which he still bore the blame for Camelot's fall (as was

---

[24] See, for instance, the "Introduction" to Robert Kellogg and Oliver Steele, eds., *Edmund Spenser: Books I and II of "The Faerie Queene," the Mutability Cantos and Selections from the Minor Poetry* (New York: Odyssey, 1965), p. 57.

argued in chapter 6): "all underneath it was hollow . . . and there ran a
prophecy that the mountain and the city on some wild morning would
topple into the abyss and be no more" (*Memoir*, 2:122–23). This is
perhaps a prophecy such as now became associated with Sulla in Tennyson's readings in Plutarch. In the adjoining stanza, there is the direct
historical equivalent. Lucretius's sensual visions

> press in, perforce
> Of multitude, as crowds that in an hour
> Of civic tumult jam the doors, and bear
> The keepers down, and throng, their rags and they
> The basest, far into that council-hall
> Where sit the best and stateliest of the land.

The Roman mobs, incited by demagogues like Sulla, despoil the best
part of man and bring freedom to an end in madness and in blood.
Lucretius mimes this end, madly spilling his own blood with a dagger,
wondering what "Duty" is (in the original reading "What matters?").
There is no God without or within.

Tennyson's gloom about "an age of lies, and also an age of stinks,"
as he said 1869 (*Memoir*, 2:75), is given in some epigrams of 1864–68.
Under an epigraph of Swinburne, "*All men born are mortal but not
man*," Tennyson chastises this optimism:

> Man is as mortal as men,
>   The cycle sweeps him away;
> I am the worm of a minute,
>   The fly will last for a day;
> Both in a minute are gone,
>   The day and the minute are one.

Some lines in the epigram "History (now-a-days)" could be the
epigraph for "Lucretius" and, indeed, for the time as Tennyson
perceived it: "the worst is the best/ And the best is the worst,/ And topsy-
turvy go all things." Similarly, in the lines from "Sadness": "Immeasurable sadness!/ And I know it as a poet,/ And I greet it, and I meet it,/
Immeasurable sadness!"[25] But this sadness is about history. Pure spirit
is another matter.

---

[25] The epigrams appear in Ricks, ed., *Poems of Tennyson*, pp. 1226–28.

X Epilogue: Beyond Clio

IN THE PREVIOUS chapter it was argued that the sixties represented the last stage in which Tennyson's philosophy of history could be said to underlay poetic structure. Such a unity of thought breaks apart in the seventies and even more so in the eighties as the three main ideas that once had composed it begin to fragment into independent units. Active providence moves to inaccessible heights "exalted, glorified, a purer spirit," as Hegel says of world spirit that consumes its worldly envelope (p. 73). The historical process functions in a hopelessly anarchical way on the plane of ordinary providence, in the barbarism that is the natural end of every cycle. The hero is moving into extinction. Where he is still within society, he is morbid and suicidal; like the society he represents, he is overwhelmed by passions. Where he leaves the "dark city," he prepares, with a certain luminous understanding, to face transcendence and to scale the heights for the last time. This fragmentation can serve as the basis for classifying some of Tennyson's work in the seventies and eighties. First, there are poems that confirm the hopeless state of present history. Then, as if breaking apart the past-present interplay that once had underwritten works like *The Princess*, there are poems that, like ancient memories, celebrate primal beginnings and attitudes. Finally, there are those poems that glorify spirit free of the historical mire: God remote on the Mount of Vision. Yet the world is noumenal with the divine presence still, and at some

164

point in the far distant future the divine part of man's nature may once more engage providential purpose in history through the resurgence of heroic spirit.

"The wheel must always move," Tennyson says in "Politics." But the state here is a wagon on natural hills. Neither uphill nor down has much historical sanguinity in it, especially given the nature of politics amok in "Freedom" (the poet's first utterance as a new peer of 1884): "Men loud against all forms of power—/Unfurnished brows, tempestuous tongues . . . Brass mouths and iron lungs!" After some coaxing by and negotiation with Gladstone, Tennyson reluctantly voted for the Third Reform Bill, "not that he deemed the time altogether ripe for such a measure, on the contrary," says Hallam Tennyson:

> But the promises of statesmen and agitators had so deeply stirred the popular mind, that delay, he thought, was no longer safe. "Perhaps," he said, "it is the first step on the road to the new social condition that is surely coming on the world. Evolution has often come through revolution. In England common-sense has carried the day without great upheavals, and I believe that English common-sense will save us still if our statesmen be not idiotic. If there is a revolution it will be world-wide, the mightiest ever known. May I not live to see it." (*Memoir*, 2:303)

"Old England may go down in babble at last," says the speaker in the 1886 "Locksley Hall Sixty Years After." Tennyson always insisted that this is a "dramatic poem"; such a poem "evolves its life" from "some event which comes to the poet's knowledge, some hint flashed from another mind, some thought or feeling arising in his own." We need a philosophical interpretation of this poem, an explanation on intellectual rather than personal grounds, for "*There is not one touch of biography in it from beginning to end,*" as Tennyson wrote irately. The Lytton letter that Hallam Tennyson reproduces as Tennyson's estimate of "valuable remarks on the drift of the poem" includes the idea that "the poem in its entirety has a peculiar historical importance as the impersonation of the emotional life of a whole generation" (*Memoir*, 2:331, 330). Old Locksley, then, like so many of Tennyson's heroes, is the "human race." He is the spirit of a people at a point in the periodic cycle of history, just as Lucretius was the "end" of Roman history. Locksley's beginnings were the beginnings of the Victorian age. "I myself have often babbled doubtless of a foolish past," says he,

"'Forward' rang the voices then, and of the many mine was one." But the present has the same relationship to this past as someone like Edith had to the long Aylmer line. No longer is the medieval ideal, the fusion of past and present, reinvigorating; now it is murderous: "hold the Present fatal daughter of the Past." Locksley is irascible with his grandson, the "vicious boy," and he raves with loathing against contemporary abuses. "Heated am I?" he asks, and in his very intemperance he mimes the age's savagery.

The past is seen as made "foolish" (meaningless) by a breakdown of will and vision in a type of epistemology the reverse of that in *In Memoriam*. It is a decorous characteristic of Locksley if he represents the time gone "back into the beast again." In the Locksley shield "the peasant cow shall butt the 'Lion passant' from his field." "Chaos, Cosmos! Cosmos, Chaos! once again the sickening game" is Lucretius's despairing "What matters? All is over." "Poor old Heraldry, poor old History, poor old Poetry, passing hence,/In the common deluge," says Locksley. Still, the "Powers of Good, the Powers of Ill" ever are present in the human mind, used either in "Strowing balm, or shedding poison in the fountains of the Will." That Locksley does the latter is only proper considering his symbolic role, but the former is ever a possibility. The "highest Human Nature is divine." So "Forward," says Locksley sardonically, "Till you find the deathless Angel seated in the vacant tomb." This will not come soon. "Let us hush this cry of 'Forward' till ten thousand years have gone," he says.

As if to seek relief from such despair, Tennyson interested himself in subjects that dealt with historical beginnings and pristine valor. He wrote what he called his "historical trilogy"—*Harold* 1876, *Becket* 1884, and *Queen Mary* 1875. As he said, it "pourtrays the making of England" (*Memoir*, 2:173). He also translated two heroic scenes from the *Iliad* and the "Battle of Brunanburh." "The Revenge," written in 1877, describes the savage heroism of the English during the time of the Spanish Armada. In 1877 Tennyson also wrote a sonnet praising the valor of the Montenegrins in their struggle against the Turk, a struggle designed to keep "their faith, their freedom, on the height,/Chaste, frugal, savage . . . smallest among peoples!" Such an effort was but a primitive remnant of heroism amidst the spiritual squalor of contemporary Europe. Not that he expected such heroic memory to reinvigorate the present (as he did in poems of the fifties). He says in the "Epilogue" to "The Charge of the Heavy Brigade at Balaclava" that he celebrates the "warrior's noble deed" because "whatsoe'er/He wrought of good or brave/Will mould him through the cycle-year/ That dawns behind the grave." This side of it, "Earth passes, all is lost . . . And deed and song alike are swept/Away, and all in vain."

Finally, there are the poems about spirit disengaging itself from the historical slough entirely. Tennyson's interest in metaphysics was strong in the seventies, and he even became the founding father of the Metaphysical Society in 1869. This gathering of thinkers discussed the great questions of the immaterial world although, as Hallam has his father saying, it "perished because after ten years of strenuous effort no one had succeeded in even defining the term 'Metaphysics'" (*Memoir*, 2:170). Theology, however, satisfied his faith in the reality of the spirit, especially after death, as the record of his interest shows. According to Emily's journal for 12 January 1871, Tennyson "reads me some of Westcott's *Gospel of the Resurrection*." On 16 January, she notes, "We talk on the subjects nearest his heart, the Resurrection of Jesus Christ and the Immortality of the Soul" (given in the *Memoir*, 2:103, as "He talked . . ."). On 14 February Emily wrote to Hallam, "In the evening Papa read me a good deal of Westcott's *Church of the Resurrection*."[1] On 18 February "We talked of the Resurrection of our Lord & of the Immortality of Man."

In "The Higher Pantheism," written 1867, immortal spirit works itself through the world as "the Vision of Him who reigns." The statement is ambiguous. Taken as man's vision of God—for "do we not live in dreams?"—the higher pantheism seems first the effort for vision and then, in failure, "broken gleams, and a stifled splendour and gloom." The 1873 "The Voice and the Peak" carries this rise and fall of man's engagement with providential purpose in terms of "voice" and of the wave imagery used, as noted above, in the *Idylls*. Spiritual energy, like the wave of the world, is drawn from the deep by the power of the prophetic height. Polluted by historical time, however, the thousand voices "roar and rave," "leave the heights and are troubled,/And moan and sink to their rest." But at the distant end of every cycle, spirit resurrects itself as a new wave "Green-rushing from the rosy thrones of dawn" (the God of the "awful rose of dawn" of the "The Vision of Sin"). Such is the future hope. The present, however, is "Swallowed in Vastness, lost in Silence," everything "drowned/In the deeps of a meaningless Past" ("Vastness") because this present is without the referent of active providence.

[1] James O. Hoge, *Letters*, p. 266.

The 1885 "The Ancient Sage" contains this same grief and hope. A "Desolate sweetness" is inherent in the ambiguous "divine farewell" that attends the progression of "A height, a broken grange, a grove, a flower." The imagery is familiar. The source of spiritual energy—the "wealth of waters"—is the summit of the Mount of Vision, for "Force is from the heights." This force descends through history and at last spills brokenly onto natural field where all is "Lost and gone and lost and gone!" This sense of loss is "The Passion of the Past" of line 219. The lines that follow often have been compared to the "Tears, idle tears" of *The Princess*; the singer of this lyric is passionate because she is "thinking of the days that are no more," a loss such as might be suggested by the ruins of the Tintern Abbey that Tennyson said inspired him to write the lyric (*Memoir*, 1:253). The Sage, too, is thinking of the "fatal sequence of this world," that loss must follow loss until there is only ruin. Yet there is also the hope that when "what we feel/Within ourselves is highest," God "shall descend/On this half-deed, and shape it at the last/According to the Highest in the Highest." In the words of "The Voice and the Peak," the "deep has power on the height,/And the height has power on the deep," in interchangeable supremacy. When man is ready spiritually, the force again will descend the Mount.

After a severe illness in 1888–89 (Tennyson died in 1892), the poet wrote "Merlin and the Gleam" in August of 1889. Hallam has his father saying that the gleam "signifies in my poem the higher poetic imagination" (*Memoir*, 2:366). Given the historical nature of the poetic imagination (as has been argued throughout), it is not surprising to find in the 1884 "Freedom" an equating of the gleam (also, "Vision") and political freedom: "O follower of the Vision, still/In motion to the distant gleam . . ." And, indeed, in addition to the manifest biographical allegory in the poem, Merlin's pursuit of the gleam is also an historical journey. Merlin wakes at sunrise and follows "In early summers" divine harmony. He passes through a "barbarous people,/Blind to the magic,/And deaf to the melody," and encounters an age of myth and fable in stanza IV. This is followed by the pastoral-agricultural stage in stanza V and the civilization of Camelot in stanza VI. Then "Clouds and darkness/Closed upon Camelot," but the "Gleam, that had waned to a wintry glimmer" draws him to the "land's/Last limit" on the "border/Of boundless Ocean" where he will die. There he sees a new "young Mariner" who will follow the gleam in a repetition of the cycle. These cycles are, in the words of "The Voice and the Peak," "raised for ever and ever."

With such poems about spirit at the last limit, Tennyson's long-developing philosophy of history comes to an end. This philosophy was a kind of sociopsychological "structure" that underwent growth, development, and decay over the period of Tennyson's life, although it retained its fundamental elements. His poems were objectifications of its imperatives. Insofar as this complex of ideas and convictions was shared by important groups, certain features of the age were also materializations of these imperatives. Something called the "Victorian age" started in the thirties. It seemed to end in the sixties. Literary historians commonly feel a "period" began in 1830 and closed in some significant shift of mind in the mid-sixties. (Bateson, for instance, says Arnold's 1865 *Essays* points to a "mid-Victorian retreat from Romanticism").[2] Politically, historians see 1830–32 as the start of the modern era and they see the death of Palmerston in 1865 as the "approaching end of the mid-century period" (with an "enormous gulf between the age of Palmerston and the succeeding decades").[3] The disjunction of the late sixties Carlyle called a type of "Shooting Niagara." So too it was indicated in the previous chapter that Clio, the muse of meaningful history, last appeared in Tennyson's major poems of the sixties.

But in another sense, this "structure" disengages itself from its own history to become part of a "living" past that can affect minds coming long after. Its imperatives continue to work when the perceiver of this past grasps it with both understanding and conviction through the same intense, divinatory empathy established as a mode of thinking in Tennyson throughout this study. Thereby is "meaning" found in this past, and in these poems. This should not imply that the poem as an historical event can be reproduced "as it really was," anymore than that the Liberal Anglican historians, quoted liberally throughout these pages, would allow that any historian could show history this way. The poem is the medium for a fusion of past and present, as this concept was traced in the age in chapter 4. To put the matter in a modern terminology, we must fuse past "meaning" and present "significance."[4] The mechanism engaged in this critical process is mysterious, but even if someone could explain it, it is not clear that we should profit from the explanation. Criticism is an art form because it is a belated engagement with the imperatives of the mental "structure" that caused the poems in the first place: in this instance, Tennyson's philosophy of history.

[2] F. W. Bateson, *A Guide to English Literature* (London: Longmans, 1965), p. 153.

[3] Anthony Wood, *Nineteenth Century Britain: 1815–1914* (New York: David McKay, 1960), pp. 254, 253.

[4] See Introduction, note 7.

It is difficult to engage the past, for, as Tennyson said in the prefatory sonnet to his play *Queen Mary*, "Guess well", "No man can send his mind/Into man's past so well, that he can form/A perfect likeness of long-vanished souls,/Whate'er new lights be let on ancient scrolls/And secular perforations of the worm./Courage, old Clio!" nevertheless. "You see the past dilated through the fog/of ages." Perhaps "Guess well" is the definitive statement of critical purpose.

Works Cited

Abrams, M. H. *Natural Supernaturalism: Tradition and Revolution in Romantic Literature.* New York: Norton, 1971.

Allen, Peter. *The Cambridge Apostles: The Early Years.* Cambridge: At the University Press, 1978.

Amiel, Henri-Frédéric. *Journal: The Journal Intime.* Translated by Mrs. Humphrey Ward. 2 vols. London: Macmillan, 1885.

August, Eugene R. "Tennyson and Teilhard: The Faith of *In Memoriam*." *PMLA* 84 (1969): 217–26.

Barnes, Harry Elmer. *A History of Historical Writing.* 2d rev. ed. New York: Dover, 1962.

Barnes, Sherman B. "The Age of Enlightenment." In *The Development of Historiography*, edited by Matthew A. Fitzsimons et al. Port Washington, New York: Kennikat, 1967.

Benziger, James. *Images of Eternity: Studies in the Poetry of Religious Vision from Wordsworth to T. S. Eliot.* Carbondale: Southern Illinois University Press, 1962.

Bishop, Jonathan. "The Unity of *In Memoriam*." *Victorian Newsletter,* no. 21 (1962), pp. 9–14.

Bradley, A. C. *A Commentary on Tennyson's "In Memoriam."* Hamden, Conn.: Archon, 1966.

Branston, Brian. *Gods of the North.* London: Thames & Hudson, 1955.

Brinton, David Garrison and Davidson, Thomas. *Giordano Bruno, Philosopher and Martyr: Two Addresses.* Philadelphia: McKay, 1890.

Brookfield, Frances M. *The Cambridge "Apostles."* New York: Scribner, 1906.

Brooks, Cleanth. "Literary Criticism: Poet, Poem, and Reader." In *Varieties of Literary Experience: Eighteen Essays in World Literature,* edited by Stanley Burnshaw. New York: New York University Press, 1962.

171

Brooks, Richard A. E. "The Development of the Historical Mind." In *The Reinterpretation of Victorian Literature*, edited by Joseph E. Baker. New York: Russell & Russell, 1962.

Brown, Alan Williard. *The Metaphysical Society: Victorian Minds in Crisis 1869–1880*. New York: Columbia University Press, 1947.

Buckley, Jerome Hamilton. *Tennyson: The Growth of a Poet*. Cambridge, Mass.: Harvard University Press, 1960.

——. *The Victorian Temper: A Study in Literary Culture*. Cambridge, Mass.: Harvard University Press, 1951.

Bultmann, Rudolf. *History and Eschatology*. The Gifford Lectures 1955. Edinburgh: At the University Press, 1957.

Bush, Douglas. *Mythology and the Romantic Tradition in English Poetry*. Cambridge, Mass.: Harvard University Press, 1937.

Carlyle, Thomas. *The Works of Thomas Carlyle*. 15 vols. New York: Peter Fenelon Collier, 1897.

Carr, Arthur J. "Tennyson as a Modern Poet." In *Critical Essays on the Poetry of Tennyson*, edited by John Killham. New York: Barnes & Noble, 1960.

Cassirer, Ernst. *Language and Myth*. Translated by Susanne K. Langer. New York: Harper & Brothers, 1946.

——. *The Philosophy of the Enlightenment*. Translated by Fritz C. A. Koelln and James P. Pettegrove. Princeton: Princeton University Press, 1951.

Chandler, Alice. *A Dream of Order: The Medieval Ideal in Nineteenth-Century English Literature*. Lincoln: University of Nebraska Press, 1970.

Chiasson, E. J. "Tennyson's 'Ulysses'—A Reinterpretation." In *Critical Essays on the Poetry of Tennyson,* edited by John Killham. New York: Barnes & Noble, 1960.

Collingwood, R. G. *The Idea of History*. Oxford: Oxford University Press, Clarendon Press, 1946.

Collins, Winston. "Enoch Arden, Tennyson's Heroic Fisherman." *Victorian Poetry* 14 (1976): 47–53.

The Correspondence of Thomas Carlyle and Ralph Waldo Emerson. Edited by C. E. Norton. 2 vols. Boston: Houghton Mifflin, 1894.

Dodsworth, Martin. "Patterns of Morbidity: Repetition in Tennyson's Poetry." In *The Major Victorian Poets: Reconsiderations,* edited by Isobel Armstrong. Lincoln: University of Nebraska Press, 1969.

Donahue, Mary Joan. "Tennyson's *Hail Briton!* and *Tithon* in the Heath Manuscript." *PMLA* 64 (1949): 385–416.

Durham, Margery Stricker. "Tennyson's Wellington Ode and the Cosmology of Love." *Victorian Poetry* 14 (1976): 277–92.

Eggers, J. Philip. *King Arthur's Laureate: A Study of Tennyson's "Idylls of the King."* New York: New York University Press, 1971.

Eliade, Mircea. *The Myth of the Eternal Return: or, Cosmos and History*. Translated by Willard R. Trask. Bollingen Series XLVI. Princeton: Princeton University Press, Princeton/Bollingen Paperback, 1971.

——. "The Yearning for Paradise in Primitive Tradition." In *Myth and Mythmaking,* edited by Henry A. Murray. New York: Braziller, 1960.

Eliot, T. S. *Selected Essays*. New York: Harcourt Brace, 1964.

Engelberg, Edward. "The Best Image in Tennyson's *Idylls of the King*." *ELH* 22 (1955): 287–92.

Fichter, Andrew. "Ode and Elegy: Idea and Form in Tennyson's Early Poetry." *ELH* 40 (1973): 398–427.

Forbes, Duncan. *The Liberal Anglican Idea of History*. Cambridge: At the University Press, 1952.

Fricke, Douglas C. "A Study of Myth and Archetype in 'Enoch Arden'." *Tennyson Research Bulletin* 2 (1974): 106–15.

Froude, James Anthony. *Short Studies on Great Subjects*. 2d ed. London: Longmans, 1867.

———. *Thomas Carlyle: A History of His Life in London 1834–1881*. 2 vols. New York: Harper & Brothers, 1884.

Gibson, Walker. "Behind the Veil: A Distinction Between Poetic and Scientific Language in Tennyson, Lyell, and Darwin." *Victorian Studies* 2 (1958): 60–68.

Gill, Richard. *Happy Rural Seat: The English Country House and the Literary Imagination*. New Haven: Yale University Press, 1972.

Gooch, G. P. *History and Historians in the Nineteenth Century*. Boston: Beacon Press, Beacon Paperback, 1959.

Gray, J. M. "Fact, Form and Fiction in Tennyson's *Balin and Balan*." *Renaissance and Modern Studies* 12 (1968): 91–107.

———. *Man and Myth in Victorian England: Tennyson's "The Coming of Arthur."* Tennyson Society Monograph no. 1. Lincoln, England: Tennyson Society, 1969.

———. "A Study in Idyl: Tennyson's *The Coming of Arthur*." *Renaissance and Modern Studies* 14 (1970): 111–50.

Green, Joyce. "Tennyson's Development During the 'Ten Years' Silence (1832–1842)." *PMLA* 66 (1951): 662–97.

Grote, George. *History of Greece*, 12 vols. 2d London ed. Reprint (as *Greece*) New York: Peter Fenelon Collier & Son, 1900.

Gunter, G. O. "Life and Death Symbols in Tennyson's 'Mariana'." *South Atlantic Bulletin* 36 (1971): 64–67.

Hales, John W. "King Alfred 'The Truth-Teller'." *Notes and Queries*. 9th Series 8 (10 August 1901): 117–18.

[Hare, Julius Charles and Augustus William.]*Guesses at Truth by Two Brothers*. London: Macmillan, 1897.

Harper, George Mills. *The Neoplatonism of William Blake*. Chapel Hill: University of North Carolina Press, 1961.

Harrison, Frederic. *The Meaning of History; and Other Historical Pieces*. London: Macmillan, 1894.

Hathorn, Richmond Y. *Tragedy, Myth, and Mystery*. Bloomington: Indiana University Press, 1962.

Hegel, Georg Wilhelm Friedrich. *The Philosophy of History*. Translated by J. Sibree. New York: Dover, 1956.

Hellstrom, Ward. *On the Poems of Tennyson*. Gainesville: University of Florida Press, 1972.

[Hinton, James.] *Man and His Dwelling Place: An Essay Toward the Interpretation of Nature*. London: Parker, 1859.

———. *The Mystery of Pain: A Book for the Sorrowful.* London: Smith, Elder, 1866.

Hirsch, E. D., Jr. *Validity in Interpretation.* New Haven: Yale University Press, 1967.

———. *Wordsworth and Schelling: A Typological Study of Romanticism.* New Haven: Yale University Press, 1960.

Hoffman, Kurt. "The Basic Concepts of Jaspers' Philosophy." In *The Philosophy of Karl Jaspers,* edited by Paul Arthur Schilpp. The Library of Living Philosophers. New York: Tudor, 1957.

Hoge, James O. "Emily Tennyson's Narrative for Her Sons." *Texas Studies in Literature and Language* 14 (1972): 93–106.

Hough, Graham. "The Natural Theology of *In Memoriam.*" *Review of English Studies* (Old Series) 23 (1947): 244–56.

Hunt, John Dixon. "The Poetry of Distance: Tennyson's *Idylls of the King.*" In *Victorian Poetry,* edited by Malcom Bradbury and David Palmer. Stratford-upon-Avon-Studies no. 15. London: Crane, Russak & Co., 1972.

Inge, William Ralph. *The Platonic Tradition in English Religious Thought.* London: Longmans, Green, 1926.

Jaspers, Karl. *The Origin and Goal of History.* Translated by Michael Bullock. London: Routledge & Kegan Paul, 1953.

———. *Tragedy Is Not Enough.* Translated by Harald A. T. Reiche, Harry T. Moore, and Karl W. Deutsch. Seeds-of-Thought Series, edited by Karl W. Deutsch. Boston: Beacon Press, 1952.

Johnson, E. D. H. *The Alien Vision of Victorian Poetry: Sources of the Poetic Imagination in Tennyson, Browning, and Arnold.* Princeton Studies in English, no. 34. Princeton: Princeton University Press, 1952.

———. "*In Memoriam*: The Way of the Poet." *Victorian Studies* 2 (1958): 139–48.

Joseph, Gerhard. "The Idea of Mortality in Tennyson's Classical and Arthurian Poems: 'Honor Comes with Mystery'." *Modern Philology* 66 (1968): 136–45.

———. *Tennysonian Love: The Strange Diagonal.* Minneapolis: University of Minnesota Press, 1968.

Kaplan, Fred. "Woven Paces and Waving Hands: Tennyson's Merlin as Fallen Artist." *Victorian Poetry* 7 (1969): 285–98.

Ker, John. *Sermons.* 7th ed. Edinburgh: Edmonston and Douglas, 1870.

Killham, John. *Tennyson and "The Princess": Reflections of an Age.* London: Athlone Press, 1958.

———. "Tennyson's *Maud*—The Function of the Imagery." *Critical Essays on the Poetry of Tennyson,* edited by John Killham. New York: Barnes and Noble, 1960.

Kincaid, James R. "Rhetorical Irony, the Dramatic Monologue, and Tennyson's *Poems* (1842)." *Philological Quarterly* 53 (1974): 220–36.

———. *Tennyson's Major Poems: The Comic and Ironic Patterns.* New Haven: Yale University Press, 1975.

Knowles, James. "Aspects of Tennyson, II (a Personal Reminiscence)." *Nineteenth Century* 33 (1893): 164–88.

Korg, Jacob. "The Pattern of Fatality in Tennyson's Poetry." *Victorian Newsletter,* no. 14 (1958), pp. 8–11.

Langbaum, Robert. "The Dynamic Unity of *In Memoriam.* In *The Modern Spirit:*

Essays on the Continuity of Nineteenth- and Twentieth-Century Literature.
New York: Oxford University Press, 1970.
——. *The Poetry of Experience: The Dramatic Monologue in Modern Literary Tradition.* New York: Random House, 1957

Langer, Susanne K. "On Cassirer's Theory of Language and Myth." In *The Philosophy of Ernst Cassirer,* edited by Paul Arthur Schilpp. The Library of Living Philosophers. New York: Tudor, 1949.

LaValley, Albert J. *Carlyle and the Idea of the Modern: Studies in Carlyle's Prophetic Literature And Its Relation to Blake, Nietzsche, Marx, and Others.* New Haven: Yale University Press, 1968.

Lecky, W. E. H. *History of European Morals from Augustus to Charlemagne.* 2 vols. London: Longmans, 1869.

The Letters of Emily Lady Tennyson. Edited by James O. Hoge. University Park: Pennsylvania State University Press, 1974.

Lounsbury, Thomas R. *The Life and Times of Tennyson.* New Haven: Yale University Press, 1915.

Löwith, Karl. *Meaning in History.* Chicago: University of Chicago Press, Phoenix Books, 1949.

Lushington, Henry. *La Nation Boutiquière; and Other Poems, Chiefly Political; "and" Points of War.* Cambridge: Macmillan, 1855.

Mackail, J. W. *Lectures on Greek Poetry.* New ed. London: Longmans, Green, 1926.

Malins, Edward. *English Landscaping and Literature: 1660–1840.* London: Oxford University Press, 1966.

Manuel, Frank E. *The Eighteenth Century Confronts the Gods.* Cambridge, Mass.: Harvard University Press, 1959.

Marshall, George O., Jr. *A Tennyson Handbook.* New York: Twayne, 1963.

Masterman, C. F. G. *Tennyson As a Religious Teacher.* 2d ed. London: Methuen, 1910.

Maurice, John Frederick Denison. *The Doctrine of Sacrifice, Deduced from the Scriptures: Sermons.* Cambridge: Macmillan, 1854.

——. *Social Morality: Twenty One Lectures.* London: Macmillan, 1869.

——. *What is Revelation? A Series of Sermons on the Epiphany.* Cambridge: Macmillan, 1859.

Mays, J. C. C. "*In Memoriam*: An Aspect of Form." *University of Toronto Quarterly* 35 (1965): 22–46.

Mermin, Dorothy M. "Tennyson's *Maud*: A Thematic Analysis." In *Texas Studies in Literature and Language* 15 (1973): 267–77.

Molesworth, Charles. "Property and Virtue: The Genre of the Country-House Poem in the Seventeenth Century." *Genre* 1 (1968): 141–57.

Moore, Carlisle. "Faith, Doubt, and Mystical Experience in *In Memoriam*." *Victorian Studies* 7 (1963): 155–69.

Moore, George. "A Critical and Bibliographical Study of the Somersby Library of Doctor George Clayton Tennyson." Dissertation, University of Nottingham, England, 1966.

Muirhead, John H. *Coleridge as Philosopher.* London: Allen & Unwin, 1930.

Mulhauser, Frederick L. "The Tradition of Burke." In *The Reinterpretation of*

Victorian Literature, edited by Joseph E. Baker. New York: Russell & Russell, 1962.

Mustard, Wilfred P. *Classical Echoes in Tennyson.* Columbia University Studies in English, vol. 3. New York: Macmillan, 1904.

Nadel, George H. "Philosophy of History Before Historicism." In *Studies in the Philosophy of History: Selected Essays from "History and Theory,"* edited by George H. Nadel. New York: Harper & Row, 1965.

Neff, Emery. *The Poetry of History: The Contribution of Literature and Literary Scholarship to the Writing of History Since Voltaire.* New York: Columbia University Press, 1947.

Nicolson, Harold. *Tennyson: Aspects of his Life, Character, and Poetry.* New York: Houghton Mifflin, 1925.

Niebuhr, Barthold Georg. *The History of Rome.* Translated by Julius Charles Hare and Connop Thirlwall. 2 vols. Cambridge: J. Taylor, 1831–32.

Paden. W. D. *Tennyson in Egypt.* Lawrence: University of Kansas Press, 1942.

Pettigrew, John. "Tennyson 'Ulysses': A Reconciliation of Opposites." *Victorian Poetry* 1 (1963): 27–45.

Pitt, Valerie. *Tennyson Laureate.* Toronto: University of Toronto Press, 1962.

Preyer, Robert. *Bentham, Coleridge, and the Science of History.* Bochum-Langendreer: Heinrich Pöppinghaus, 1958.

Priestley, F. E. L. *Language and Structure in Tennyson's Poetry.* The Language Library. London: Andre Deutsch, 1973.

——. "Tennyson's *Idylls.*" In *Critical Essays on the Poetry of Tennyson,* edited by John Killham. New York: Barnes and Noble, 1960.

Reade, William Winwoode. *The Martyrdom of Man.* 12th ed. London: Trubner, 1887.

Reed, John R. *Perception and Design in Tennyson's "Idylls of the King."* Athens: Ohio University Press, 1969.

Ricks, Christopher, ed. *The Poems of Tennyson.* London: Longmans, 1969.

——. *Tennyson.* New York: Macmillan, 1972.

Rollin, Charles. *The Ancient History of the Egyptians, Carthaginians, Assyrians, Babylonians, Medes and Persians, Macedonians, and Grecians.* 7 vols. 5th ed. London: J. Rivington, 1768.

Roppen, Georg. "'Ulysses' and Tennyson's Sea-Quest." *English Studies* 40 (1959): 77–90.

Rosenberg, John D. *The Fall of Camelot: A Study of Tennyson's "Idylls of the King."* Cambridge, Mass.: Harvard University Press, Belknap Press, 1973.

——. "The Two Kingdoms of *In Memoriam.*" *Journal of English and Germanic Philology* 58 (1959): 228–40.

Rosenberg, Philip. *The Seventh Hero: Thomas Carlyle and the Theory of Radical Activism.* Cambridge, Mass.: Harvard University Press, 1974.

Rosenmeyer, Thomas G. *The Green Cabinet: Theocritus and the European Pastoral Lyric.* Berkeley: University of California Press, 1969.

Ryals, Clyde de L. *From the Great Deep: Essays on "Idylls of the King."* Athens: Ohio University Press, 1967.

[Seeley, Sir John Robert.] *Ecce Homo: A Survey of the Life and Work of Jesus Christ.* London: Macmillan, 1866.

Sewall, Richard B. "The Tragic Form." *Essays in Criticism* 4 (1954): 345-58.

Shaw, W. David. "The Idealist's Dilemma in *Idylls of the King.*" *Victorian Poetry* 5 (1967): 41-53.

——. "*Idylls of the King:* A Dialectical Reading." *Victorian Poetry* 7 (1969): 175-90.

——. "Imagination and Intellect in Tennyson's 'Lucretius'." *Modern Language Quarterly* 33 (1972): 130-39.

——. "*In Memoriam* and the Rhetoric of Confession." *ELH* 38 (1971): 80-103.

Shinn, Roger Lincoln. *Christianity and the Problem of History.* New York: Scribner, 1953.

Smith, Elton Edward. *The Two Voices: A Tennyson Study.* Lincoln: University of Nebraska Press, 1964.

Solomon, Stanley J. "Tennyson's Paradoxical King." *Victorian Poetry* 1 (1963): 258-71.

Stange, G. Robert. "Tennyson's Garden of Art: A Study of *The Hesperides.*" In *Critical Essays on the Poetry of Tennyson*, edited by John Killham. New York: Barnes & Noble, 1960.

Stanley, Arthur Penrhyn. *The Life and Correspondence of Thomas Arnold, D.D.* 12th ed. 2 vols. London: John Murray, 1881.

Stedman, Edmund Clarence. *Victorian Poets.* Boston: Houghton Mifflin, 1903.

Stevenson, Lionel. "The 'High-born Maiden' Symbol in Tennyson." In *Critical Essays on the Poetry of Tennyson*, edited by John Killham. New York: Barnes & Noble, 1960.

Templeman, William Darby. "Tennyson's *Locksley Hall* and Thomas Carlyle." In *Booker Memorial Studies: Eight Essays on Victorian Literature in Memory of John Manning Booker*, edited by Hill Shine. Chapel Hill: University of North Carolina Press, 1950.

Tennyson, Sir Charles. *Alfred Tennyson.* New York: Macmillan, 1949.

——. "The Dream in Tennyson's Poetry." *Virginia Quarterly Review* 40 (1964): 228-48.

[Tennyson, Hallam, Lord.] *Alfred Lord Tennyson: A Memoir by His Son.* 2 vols. London: Macmillan, 1897.

Tennyson in Lincoln: A Catalog of the Collections in the Research Centre. vol. 1. Edited by Nancie Campbell. Lincoln, England: Tennyson Society, 1971.

Tennyson: The Critical Heritage. Edited by John D. Jump. London: Routledge & Kegan Paul, 1967.

Tillich, Paul. *The Protestant Era.* Abridged ed. Translated by James Luther Adams. Chicago: University of Chicago Press, Phoenix Books, 1957.

Toynbee, Arnold J. *A Study of History.* 12 vols. London: Oxford University Press, 1933-61.

Trilling, Lionel. *The Liberal Imagination: Essays on Literature and Society.* New York: Viking, 1950.

Vico, Giambattista. *The Autobiography of Giambattista Vico.* Edited by Max Harold Fisch and Thomas Goddard Bergin. Ithaca, N.Y.: Cornell University Press, 1944.

——. *The New Science of Giambattista Vico.* Edited by Thomas Goddard Bergin and Max Harold Fisch. Ithaca, N.Y.: Cornell University Press, 1968.

Walsh, W. H. *Philosophy of History: An Introduction.* Rev. ed. New York: Harper & Row, Harper Torchbook, 1968.

Wellek, René. "The Concept of 'Romanticism' in Literary History." *Comparative Literature* 1 (1949): 1–23, 147–72.

——. *Confrontations: Studies in the intellectual and literary relations between Germany, England, and the United States during the nineteenth century.* Princeton: Princeton University Press, 1965.

Welsh, Alexander. *The Hero of the Waverly Novels.* Yale Studies in English, vol. 154. New Haven: Yale University Press, 1963.

Westcott, Brooke Foss. *Essays in the History of Religious Thought in the West.* London: Macmillan, 1891.

Willey, Basil. *The Seventeenth Century Background: Studies in the Thought of the Age in Relation to Poetry and Religion.* London: Chatto & Windus, 1934.

Williams, Raymond. *Culture and Society: 1780–1950.* New York: Columbia University Press, 1958.

Wilner, Ortha L. "Tennyson and Lucretius." *Classical Journal* 25 (1930): 347–66.

Wilson, Hugh H. "Tennyson: Unscholarly Arthurian." *Victorian Newsletter*, no. 32 (1967): 5–11.

Index

Adultery ("sin"), 119, 133–35, 140–42, 161

"Alexander," 10

Allen, Peter, 13 n. 1

"All Things Will Die," 47

"All thoughts, all creeds, all dreams are true," 47

Amiel, Henri-Frédéric, 123, 141, 142, 143

"Ancient Sage, The," xii n. 4, 168

Apocalypse: as conquest (war), 6, 29, 36, 40, 47, 99, 108, 111, 118, 150; as divine judgment, 23, 28; as "fire birth," 89–90, 92; as millennium, 5–6, 100; as revelation (epiphany), 23, 46, 80, 95–96, 101, 112, 150; as revolution, 39–40, 70, 72–74. *See also* History; Irony; War

"Apostles," the Cambridge, 5, 13, 14–15, 18, 19, 20, 21, 24, 25 n. 55, 30, 32, 33, 40, 45, 46, 54, 71 n. 1, 73, 78, 116 n. 8, 122, 146

Archetype (paradigm): apple, 29–30, 36, 37; city, 24–26, 40, 41, 57; house, 51, 53, 56–66 passim, 70–78 passim, 98, 106, 150, 154–55; mount (height, tower), 25, 30–37 passim, 40, 48, 50–51, 53, 58, 75–76, 138, 164, 167, 168; phoenix, 73–76, 89, 143, 148; tree (vine), 25, 29–31, 49, 51, 85, 86; voyage (pilgrimage, quest, wandering), 29, 36, 90, 94, 108, 138–39, 146, 168. *See also* Imagery; Myth

"Armageddon," 1, 5, 11, 18, 24, 28, 46, 47, 72, 75, 100

Arnold, Matthew, xi, 17 n. 20, 80, 169

Arnold, Thomas, 15, 16, 21, 39, 55, 64, 75, 90

"Audley Court," 59

August, Eugene R., 96, 97

Augustine, Saint, 18, 22 n. 37

"Aylmer's Field," 150, 154–55, 166

Bagehot, Walter, 153, 158

"Battle of Brunanburh," 166

Becket, 166

Benziger, James, 17

Bishop, Jonathan, 77 n. 11, 83 n. 25

"Boadicea," 151

Bradley, A. C., 84, 86, 94

Brookfield, Frances M., 14 n.6
Browne, Sir Thomas, 7, 124
Browning, Robert, 17 n.20, 23 n.46, 141
Bruno, Giordano, 16, 141
Bryant, Jacob, 2, 12, 40, 73
Buckle, Henry Thomas, 126 n.26
Buckley, Jerome Hamilton, 13, 19 n. 27, 24 n.51, 26, 28 n.59, 59 n.17, 67, 74 n.5, 79 n.13, 117 n.9, 144, 155–56
Bultmann, Rudolf, 97
Bulwer, Edward, Lord Lytton, 165
Burke, Edmund, 15 n.9, 19, 21, 35
Bush, Douglas, 38 n.6, 155 n.15, 158 n.21
Byron, George Gordon, Lord, 2, 17 n. 20, 45

Carlyle, Thomas, 4, 17, 54, 55, 56, 63, 66, 68, 71 and n.1, 72, 74, 86, 87, 89, 97, 99, 169
Carr, Arthur J., 45
Cassirer, Ernst, 18 n.21, 20 n.29
Chandler, Alice, 56, 63, 68
"Charge of the Light Brigade, The," 102–3
Chiasson, E. J., 42 n.10
Class: classless (humanity, "people"), 20, 22, 23, 33–34, 43, 70, 81, 90, 103, 158, 162; lower, 71, 99, 155, 157–58; middle (commercial), 33, 40, 43, 54, 66, 71, 72, 99, 104–5, 110, 151–53; upper, 31, 33, 37–40 passim, 43, 50, 54, 58–59, 64–65, 71, 76, 154. See also Man
Clough, Arthur Hugh, 157
Coleridge, Samuel Taylor, 14, 15 n.9, 21, 50, 146
Collingwood, R. G., 18 n.21
Collins, Winston, 153 n.8
"Coming of Arthur, The," 104
Comte, Auguste, 126 n.26
Croker, John Wilson, 29, 37

Davies, Edward, the Reverend, 2, 114
De Vere, Aubrey, 38

Dodsworth, Martin, 153 n.9
Donahue, Mary Joan, 24 n.49
"Dora," 53
Dramatic monologue, 36, 68
"Druid's Prophecies, The," 7, 8, 9
Durham, Margery Stricker, 100

"Edwin Morris," 59
Eliade, Mircea, 30, 63, 84
Eliot, T. S., 51, 59 n.17, 77 n.11, 82
Emerson, Ralph Waldo, 66, 136
Engelberg, Edward, 145
"Enoch Arden," 150, 151–53
"Epilogue" to "The Charge of the Heavy Brigade," 166
"Expedition of Nadir Shah into Hindostan, The," 7, 9

Faber, George Stanley, 2, 12, 47
"Fall of Jerusalem, The," 6, 9
Fichter, Andrew, 35 n.3
Fitzgerald, Edward, 14, 69
Forbes, Duncan, 20–21
"Freedom," 165, 168
Fricke, Douglas C., 151 n.3
Froude, James Anthony, 126

"Gareth and Lynette," 161
Gibbon, Edward, 2, 3, 4
Gibson, Walker, 96
Gilbert, W. S., 65, 66
God: definition of, xiii; as judge, 21, 23, 28, 29, 31, 41, 46; as unknowable, 6, 8, 28, 70, 79–80, 82–83, 148. See also Providence, active; Providence, ordinary
"God's Denunciations against Pharaoh-Hophra," 6, 8, 27–28
Goethe, Johann Wolfgang von, 14, 18 n. 21, 141
"Golden Year, The," 54, 68, 80
Gray, J. M., 68, 124 n.21, 132 n.1
Green, Joyce, 28
Grote, George, 22, 124
"Guess well, and that is well. Our age can find," 170

Gunter, G. O., 51

"Hail Briton!" 39, 92, 101
Hallam, Arthur Henry, xii n.4, 15, 21, 43, 56, 76, 77 n.11, 81, 85, 86, 87, 88, 89, 92, 93, 94, 95, 96, 101, 104
"Hands All Round!" 102
Hare, Julius Charles, 14, 15, 17, 19, 20, 22, 25, 26, 27, 75, 116 n.8, 122 n. 14, 124, 150
Harold, 166
Harrison, Frederick, 148 n.29
Hegel, Georg Wilhelm Friedrich, 23, 71 and n.1, 81, 112–49 passim, 164
Hellstrom, Ward, 108, 117 n.9
Herder, 55, 63
Herodotus, 2
"Hesperides, The," 14, 24, 28–31, 33, 36, 37
"Higher Pantheism, The," 167
"High-Priest to Alexander, The," 6
Hinton, James, 127, 140
"History (now-a-days)" ("The cursed will be blessed"), 163
History: anarchy (chance, fortune) in, 92, 98, 99, 103, 110, 118, 124, 150– 52, 154, 160, 164; barbarism (savagery) in, 26–27, 75, 129, 148–49, 150, 151, 155, 164, 166; "challenge and response" (opposition) in, 23, 29–31, 36, 41, 117–18, 128, 131, 132, 141; cycle in, 7–8, 11, 13, 19, 20, 21, 28, 39, 40, 70, 72, 76, 77 n. 11, 115–18 passim, 144, 156, 167; definition of, xiii; determinism in, 19, 20, 73, 74, 80, 92, 96, 125; dialectic (contradictions) in, 32, 39, 47–52 passim, 116 n.5, 118, 131, 144; discovery in, 21–22, 26–27, 34–35, 49; evolution (culture) in, 4, 23, 33, 35, 65, 72–73, 77–78, 77 n.11, 80, 95, 96–97, 117 and n.8, 156, 165; freedom in, 8, 11, 19, 20, 21, 23, 29, 30, 33, 80, 86 n.31, 92, 96, 117, 118, 122–23, 125, 126, 132, 141–43, 163; progress in, 13, 19, 20–21, 20 n.31, 33–35, 47, 49,

71–75 passim, 76–78, 77 n.11, 97, 100, 126, 148 n.29; revolution in, 15, 39, 65, 70, 71, 75, 81, 87–88, 89, 93, 154–55, 160, 165. *See also* Apocalypse; Irony; War
History, philosophy of: definition of, xi–xiii, 1–2, 150; "meaning" in, xii, 18, 42–43, 82, 87, 93, 97; mythic mode in, 11–12, 18 and n. 21, 22, 63, 84; as "structure," xiv, 169
History, philosophy of, Tennyson's: in the Cambridge poems, early, 13–14, 24; in the Cambridge poems (1830–33), 32–33, 52; in the English idyls and *The Princess*, 53– 54, 98, 112; establishment of, xi– xiii; in the *Idylls of the King*, 112– 13, 117–18; in *In Memoriam*, 70–71, 78–80, 89, 98, 112; in the late poems (1860s), 150; in the late poems (1870s, 1880s), 164–65; "meaning" in, 73, 76, 77–80, 85, 86–87, 88, 89, 91, 92, 93, 94, 95, 107, 150, 153, 166, 169; in the political poems and *Maud*, 98–99, 112; six-stage development of, xiv–xvi; in the Somersby poems, 1, 11. *See also* God; History; Intuitionalism; Man
History, written: by the Cambridge "Apostles," 14–15; characteristics of eighteenth century, 3–4, 93; characteristics of Romantic, 3–4, 10–11, 23; as education in early nineteenth century, 2–4; Tennyson's readings in, at Somersby, 2; Tennyson's readings in (1840s, 1850s), 115–16
"Holy Grail, The," 161
Hough, Graham, 79 n.13
Hume, David, 2, 3, 4
Hunt, John Dixon, 82 n.20

"Idealist, The," 16
Idyl (idyll), 55–57, 59–60, 63, 67
Idylls of the King, 33, 40, 41, 44, 55, 71, 103, 112–49, 156, 158, 159, 167. *See also individual idylls*

"I loving Freedom for herself," 34, 35, 54

Imagery: animal (bird), 50, 51, 85–87, 99, 104, 106, 145, 155, 166; fire, as mind, 11, 17–18; fire and water, 89 n.32, 120, 129–31, 137–39, 159; mechanical (artifact), 80, 89, 91, 93, 95, 109; organic (vegetation), 9, 19, 35, 37, 54, 63, 80, 86, 96, 142, 145; seasonal, 88, 90, 144; water, 145, 148–49, 167. *See also* Archetype; Myth; Nature

"In deep and solemn dreams," 5, 16

Inge, William Ralph, 17, 22 n.42

In Memoriam, 33, 37, 71, 75, 76–97, 101, 103, 104, 106, 107, 111, 112, 117, 120, 130, 145, 148, 158, 166

Intuitionalism (divination, empathy, prophecy, vision): as dream (sleep), 5, 16, 29, 36, 37, 47, 110, 125, 152, 159–61; in hero, 24, 39, 42; in historian, 3–4, 15–16, 17, 54–55; in poet, 1, 4–5, 13, 24, 28, 38, 48, 52; in prophet (holy man), 6–7, 7–8, 10, 30, 61; in Tennyson, 5–6, 15–17, 47, 49, 54, 79–80, 79 n.13, 83; as vestigial faculty, 53, 65. *See also* Neoplatonism; Will

Irony, 8, 36, 37, 38, 42, 43, 71 n.1, 116 n.8, 117, 121, 126, 133, 136–37, 139 n.6, 143, 144, 145, 150, 153

"Jack Tar," 151

Jaspers, Karl, 20 n.31, 44–46, 67

Jesus Christ, 11, 87, 92, 97, 121, 123, 126, 148, 154, 167

Johnson, E.D.H., 24 n.51, 26, 42 n.10, 94 n.37, 119, 155 n.14, 159 n.22

Joseph, Gerhard, 23, 67

Jowett, Benjamin, 2 n.3, 15, 17, 71, 81

Kant, Immanuel, 14

Kaplan, Fred, 132 n.2

Keats, John, 56

Kemble, John, 13, 14, 15, 32

Ker, John, 140–41

Killham, John, 21 n.33, 61, 72, 111 n. 14

Kincaid, James R., 42, 52, 117 n.10

"King Charles's Vision," 10

Kingsley, Charles, 59, 77, 99

Knowles, James, 43, 114

Korg, Jacob, 45 n.17

"Kraken, The," 47

"Lady Clara Vere de Vere," 58, 154

"Lady Clare," 58

"Lady of Shalott, The," 47, 50–51, 61

"Lamentation of the Peruvians," 7, 8

Langbaum, Robert, 38 n.6, 68, 79 n. 13

"Last Tournament, The," 160 n.23

Lecky, W.E.H., 127, 139

"Liberal Anglican" historians, 15, 18, 19, 20, 38, 54, 90, 169

"Lines on Cambridge of 1830," 13

"Locksley Hall," 53, 54, 64, 71–75, 76, 77, 78, 89

"Locksley Hall Sixty Years After," 165–66

"Lord of Burleigh, The," 58

"Lotos-Eaters, The," 32, 36–38, 40, 46, 47, 50, 51, 102, 105, 151–52, 161, 162

Lounsbury, Thomas R., 12 n.3, 24

"Love thou thy land, with love far-brought," 33, 53, 72

Lowell, James Russell, 108 n.10

Löwith, Karl, 1, 42

"Lucretius," 150, 155–63, 165, 166

Lushington, Henry, 142

Lyell, Sir Charles, 73, 89

Macaulay, Lord, 3, 116

Malory, Sir Thomas, 12, 39, 45, 113

Man: definition of, xiii–xiv; as family unit, 58, 62–63, 118, 125–26, 158–59; as God's agent, 6–7, 8–11, 34, 38, 71 n.1, 117, 118, 123; as martyr (sacrifice, scapegoat), 41, 92, 103, 105, 148, 149, 153–54; as obsolete, 31, 33, 36–37, 40, 50, 51, 52, 56, 70, 134, 152, 153; passions in, 112,

118–19, 121–23, 125, 128, 131–32, 134–35, 145–46, 156, 158, 161, 164; as suicide, 42, 104, 105, 134, 152–55, 158, 160, 162–63, 164. *See also* Class; Vows

Mandeville, Bernard, 21 n.36, 116 n.8

"Man is as mortal as men," 163

"Mariana," 51, 106

Marshall, George O., Jr., 38 n.6, 79 n. 12

Masterman, C.F.G., 91 n.36

Maud, 71, 103–11, 112, 124, 151, 152, 153

Maurice, John Frederick Denison, 5, 14, 17, 22, 99, 115, 121, 122–23, 125, 126, 140, 142

Mays, J.C.C., 90 n.36

"Mechanophilus," 26, 34–35, 53

Merivale, Charles, 14

"Merlin and the Gleam," 168

"Merlin and Vivien," 103, 104, 105, 109, 161

Mermin, Dorothy M., 110

Metaphysical Society, 123 n.14, 148 n. 29, 167

Mill, John Stuart, 31

Milman, H. H., 15, 115

Milnes, Richard Monckton, 73 n.2

Milton, John, 2, 6, 8, 45, 50, 94, 141, 142

"Mithridates Presenting Berenice with the Cup of Poison," 9, 156

"Montenegro," 166

Moore, Carlisle, 77 nn.13, 14, 89 n.32

"Morte d'Arthur," 32, 39–44, 114, 134

Motley, J. L., 3

Mustard, Wilfred P., 155 n.13

"Mystic, The," 5, 26, 27

Myth: as "fable," 25, 148; as historical symbolism, 13, 22, 30, 45, 47; Nordic, 25, 30, 86. *See also* Archetype; Imagery

"Napoleon's Retreat from Moscow," 10–11, 103 n.7

"National Song," 32

Nature: fallen (Original Sin), 19 and n.

28, 27, 45, 48; as organicism, 19, 20, 35, 37, 54, 71 n.1, 73, 74, 77–78, 86, 87, 96, 117. *See also* History, evolution (culture) in; Imagery, organic

Neoplatonism, 16–17, 22 n.37, 29, 31, 45, 80. *See also* Intuitionalism; Will

Newman, John Henry, 86

Nicolson, Harold, 24 n.51

Niebuhr, Barthold Georg, 14–16, 18, 20, 22, 54

"Northern Farmer, New Style," 155

"Nothing Will Die," 47

"Ode: O Bosky Brook," 35

"Ode on the Death of the Duke of Wellington," 37, 100–101, 102, 103, 110, 112, 118

"Ode to Memory," 35

"Oenone," 18, 29

"Of old sat Freedom on the heights," 33

"Old Chieftain, The," 10

"Old Sword, The," 9

Paden, W. D., 2, 9, 11, 30, 40, 47

"Palace of Art, The," 50

Palgrave, Francis T., 115

Past, in the present: as medievalism, 54–66 passim, 71, 94, 98, 156, 166; power of, 11, 37, 54–57 passim, 68, 73, 86, 91–93, 98–101, 103, 106–7, 110, 117, 156, 166

"Pelleas and Ettarre," 160 n.23, 161

"Penny-Wise, The," 99

"Perdidi Diem," 48–49

"Persia," 7

Pettigrew, John, 45

Pitt, Valerie, 77 n.11

Plato, 17, 22, 31, 122 n.14, 162

Plotinus, 17, 80

Plutarch, 157, 160, 163

"Poet's Mind, The," 31

"Politics," 165

Preyer, Robert, 15 n.9

Priestley, F.E.L., xi, 117 nn.9, 10, 153 n.8

Princess, The, 33, 34, 53, 55, 57, 59–68, 70, 75, 76, 78, 84, 94, 97, 98, 99, 106, 110, 112, 117, 154, 156
"Progress of Spring, The," 35
Providence, active: anthropomorphism of, 6, 24, 25, 28, 29, 36, 38, 40, 46, 48, 50, 70, 72, 80–81, 91, 120, 161; as Biblical God, 1, 6–7, 13, 18–25 passim; as historical "purpose," 11, 24, 33, 36–37, 46, 48, 53, 71–72, 111, 117 n.8, 122, 130, 167; as power (potentials), 19, 48, 92, 100, 103; withdrawal of, 76, 150, 152, 153, 164, 167, 168; as world spirit, 81, 118, 144, 148. *See also* God; History, "challenge and response" in
Providence, ordinary: anthropomorphism of, 29, 33, 36, 38–41, 46, 50, 58, 105–6, 134, 152; as natural law, 13, 18–19, 35–38 passim, 51, 74–75, 85, 118, 132–33, 150, 152, 155. *See also* God; History, anarchy in
Pythagoras, 31

Queen Mary, 166

Reade, William Winwoode, 136, 143, 148
Reed, John R., 123 n.15, 149 n.31, 153
Reform Bill: First (1832), 33, 38, 58, 64; Second (1867), 157–58; Third (1884), 165
"Remorse," 48
"Revenge, The," 166
Ricks, Christopher, 24 n.49, 47, 50, 51, 73 n.4, 74, 75 n.8, 111 n.14, 152, 153 n.9
"Rifle Clubs!!!" 99
"Riflemen Form!" 151
Robertson, William, 3, 4
Rollin, Charles, 2, 6, 7, 10
Roppen, Georg, 139 n.5
Rosenberg, John D., 32 n.1, 77 n.11, 96, 117 nn.9, 10, 140, 147
Ruskin, John, 152
Ryals, Clyde de L., 19 n.28, 59 n.17, 117 n.9, 139 n.6, 143 n.18

"Sadness," 163
Saint Simonists, 21, 72, 73
Scott, Sir Walter, 2, 3, 4, 34, 68
Sedgwick, Henry, 77
Seeley, Sir John Robert, 121, 126, 140, 141, 143
"Semele," 74
Shakespeare, William, 2, 45, 46, 67
Shaw, W. David, 79 n.13, 144, 155 n.14
Shelley, Percy Bysshe, 5, 56, 90, 92
"Sir Galahad," 58
Smith, Adam, 21 n.36, 116 n.8
Smith, Elton Edward, 28 n.59
Solomon, Stanley J., 144
Spedding, James, 19 n.27
"Splendour falls on castle walls, The," 110
Stange, G. Robert, 28 n.59, 30
Stanley, A. P., 15, 19, 90 n.34
Stedman, Edmund Clarence, 55–56, 59
Sterling, John, 14, 15
Stevenson, Lionel, 50
Strauss, D. F., 15
Suetonius, 2
"Suggested by Reading an Article in a Newspaper," 99, 104
"Supposed Confessions of a Second-Rate Sensitive Mind," 48, 144
Swinburne, Algernon, 163

Tacitus, 2, 3
"Tears, idle tears, I know not what they mean," 61, 168
Templeman, William Darby, 71 n.1
Tennyson, Emily, Lady (wife), 3, 60, 78, 97, 114 n.2, 115, 116, 125, 126, 142 n.16, 157, 167
Tennyson, George Clayton, the Reverend (father), 2
Tennyson, Hallam, Lord (son), 73 n.2, 102, 153, 165
Tennyson, Sir Charles (grandson), 2, 14 n.2, 17, 29, 66 n.26, 99, 103, 110, 126–27, 136, 157
Tennyson d'Eyncourt, Charles (uncle), 61, 66

Theocritus, 55–56, 156

Thirlwall, Connop, 14, 15, 21, 25 n.55, 116 n.8

"This Earth is wondrous, change on change," 34

Thucydides, 27

"Timbuctoo," 13, 18, 24–28, 30, 31, 33, 34, 37, 47, 48, 51, 57, 73, 82

"Time: An Ode," 27

"Tiresias," 32, 39–44, 92

"Tithon," 32, 40–44

"Tithonus," 41, 42

"To J.M.K.," 15

Toynbee, Arnold J., 20 n.31, 23

Tragedy, 8, 45–46, 144, 153

"Two Voices, The," 47, 49–50, 73, 75, 111 n.14

"Ulysses," 32, 36, 40–45, 47, 152–53

"Vale of Bones, The," 9

"Vastness," 167

Vico, Giambattista, 21–23, 116 n.8

"Vision of Sin, The," 53, 75–76, 102, 167

"Voice and the Peak, The," 167, 168

Voltaire, 2, 20

Vows, 118, 119, 120–21, 122, 134, 135–36. *See also* Man

"Walking to the Mail," 57

War: civil (fratricide), 39–40, 103–5, 107, 118, 124, 132, 143, 156, 158, 160; predisposition to, 9–10, 72, 118–19, 125, 127, 136; against "self," 105, 131, 137, 143; between states, 6–7, 72–73, 75, 100–105, 110–11, 119, 124, 136, 143. *See also* Apocalypse; History; Irony

Westcott, Brooke Foss, 22, 25, 167

Whately, Richard, 15

Whitman, Walt, 141

Will (effort, choice): ascendent, 10–11, 20, 22 n.37, 23–25, 29, 42, 45, 80, 85–86, 90–92, 95–97, 100–102, 108, 117, 140, 142, 143; failure of, 19, 28, 99, 106, 109, 128, 133, 140, 142, 143, 166. *See also* Intuitionalism; Neoplatonism

"Will," 101–2

"Will Waterproof's Lyrical Monologue," 53, 69 n.32

Wilner, Ortha L., 155 n.13

Wilson, Hugh H., 114

Wordsworth, William, 14, 16, 27, 70, 90

"Written During the Convulsions in Spain," 15

Xenophon, 2

"You ask me, why, though ill at ease," 32, 33

The Johns Hopkins University Press

This book was set in IBM Selectric Aldine Roman by Horne Associates, Inc. from a design by Charles West. It was printed on 50-lb. Bookmark paper and bound by Thomson-Shore, Inc.

Library of Congress Cataloging in Publication Data

Kozicki, Henry, 1924–
    Tennyson and Clio: history in the major poems.

    Bibliography: pp. 171–78
    Includes index.
    1. Tennyson, Alfred Tennyson, Baron, 1809–
1892–Criticism and interpretation.
2. Tennyson, Alfred Tennyson, Baron, 1809–1892–
Philosophy. I. Title.
PR5588.K6   821'.8   79–10979
ISBN 0–8018–2197–5